RALPH WALDO EMERSON

R. Waldo Emerson

RALPH WALDO EMERSON

Portrait of a Balanced Soul

EDWARD WAGENKNECHT

> A man is a golden impossibility. The line he must walk is a hair's breadth. The wise through excess of wisdom is made a fool.
>
> RWE: "EXPERIENCE"

NEW YORK   OXFORD UNIVERSITY PRESS   1974

For GERALD WARNER BRACE
with affection and respect

CONTENTS

RALPH WALDO EMERSON

WHAT EMERSON WAS NOT

Emerson, The Wisest American—such was the title of a popular biography published as late as 1929. Though not all would have agreed, the label attached to the name was still eloquent of the position the Concord writer had come to occupy in the minds of many of his countrymen. Though they might never have read much of Emerson themselves, nor cared to read him, their reaction to Philip Russell's title was still very different from what it would have been had he been writing about Longfellow or Whittier or Lowell—or, at that time, even Thoreau. Some years before, John Burroughs had startled his biographer, Clara Barrus, by telling her that there had never been a man whom he had reverenced like Emerson. She asked at once, "More than Whitman?" and Burroughs replied, "In a different way— Emerson was more astral—more like a star toward which I gazed. Walt, with all his cosmic qualities, was a comrade." [1]

Much humbler people than Burroughs would have agreed, and the Emerson legend, as distinct from his direct influence, cannot be fully apprehended if we confine ourselves entirely to serious or qualified investigators. I am sure I myself first heard of Emerson (and very likely of Boston and of Harvard University too) as a very small child, when in 1905–6 Seymour Eaton's *The Roosevelt Bears: Their Travels and Adventures* was published first in a chain of American newspapers and then as a book. This engaging verse chronicle, which reflected the con-

temporary obsession with President Roosevelt, recorded the doings of two Western bears, Teddy B and Teddy G, on a tour of
the United States. Several installments were devoted to the
Boston area, and when the bears reached the Public Library
there,

> They took the books and down they sat
> To study Emerson and the Autocrat.

In the book version there is a wonderful picture of them,
against what is unmistakably a Boston Public Library background, one reading a green volume labeled Emerson, the other
absorbed in a tan one marked *The Autocrat*. The incomplete
title did not stick in my childish mind, probably because no
author was named, but Emerson then and there became what he
remained to me for many years, a symbol of the frozen heights
in literature and in thought, and I am not quite sure that either
I or my countrymen have completely recovered from this impression even yet. At the same period, one of the pioneer creators
of the American comic strip, R. F. Outcault, was busily engaged, every Sunday, with the adventures of Buster Brown.
His main preoccupation was the staple fare of the American
comic strip at that time, the high jinks perpetrated by a mis-
chievous small boy, but Outcault was an incorrigible moralist,
and he always gave his last panel to Buster's posted "resolutions,"
which had no influence whatever upon his conduct and often
only the loosest possible connection with the preceding action.
On October 25, 1905, there was a tirade against card playing, in
the course of which Outcault managed to ring in Shakespeare,
Newton, Napoleon, and Emerson, whom Buster described as
the greatest mind America had produced.

   It would be easy to dismiss such writers as Seymour Eaton
and such artists as Outcault on the ground that they did not

know what they were talking about, but this would be a superficial view. Very few of the people who create popular fame know what they are talking about. Mark Twain was quite right when he argued that the adjective "famous" could not properly be applied to any man who was known only to those capable of judging him. Certainly it cannot apply to any author whose name is familiar only to those who have seriously read him. But the accuracy of the image which survives in popular fame is another matter.

In Emerson's case, the "wisest American" label is at least an improvement over some he was asked to wear during his lifetime, when all too many newspapers regarded him as a butt or a figure of fun, and when the average "right-thinking" American who was not a transcendentalist himself tended to think of him as a good, but utterly impractical, man, whose strange notions would be certain to wreck society if they could possibly be activated; fortunately, such persons generally added, this could never be. Nevertheless the popular twentieth-century estimate, besides being inaccurate, in some respects does Emerson considerable injustice. To think of him as a philosopher and a scholar, or to cause him to occupy common ground with Kant or Locke, is only slightly less absurd than to undertake a similar interpretation of, say, Oliver Wendell Holmes, for Emerson was a hopelessly unsystematic thinker, a crow who had followed many plows, and an idea which he had taken from some great thinker through the medium of a popular summary of his thought in an encyclopaedia or newspaper article might well be quite as important to him as something he had dug out for himself from the heart of the man's work. To everything that goes under the name of historical scholarship he was profoundly indifferent. What interested him was the value of an idea for himself (he did not care where it came from); when he visited a great library, he came away thinking he had all the best of it at home. He called illusion, temperament, succession, surface, reality, and subjectivity "the lords of life," but he added that temperament was "the iron wire on which the beads are strung." So it was, beyond question, for himself. External authority meant nothing to him; his witness was within.

Because he wrote much less poetry than prose, and because ideas are important in his verses and their metrics often rough and imperfect, some have thought Emerson a moralist who wrote sermons and covered them over with beauty like a veneer. Nothing could be further from the truth. His mind was a poet's mind always, as much in his prose as in his verse. It is true that John Dewey and some other good judges have been willing to accept him as a philosopher despite his neglect of formulations, yet it seems something of a joke that, in his old age, he should have served on a subcommittee on philosophy at Harvard. Perhaps the fact that he did not do notably well in his philosophy courses in college was not so important as George Edward Woodberry thought; perhaps even the contempt he sometimes expressed for systematic philosophy may be discounted—"Every man knows all that Plato or Kant can teach him"—for he made extreme statements about many things. When all allowances have been taken, however, Bronson Alcott was still right when he said that his friend's categories were those of the imagination, not the reason. Emerson *perceived* truth and proclaimed it; he did not reason or winnow it out; and when he changed his mind, it was simply because he had perceived or intuited further or differently. Had he been a less sane man than he was, he might have attributed changing views to fresh revelations. He never did this, but he trusted his intuitions as heroically as ever did prophet who proclaimed, "Thus saith the Lord." If he had more sympathy with poets than with philosophers, the reason was that he thought the poet had a more natural affinity for faith, since to him it came naturally and spontaneously, while the philosopher had to work it out systematically and could not sustain it without intellectual scaffoldings. Emerson did not exhort or argue or propagandize. In this respect, as Samuel McChord Crothers observed, he was more sage than prophet. He expessed what came to him. What his hearers did with it was their concern, not his.

His image has also been obscured for posterity by what is called his transcendentalism. Since Emerson did not at any time feel himself confined to a particular system of thought, and since this book is a character study and not a philosophical essay, no technical or detailed consideration of transcendentalism need be undertaken here. Like many of our power words—classical, romantic, Christian, and others—transcendental and transcendentalism are always in danger of meaning all things to all men. The Concord transcendentalists of whom Emerson was one were all such pronounced individualists that many will find it difficult to find anything besides a generally idealistic outlook that they held in common.

In a way, the term "transcendentalism" is even misleading to those who have any knowledge of systematic theology. In the Christian religion, God is both transcendent and immanent. Insofar as He manifests Himself in the world, through nature and human consciousness and the normal processes of human life, He is immanent. But if God were wholly immanent, He would be swallowed up in the world that He has made; we should all be obliged to become pantheists, and sooner or later we should find ourselves worshipping a cyclone. The Christian God, therefore, is transcendent as well as immanent; He is in the world and outside of it at the same time. God in His Heaven (with whatever accent one chooses to read that word) is a transcendent God.

Both these elements appear (to repeat) in all sound Christian theology, but the emphasis shifts notably from one aspect to the other. It is much easier to believe in the Divine Immanence when things are going pretty well than it is in times of war or natural calamity. Nevertheless, God cannot become wholly a "Divine Otherness" without destroying religion itself, for religion is much less concerned with God in His heaven than with God in His relationship to man. If there is no such relationship, a religious philosophy may survive, but not a religion.

It must not, therefore, be supposed that the Concord transcendentalists emphasized God's transcendence at the expense of His immanence. Quite the contrary was the case. They were as much given to finding manifestations of God in nature as any nineteenth-century poet, and the audacity of their determination to find Him in every man equaled that of the Quakers.

The intellectual backgrounds of Concord transcendentalism were highly respectable. Though John Locke thought of himself as a good Christian, he saw the senses as the only sources of human knowledge. Kant denied Locke's assumption that the baby's mind was a *tabula rasa* at birth, without independent knowledge; he believed, on the contrary, that the mind possessed in its own right certain ideas or categories and that Divine Reality was directly accessible through conscience or the categorical imperative. Fichte, Schelling, Hegel, and others developed these ideas in a way that made German philosophy an important influence not only upon the Concord transcendentalists, but also upon the English Romantics, with whom they had much in common. And by so doing they established or re-established the intellectual respectability of an intuitive approach to moral and spiritual knowledge through means *transcending* that which could be apprehended through the five senses.

None of this means, however, that Emerson, or any of the transcendentalists, consciously or deliberately took upon themselves the task of introducing German philosophy into the United States. They were much too independent-minded for that. Emerson in particular read "for lustres," that is, for inspirational power; he is the perfect type of the man who never did finish reading the book because it started him thinking. Above all, he had the gift of finding what he sought in his reading, or that which interpreted him to himself; that which did not serve these ends he simply ignored. It is no wonder, therefore, that Frederic Ives Carpenter should have been able to employ so many different philosophical terms in trying to describe him:

Emerson's philosophy may perhaps be described as a Pragmatic Mysticism. It is idealistic in that it puts the mystical experience first. It is dualistic in that it looks both ways from its position on the bridge between the soul and nature. It is monistic in that it maintains that this bridge is the only reality. But it is pragmatic in that it tests all truths (including the mystical belief in the value of life) by experience.[2]

Emerson used all these lines of approach, but he committed himself to none of them. If the wise Frenchman declared that there were exceptions to all rules *including this one*, Emerson saw reality as larger than any possible definition of it, including his own. Nor did he confine this point of view to philosophical matters; for him all human institutions, including government, took on an aspect of fluidity—forever dissolving, forever becoming—with no institution, no creed, and no moral code an end in itself. This was what the composer Charles Ives meant when he declared that "the inactivity of permanence" was the one thing Emerson would not permit. "Emerson wrings the neck of any law that would become exclusive and arrogant, whether a definite one of metaphysics or an indefinite one of mechanics."[3]

Inevitably, then, he gloried in multitudinous surface inconsistencies. Underneath them all, he was profoundly consistent. He was deeply impressed by the thought that all men who have thought deeply and truly are in fundamental agreement with

one another; he stressed this agreement; for all his love of rhetorical overstatement and occasional provocativeness, he tended
to ignore the areas of disagreement and thus became a powerful
force toward conciliation. But he never envisaged harmony in
creedal terms. "He may have no system," wrote Prosser Hall
Frye, many years ago, "but he has a disposition." [4]

This disposition is the concern of this book. But first we
must remind ourselves briefly of the facts of his outward experience.

BIOGRAPHY

Ralph Waldo Emerson was born in Boston on May 25, 1803. It has often been remarked, sometimes with horror and sometimes with fervent admiration, that he came of seven generations of Puritan clergymen. This is not the whole story, however. The American founder of the Emerson family, Thomas Emerson, who came to America in 1635, was a baker, and though his son became a clergyman, his grandson, Edward, was a merchant. The father of Emerson's mother, Ruth Haskins, was a distiller who had been a cooper and a privateer and a captive of both the Spanish and the French. The famous Reverend Samuel Ripley of Concord, whom Emerson commemorates in his *Lectures and Biographical Sketches*, was only a step-grandfather, having married Phebe Bliss Emerson after her fiery young clergyman-husband, the builder of the Old Manse, who had come very close to participating in the battle under his windows on April 19, 1775, ran off to join Washington's army as chaplain and to die, leaving Ripley to be invested with his house, his charge, and his wife.

Emerson's own father, William, pastor of the First Church in Boston, died in May 1811, just before Ralph's eighth birthday, leaving his widow to keep a boardinghouse and bring up her sons in poverty. Emerson does not seem to have had any exaggerated regard for him, and he is often regarded as something of a lightweight, but he did not lack either intelligence or sensibility, and he certainly knew all the "right" people, for his funeral was attended by sixty coaches and the Ancient and Honorable Artillery Company. He was also an editor of *The Monthly Anthology*, out of which grew the Boston Athenaeum.[1]

Ralph Waldo was the fourth child to be born into the Emerson family, but the first, Phebe Ripley, had lived only two years, dying in 1800, and the second, John Clarke, was to die in 1807. After his fourth year, therefore, Emerson was to have only one older brother, William, who, after an abortive attempt at theology in Germany, became a successful lawyer in New York and continued to practice there until his death in 1868. Ralph acquired a sister, Mary Caroline, in the year of his father's death, but she had only one more year of life than Phebe and died in 1814. Emerson had three younger brothers, however, though he was to bury all of them in time. Robert Bulkeley (1807–59) was what is now called "retarded," and though both Edward Bliss (1805–34) and Charles Chauncy (1808–36) were at first considered more brilliant than Ralph, they turned out to be too delicately attuned for great staying power; both experienced breakdowns and died young.

Childhood was arduous, poverty-stricken, and "deprived." The boys labored hard to relieve their overburdened mother; one winter Ralph and Edward had only one overcoat between them. It is generally said that they pastured their cow on Boston Common, but Frank Sanborn says it was not on the Common itself, but beyond it, where the Providence Station was later to stand. That Emerson roamed over the Common spouting Scott and Campbell seems certain however; that he also possessed the "sluggish" mind with which he credited himself is harder to believe.

Yet, as that fantastically eccentric woman of genius, Aunt Mary Moody Emerson, perceived and proclaimed, the Emerson boys were "born to be educated." Educated and challenged too, with visions of heroic achievement held up before them and no acknowledgment that anything good or desirable might be impossible.[2] We may omit the dame schools which began when the child was three. At one period the pinch grew so tight that the family had to leave Boston and take refuge with Dr. Ripley in Concord. From 1813 to 1817, however, Emerson attended the Boston Latin School, which, if some of the stories we hear are true, may not have been much better than the humbler institutions. In 1817 he began working his way through Harvard, serving as "president's freshman" and waiting on tables. He was graduated in 1821 (by this time he had decided that he wanted to be called Waldo, not Ralph), but though he was Class Poet and had received some honors, he was barely in the upper half of his class and was apparently not considered for Phi Beta Kappa.

Though in later years Emerson was sometimes willing to grant some value to mathematics and drill in Latin grammar on the ground that they trained the student in exactitude, he also saw the classical education as a forced survival, quite as artificial as chignons, and mathematics as a useless burden, of no practical value to more than four-fifths of a college class, taking up to two-thirds of a student's time during his first two years, robbing him of the joy of his education, and tempting him to unworthy amusements by way of relief. Aside from his admiration (later quite outgrown) for Edward Everett and a few other professors, his college years would not seem to have been of much value to him, and it is not surprising that President Eliot should later have found in his writings "all the fundamental motives and principles of my hourly struggle against educational routine and tradition." [3] The ideas Emerson developed in this area were indeed advanced for his time; he disbelieved in grades and in compulsory attendance and even suggested that "the class shall have a certain share in the election of the professor."

Whatever his views were at this time, he soon had a chance to test them out, for he taught in his brother William's school and elsewhere. As a matter of fact, he had already taught, during vacations, at his uncle's school in Waltham. He did not enjoy teaching, nor did he feel that he did it well, but his more sensitive pupils seem to have rated him more highly. Apparently somewhat in awe of the girls, he was not inclined to fraternize with his pupils, but he maintained order without the necessity of seeming to insist on it, and there was no harsh discipline nor ill temper.

In February 1825 Emerson went back to Cambridge to study divinity, but illness and eye trouble soon caused him to withdraw. His teaching career was not yet quite over; there was also a spell, for health reasons, on Uncle Ladd's farm in Newton. Nevertheless he was "approbated to preach" by the Middlesex Association of Ministers on October 10, 1826.

He preached his first sermon at Waltham in October, but health was still a problem, and on November 25 he sailed for Charleston, South Carolina. Between January and June 1827 he preached in various Southern and Middle Atlantic cities; after his return to the Boston area he continued his preaching in New England, and in August he took a Master's degree at Harvard. On December 6 he supplied the pulpit in Concord, New Hampshire, where he met a seventeen-year-old beauty named Ellen Louisa Tucker. Early in 1829 he became the junior colleague of the Reverend Henry Ware, Jr., at Boston's Second Church (circumstances were soon to leave the junior minister in full charge), and on September 30 he and Ellen were married. Both his personal and his professional future now seemed assured. But on February 8, 1831, Mrs. Emerson died (she had been, and she was to remain, much more important in his life than the short time she lived with him might indicate), and the next year her widowed husband resigned his pulpit out of conscientious scruples. On Christmas Day he sailed alone for Malta.

John Jay Chapman's grandmother first heard Emerson's name when a neighbor said to her, "Oh, have you heard? The new minister of the Second Church has gone mad." The particular form which Emerson's lunacy took was that he felt he could no longer administer the sacrament of the Lord's Supper, having become convinced that Jesus "did not intend to establish an institution for perpetual observance when he ate the Passover with his disciples." But there was more to it than that. The spontaneity which for Emerson was the heart of the religious life was becoming increasingly difficult under ecclesiastical forms and a prescribed service. He even came to dislike offering prayer at stated times without reference to the prompting of the Spirit. In this respect, as he himself recognized, Emerson moved very close to the Quaker position, but he never formally severed his tie with the Unitarians. He continued to appear frequently as a guest preacher until about 1840, notably at New Bedford and for three years at East Lexington; after that he may be said to have made his own pulpit out of the lecture platform.

Emerson remained in Europe (Malta, Sicily, Italy, France, England, Scotland) until the autumn of 1833, meeting Landor, Coleridge, Wordsworth, and, above all, Carlyle, with whom he established a lasting friendship, not entirely untroubled by doubts on either side. He thanked God for these opportunities, particularly, it would seem, because they increased his sense of self-reliance. "I shall judge more justly, less timidly, of wise men forevermore. . . . Especially are they all deficient, all these four —in different degrees, but all deficient,—in insight into religious truth." On October 7 he landed in New York and moved to rejoin his mother, who was now living in Newton Upper Falls. A year later they went again to Concord, to live in the Old

Manse with Dr. Ripley, and in the summer of 1835, having become engaged to Lydia Jackson of Plymouth, Emerson bought the Coolidge house in Concord, which was to remain his home for the rest of his life and which survives as a shrine to his memory. Emerson and Lydia were married on September 14.

This second marriage produced four children: Waldo (1836); Ellen Tucker (1839); Edith (1841); and Edward Waldo (1844). Waldo's death in 1842 (the occasion of "Threnody"), was a lasting grief; all Emerson's other children, along with his wife, outlived him.

Professional lecturing (i.e. lecturing as distinct from preaching and as a calculated means of livelihood) may be said to have begun at the Masonic Temple in Boston in November 1833, oddly enough with a lecture on natural history, and continued throughout the rest of Emerson's life. In time he would spend a good deal of time on the road, sometimes encountering great hardships. Some of this will be considered in other connections. Here one need only check off certain highlights of his career as a public speaker: his address at Concord's Second Centennial celebration in 1835; the Phi Beta Kappa oration at Harvard (1837), which has been called an American intellectual Declaration of Independence; the Divinity School address the next year, which caused even Unitarians to call him an atheist and an infidel; the antislavery oration at Boston in January 1855; and his address at the Harvard Civil War commemoration in the summer of 1865 and the second Phi Beta Kappa oration in 1867. In 1866 Harvard had given him an LL.D. and made him an Overseer, and in 1870 and 1871 he gave there the lectures afterward published as "Natural History of Intellect." From 1842 to 1844 he edited the transcendentalist organ, *The Dial*, after Margaret Fuller had given it up.

Emerson's first book, *Nature* (1836), sounded most of the themes he was to elaborate through the years. *Essays*, First Series and Second Series, followed in 1841 and 1844, and he collected his *Poems* in 1846. There followed *Representative Men* (1850); *English Traits* (1856), always the favorite Emerson book of those who do not care much for Emerson; *The Conduct of Life* (1860), perhaps his last completely first-rate prose work; *May Day* (1867), his second and last collection of poems; and *Society and Solitude* (1870), which was made up largely of papers written some time before and which showed Emerson in a somewhat relaxed mood. In 1852 he collaborated with William Henry Channing and James Freeman Clarke to produce the *Memoirs of Margaret Fuller*, and in 1874 he brought out *Parnassus*, an immense poetic anthology with which he had amused himself for some years.

Emerson made a second trip to Europe in 1847–48. In 1865 his daughter Edith married William Forbes, son of a prominent railroad man, and this led to a very happy excursion by rail to California in 1871. The following summer, Emerson's house was partially destroyed by fire, whereupon his friends and neighbors not only raised funds to restore it, but sent him and his daughter Ellen, who had become his right-hand man, to Europe while the work was being done. He went as far as Cairo this time, renewing old contacts and meeting new celebrities. Concord welcomed him and Ellen home with a triumphal arch, the tolling of bells, and other honors generally reserved for those who have engineered murder on a grand scale.

Cushioned though the shock of the fire had been, it still seems to have taken its toll, and Emerson's mental decline is generally dated from this event. *Letters and Social Aims* (1875), the last book to appear during his lifetime, was put together by James Elliot Cabot, who became his biographer, and who was also responsible for the three posthumous collections: *Miscellanies* (1883), *Lectures and Biographical Sketches* (1884), *and Natural History of Intellect and Other Papers* (1893). After

1876 Emerson was no longer able to make entries in his journal, and though he was always perfectly rational, his memory failed rapidly. When he attended Longfellow's funeral in March 1882, all he knew was that the man being buried had a beautiful soul, but he could not say his name. He himself had only a month to live, until April 27, 1882.

CHAPTER ONE

SELF-RELIANCE

I

Emerson was tall and slender, six feet or a trifle under; in 1830 he tipped the beam at 157 pounds, but by 1871 his weight had fallen to 140½. He himself said that his friends always greeted him after absence with the observation that he was a little thinner than they had remembered him. His head was long, narrow, and high, his hat size 6⅞. His shoulders sloped markedly (Mrs. Longfellow speaks, with unwonted sarcasm, of "his falling voice and shoulders"),[1] and he walked rapidly, carrying one shoulder slightly higher than the other. His eyes—"eagle eyes" Emma Lazarus called them[2]—were a very bright blue, his nose accipitrine, his mouth wide, his chin firm, and his lower lip rather prominent. His hair remained thick and brown until he was fifty, but when his daughter told him she was glad he had never worn a beard, he replied that he had had none to wear.

Oliver Wendell Holmes, Daniel Chester French,[3] and others have left us rather detailed descriptions and interesting impressions of Emerson's appearance. Apparently there was always something of the countryman about him, even on the lecture platform, but for those capable of feeling it, the radiance he exuded made this unimportant; David Scott was, I think, exceptional in finding him "severe, and dry, and hard." In his

Latin School days, Rufus Dawes, a classmate, thought him "spiritual-looking," "angelic and remarkable," and this impression was shared later by the journalist Charles Taber Congdon, who first saw him, in the pulpit at New Bedford, as "the most gracious of mortals, with a face all benignity, who gave out the first hymn and made the first prayer as an angel must have read and prayed." Elizabeth Hoar felt much the same way when she encountered him as a teacher (it was, she said, "as if angel spoke"), and the more critically inclined Jane Carlyle used much the same figure, while George Eliot described him as "the first man I have ever seen." If these ladies seem over emotional, Nathaniel Hawthorne was not, for he and Emerson never achieved a really satisfactory understanding, yet Hawthorne thought his neighbor had a "pure intellectual gleam diffused about his presence like the garment of a shining one." It is true that Hawthorne's son Julian thought Emerson ugly, misshapen, awkward, and shambling, and absurdly compared him to Socrates and Mirabeau, but even Julian admitted that he gave the impression of beauty, like sunlight coming into a room, and he contradicted himself altogether when he gave Emerson "the grace and movement of a natural king." [4] In the light of these testimonies, it is almost shocking to learn that when Emerson's wife-to-be, Lydia Jackson, first glimpsed him in the pulpit, she was most of all impressed by the length of his neck!

It seems generally agreed upon that Emerson's smile and his voice were especially attractive. George William Curtis says that the smile broke like the coming of day itself—"at Emerson's house it is always morning"—and John W. Chadwick found that "the whole street seemed to be lighted up and cheered and brightened with the ineffable sweetness of his face." This sweetness was in no way associated with weakness, however, for John Burroughs speaks of his "serene, unflinching look," and though he was almost a broken man when Herman Grimm met him, the German was still impressed by his bright coloring and thought he looked more fifty than seventy. As for the voice as an organ, it seems to have been as beautiful and melodious as Longfellow's, though E. P. Whipple insists that there was nothing sensuous about it, but rather the suggestion of "an impersonal character, as though a spirit was speaking through him." In conversation it was quiet and unassertive; you had to listen if you wished to hear what he was saying, but, for that very reason, it was obvious that he was a man who was accustomed to being listened to. Alexander Ireland called Emerson's voice "the sweetest, the most winning and penetrating" he had ever heard, and Nathaniel Parker Willis says it had much more body than might have been expected from so slight a man.

Finally, it is interesting to note Daniel Chester French's professional impression that there was "nothing slurred, nothing accidental" in Emerson's features, but rather the perfection of detail to be looked for in great sculpture, strangely coexisting with "an almost child-like mobility that admitted of an infinite variety of expression." Says Bliss Perry:

Seen from one side, . . . [his] was the face of a Yankee of the old school, shrewd, serious, practical; the sort of face that may still be observed in the quiet country churches of New England or at the village store. Seen from the other side, it was the face of a dreamer, a seer, a soul brooding on things to come, things as yet very far away. I once asked Daniel Chester French . . . if this well known characteristic of Emerson's features did not increase the difficulty of the sculptor's task. Not at all, he replied: all that he had to do was to project the planes of each side until they met at a point beyond the face itself.

French was a pretty good transcendentalist himself!

II

The body was not robust; the family history being what it was, this could hardly have been expected. In 1838 Emerson wrote his brother William that only two or three of the Emersons had sound health. Even in youth he lamented a certain lack of animal spirits.

> I bear in youth the sad infirmities
> That use to undo the limb and sense of age.

"I come to you in weakness, and not in strength," he wrote to Second Church when accepting their call. "In a short life, I have yet had abundant experience of the uncertainty of human hopes." And in 1841 he wrote Margaret Fuller that he operated within narrow limits and did not dare to o'erpass them.

In early life he suffered from rheumatism, eye trouble, and the lung condition which threatened him with tuberculosis and sent him south in 1827. One eye was operated upon, but he did not buy his first pair of glasses until he was nearly fifty. Beginning in 1825, a bad hip troubled him until December 1829, when, after having dismissed his regular physician, he was cured in two hours by a "quack." In 1827 his health was so bad that he wondered seriously whether he was going to be able to go on with his plans for the ministry, and in 1828 he was "treading on eggs" and battling "betwixt life and death." He carried a cane to his wedding, and in October 1829 he was preaching from a chair. But though Cabot says that "tenderness of lungs" and "fits of languor" troubled him until he was forty, his ocean voyage to Europe in 1832 seems to have been wonderfully beneficial, and his later life was apparently that of one of those never robust men who, while they develop no great physical strength, yet manage to adjust their resources to their obligations and thus live on a rather remarkably even and comfortable keel.

In 1859 he sprained his ankle badly on Wachusett Mountain and spent two or three months on crutches, which hurt his arm and deprived him of his customary exercise with generally debilitating effects, causing him to remark that if King Lear had ever suffered this injury, he would have learned that there are worse afflictions than unkind daughters. He may have had chicken pox on his first ocean voyage and measles after the return from his second. Once, at least, a Concord summer was too hot for him, for he complained that the sun felt like a burning glass and even the slugs were broiled. Generally speaking, however, he loved summer's "rivers of heat" and disliked cold, though, oddly enough, he also disliked wearing an overcoat and took a cold bath every morning, winter and summer. On his lecture tours, he preferred hotels to private homes because he thought he had a better chance to keep warm there, and he would beg the innkeeper to make him "red-hot." He also found heat useful to put him back into shape when he was sick. He enjoyed sound, unbroken sleep throughout his nights, and, since he was hopelessly addicted to the old New England habit of pie for breakfast, his digestion must have been sound.

Like Jonathan Swift, Emerson died from the head down. It seems odd that a man of such ebullient temperament, and with such enthusiasm for youth, should have begun calling himself an old man in his forties. (Contrariwise, as late as the time he wrote "Terminus," he found no "wrinkles and used heart" within himself, but "unspent youth.") Moncure D. Conway recorded Emerson's having told him that, the morning after the fire, he felt something snap in his brain. During his last years he forgot words and names, restored dead friends to life, went out to take the obelisk instead of the omnibus, called Moody and Sankey "Mosely and Sukey," and in the midst of a conversation with a distinguished visitor, he would apply to his daughter to find out to whom he was speaking. He was not unaware of the disadvantages involved in all this. In 1876 he wrote Emma Lazarus that he now tended to avoid social contacts and had even grown silent in his own house, for fear of distressing his family; later, he hesitated about going to stay with Edith and her husband because he might lose his wits from day to day. Yet there are indications that his infirmities disturbed his daughter Ellen, upon whom most of the burden of filling up his deficiencies fell, more than they did him; in some moods at least, he was quite capable of being amused by them. When he died, she wrote Lowell that the family were thankful and that neither he nor they could have endured going on much longer.[5]

More interesting than all this is Emerson's own attitude toward health and sickness. He quoted with apparent approval Dr. Johnson's statement that "every man is a rascal as soon as he is sick." Life was ecstasy. Health was genius. Sickness was a "cannibal," making it impossible for a man to sustain a proper relationship to himself or to the universe. He insisted upon the duty of keeping well as Stevenson was to insist upon the duty of being happy, and as a matter of fact, he insisted upon that too. "It is observed that a depression of spirits develops the germs of a plague in individuals and in nations." When he was in Rome in 1833 he felt stronger than he had since his college days; one could not afford to be sick in Rome, where there was so much to see and to do! But he would not "lie by" when he grew "thin and puny" either; were he to do this, he would lose all his "best days."

He was almost a fanatic on the subject of not allowing sickness to be discussed at the table or in social gatherings; once he even wrote a correspondent that he was not a "good sympathizer" and came pretty close to declaring that all individuals, including herself, were responsible for the ills which beset them.[6] His letters to the ailing John Sterling in England are not really out of line with this; if they are not unsympathetic, they are a bit astringent to send to a dying man. Yet Emerson had plenty of sickness around him in his own household, and he does not seem to have been heartless in dealing with it. Even Edward Waldo had to be withdrawn from Harvard for health reasons in the fall of his freshman year, with a view to being re-entered a year later; meanwhile he departed for the West to embrace strains and hardships compared to which anything Harvard might have had to offer him must have been slight, and when he came back worn out, he talked about going into the army! And in 1864, when Edith was ailing, her father, though worried about her aversion to hydropathy and other remedies, did not seek to force his own ideas upon her.

From time to time Emerson speculated about the possibility of the mind establishing such control over the body that all sickness would disappear. On this basis Paul Elmer More attacked him as a kind of Christian Scientist,[7] and John Burroughs functioned in the same climate of opinion when he said that if Emerson's ideas could be reduced to jelly, and all the iron and lime taken out of them, you would have New Thought! It would not be difficult to find Emersonian utterances which bring him close to Eddyism. Like medieval men (and Nathaniel Hawthorne), he thought doctors likely to be materialists, and in 1873 his anti-sickness mania went to the extent of his telling Charles Eliot Norton that he had never been sick for a whole day in his life, a statement which was obviously untrue.[8] Yet when Mrs. Eddy tried to enlist his interest in Christian Science, she got no response whatever from him; for a man as courteous and sympathetic as he was habitually, he might even be said to have treated her somewhat summarily.[9]

However this act be judged, the impulse behind it was predictable and not uncharacteristic. Emerson always shied from extremes; he never went too far. Idealistic as he was, therefore, he never denied the existence and reality of matter upon its own ground. This is the point at which those who do not admire Emerson always sacrifice him to Thoreau, who was much more of a come-outer; they mistrust Emerson because they think he played it safe. Admire it or curse it, there can be no question that moderation, or the ideal of balance, was there, nor that it was a basic element in his character and temperament. As the subtitle of this volume will already have warned the reader, we shall find it emerging again and again in various connections as we proceed.

III

If Emerson lacked what he calls animal spirits, he was certainly not deficient in either ardor or cheerfulness. "What is a man good for without enthusiasm?" He was a prophet of joy, respecting the pursuit of happiness far beyond most moralists, and he is said to have rebuked Ruskin himself for his pessimism. He discerned no special gift for suffering in his own makeup; neither was he anxious to cultivate it. For him the spiritual world was in harmony with human aspirations; to doubt this would be to blaspheme life itself.

In youth and in age, he had a marked capacity for hero-worship, embracing at different times Everett, Webster, Lincoln, Carlyle, Michelangelo, and many others. "Others laugh, weep, sell, or proselyte; I admire." He objected to over-asseveration for very much the same reason Quakers reject oaths, but his tendency to overstatement betrays him and his inner temperature very often. It has sometimes been said that he lived only in the ecstasy of the moment; this is an exaggeration. But he valued the moment nevertheless and surrendered himself to it whenever possible.

He himself speaks of his "silliness" and his "cardinal vice of intellectual dissipation." "In writing, as in all things else," he says, "I follow my caprice." In 1841 he begged Margaret Fuller for some good verses in the next number of *The Dial*, "for we must have *levity* sufficient to compensate the morgue of Unitarianism and Shelley and Ideal Life and Reform in the last number." This "silliness," which Cabot calls humor or detachment, was inherited from his father. Opinions as to Emerson's humor have always differed. Oliver Wendell Holmes, who was a good judge, credited him with a good deal, but "The Comic" is one of his least rewarding papers. He did not care for laughter and disliked being made to laugh, but this may have been because he found it physically uncomfortable. In his youth he had been embarrassed socially by a nervous tendency to giggle. Whatever the origin of his "levity," it was valuable to him and may well have saved him from the breakdowns experienced by two of his brothers.[10]

Emerson professed not to admire action for its own sake. "Physical force has no value where there is nothing else." Yet, on one side, he was clearly attracted to it. Like George Eliot, he committed himself to the proposition that any decision is better than no decision, which is nonsense unless action itself has an inherent value, and, as we shall see when we come to deal with his attitude toward politics and practical affairs, the allowances he was willing to make for men of action were sometimes very large. Moreover, he saw the artist himself in this light. "Art delights in carrying thought into action. Literature is the conversion of action into thought. The architect executes his dream in stone. The poet enchants you by idealizing your life and fortunes."

It was not surprising, then, that all his tastes in art should have been "vital and spermatic." Poetry was "the *gai science.*" He had no use for grisly subjects. Death was never effective in literature. Sir Thomas Browne smelled of the charnel house; even some of the masters of Italian sacred painting erred in this regard. *The Bride of Lammermoor* and the story of Patient Griselda were the only sad stories he ever liked; he told Mrs. Fields that *The Divine Comedy* was too terrible to finish (unfortunately, all the terribleness is at the beginning).

His optimism and his faith in life have never been questioned. In his eyes nothing divine ever died and all good was eternally reproductive. As to what is called fate, a man can live only by ignoring it; to do anything else is to invite the evils you fear. Belief in predestination or original sin he called "the soul's mumps and measles and whooping coughs." In this aspect, the idealistic transcendentalist Emerson was as pragmatic as the Dr. Johnson who demonstrated the reality of matter by kicking his toe against a stone.

Some of the applications Emerson made of his optimism seem very extreme today. At the end of the Civil War he believed "that the day of ruling by scorns and sneers is past; that good sense is now in power, and *that* resting on a vast constituency of intelligent labor, and, better yet, on perceptions less and less dim of laws the most sublime." He was familiar with the Malthusian nightmare, but brushed it off on the assumption that man's ingenuity would suffice to solve the problem posed. He did not think flying machines would come until the race was ready for them, since men would not be allowed to acquire more power than they could be trusted with. Every man has the wisdom to steer his own boat, he declared, though he must certainly have known that many wreck them on the rocks, and he made such amazing statements as that merit is always welcomed as soon as it is recognized, that the man who knows most will always command the ear of the company in which he finds himself, and even that courtroom audiences are impartial, desiring only to learn the truth and see justice done. "It does not hurt weak eyes to look into beautiful eyes never so long," he says, yet he must surely have known that sexual attraction has its sinister aspects. He even had the idea that ugly buildings in American cities are soon destroyed, "but any beautiful building is copied and improved upon, so that all masons and carpenters work to repeat and preserve the agreeable forms, while the ugly ones die out," a view which, if he could come back, could hardly survive a walk through any American city or a leafing through the pages of such books as Nathan Silver's *Lost New York* or Constance M. Greiff's *Lost America*.[11]

In the famous "Compensation," Emerson seems to carry his optimism to fantastic lengths, for we read here that "a certain compensation balances every gift and every defect. A surplusage given to one part is paid out of a reduction from another part of the same creature. If the head and neck are enlarged, the trunk and extremities are cut short." Again: "Every excess causes a defect; every defect an excess. Every sweet hath its sour; every evil its good. . . . For every grain of wit there is a grain of folly." And finally: "Every secret is told, every crime punished, every virtue rewarded, every wrong redressed, in silence and certainty." Nor was Emerson quite incapable of matching this in other connections. When Margaret Fuller was drowned, he wrote Carlyle that her death was fortunate in view of her diminished health and powers and the fact that her marriage would have taken her away from her friends!

Skeptics may well ask what was taken away from Shakespeare that the common men of his time possessed, and what is given to the man (whose name is Legion) who is little all over. If Emerson is to be taken literally, the wisest men are also the most foolish and the best the worst. But this is no more wholly optimistic than pessimistic, for in such a world as he has suggested, if you cannot lose, you cannot win either. *The House of the Seven Gables* has often been taken as Hawthorne's answer to transcendentalist nonsense; Clifford Pyncheon is a consistent loser; for him there is no compensation. And in "Circles" Emerson himself carries the argument of "Compensation" to an almost Mephistophelian indifference. He is not careful to justify himself, he says, and sets no value on what he does or says. "No facts are to me sacred; none are profane; I simply experiment, an endless seeker with no Past at my back." [12]

But no doubt it would be unwise to take him too literally, here or elsewhere. If Hawthorne had his Clifford Pyncheon, Emerson had his own brother Bulkeley, for whose benefit he recognized that the law of compensation had not functioned. Moreover he himself, returning from Europe in 1833, when he did not yet know what God wanted him to do with his life (though he believed he would be shown), thought that if the ship should founder, he might regret it less than many of his fellow passengers. He once declared that "despondency comes readily to the most sanguine," and he was not exactly a cheerful idiot when he said that the way to win was to expect nothing, thus putting yourself into a position where any possible good was clear gain, nor yet when, upon the death of Louisa Hawthorne in a steamboat accident, his letter to Sophia took the not quite exuberant form of being unable to decide which method of leaving such a world as this was best. Emerson did not cultivate what Henry James was to call "the imagination of disaster," but he understood it nevertheless. "Can this hold?" he asked Aunt Mary when he was most happily situated, with his Ellen and his church. After he died, Edith wrote Carlyle that he had awakened every morning in a joyful mood and had always been in good spirits, and she quoted her mother as saying he was the happiest person she had ever known. Certainly there is truth in this. But Emerson's own saying that every awakening after the age of thirty was sad is not deprived of all significance by her (or his daughter's or Edith's) report.

We shall not understand much of what Emerson had to tell us unless we understand that it is to be taken, if not in a Pickwickian, certainly in an Emersonian sense. Rejecting automatic progress, he believed in the goodness and holiness and perfection of mankind only potentially (though he did not always make these distinctions clear), and he recognized the importance of discipline, which gets a main heading even in *Nature*. He speaks of the "fool-part" of mankind and finds "imbecility" in many human activities, and he sounds much like Carlyle when he says that the masses need to be schooled, not flattered. Moreover, he does not stress the idea that the good man will be sure to escape calamity, but merely that he can be made equal to it; hence his references to "the death of a dear friend, wife, brother, lover" as essentially dead or powerless circumstances need not cause us to conclude that he did not feel such calamities. He did not pretend to possess a charmed life or special insight either, for after Waldo's death he wrote, "I am defeated all the time; yet to victory I am born." And Christians at least ought to be able to understand this, for have they not made that hideous supergallows, the Roman cross, the very symbol of their faith?

IV

Emerson was sanguine, then, and he was hopeful. Was he also, as might have been expected, ambitious? He called ambition the leprosy of the Emersons and urged William not to overwork himself and die of it, and he admitted that whatever he admired inspired him with the desire to do it himself. Yet the incentives which inspire the ambitions of most men passed him by. Power did not attract him. He aspired to eminence as an orator and a writer, but even here he had no desire to dominate men's minds; what he wanted to do was to awaken their own powers and inspire them to think for themselves. Nor was he ever interested in the accumulation of money, and we may glance at the economic aspects of his life before we pass on to more important matters.

As we have seen, his childhood was impecunious; one of his most vivid childhood memories was of his anguish while searching for a dollar he had lost in some poplar leaves when sent out to buy a pair of shoes. Once he and Edward gave their only loaf of bread to a destitute person and Aunt Mary tried to still the rumblings in their stomachs with tales of heroism!

The interesting thing is that the memory of these early hardships did not cause Emerson to be penurious in later life. With his marriage to Ellen Tucker, his financial status was considerably improved ("I do not wish to hear of your prospects," she had told him), and though her money was not the cause of his leaving the ministry, it certainly cushioned the transition. His claim to a share in her estate was disputed, however, and though the matter was finally decided in his favor, this was not until after it had gone before the Supreme Judicial Court in Boston. In 1838 he wrote Carlyle that he had $22,000 besides his house, yielding him an annual income of 6 per cent.

He made more money from lectures than from books (during the Civil War the book royalties virtually collapsed). He called his $1000 check for *Parnassus* the largest he had ever had from writing. When William Henry Furness paid him $1200 for six lectures in Philadelphia, he exclaimed, "What a swindle!" but he did even better than that on the courses James T. Fields managed for him in Boston. Such earnings were exceptional, however, for there were times when he received only $10 for a lecture, or even less.

He professed no "genius in economy" nor capacity to under-stand accounts, and his son did not think him a wise bargainer in his own behalf. When he tried to bargain he felt cheap after-ward, and even in 1870 he said that he always spent more than he earned. Yet he had his triumphs. He lost money on railroad stock, and it is said that he would have been pinched during his last years without the wise management of his son-in-law, William H. Forbes. On the other hand, he spent $3500 to buy a house which is said to have cost $7800 to build, afterward increasing his land holdings considerably (in 1844 he bought eleven acres on the shore of Walden Pond at $8.10 an acre), and in 1848, when he asked the Fitchburg Railroad to pay for the destruction of a woodlot which he believed had been fired by sparks from a locomotive, they did it!

Emerson abjured all otherworldly cant about money. He wished, and he thought any man who respected himself must wish, to be "self-sustained." In his eyes poverty was demoraliz-ing, and to spend without earning was the "doctrine of the snake." A man must earn a living because it was incumbent upon him to be a producer as well as a consumer. Sane men do not desire gold for its own sake, but for the sake of the benefits it can procure, among them freedom and beauty.

Success consists in close appliance to the laws of the world, and since those laws are intellectual and moral, an intellectual and moral obe-dience. Political Economy is as good a book wherein to read the life of man and the ascendency of laws over all private and hostile influences, as any Bible which has come down to us.

He believed that we ought to spend our money on what in-terests us, "buying *up* and not *down*," never subscribing at the insistence of others and never giving where we do not wish to give. His "Are they *my* poor?" in "Self-Reliance" is brutal, but in practice Emerson generally answered in the affirmative. In his eyes a "rich" man was, among other things, one capable of assisting his friends. Emerson was never a sentimentalist, but few men of his limited means can ever have given more generously.

Furthermore, he knew how to receive graciously as well as to give. Abel Adams sent Edward to college because he thought he had given his father bad advice about investments, but the great gift Emerson received was after the burning of his house. He had always been wary of such things. "It is not the office of a man to receive gifts. How dare you give them? We wish to be self-sustained . . . to bestow." Now the flow was in the other direction for a change, and, with one eye on the Great Fire of 1871, he wondered whether he and his family had become another Chicago! But he accepted gracefully, without servility and without hauteur—"Are my friends bent on killing me with kindness?"—and he seems to have had no more financial worries during the last decade of his life.

V

Emerson's real ambition, however—if the word can be used in this sense at all—was for spiritual insight, and neither his attitude toward himself nor his famous gospel of Self-Reliance can be understood without some grasp of his attitude toward intuition. Like Meister Eckhardt, he might have said, "I have a power in my soul which enables me to perceive God." This power—the "ark of God" in every human breast, transcending the rational understanding—was non-material, co-existent with mind itself, and the basis of all moral sensitivity. Certainly Emerson believed in it long before he ever heard of transcendentalism, which was a word he never cared for much anyway; he was amused when one man defined it as "operations on the teeth," while another thought it was a nickname given by those who stayed behind to the others who had gone on ahead.

Of course this does not mean that his perceptions functioned in a vacuum. He made the extreme statement that everything done naturally was well done, and he tended to value the testimony of tradition less than the apprehension of the moment because the witness of the latter was immediate and in that sense of unquestionable authenticity.

> This shining moment is an edifice
> Which the Omnipotent cannot rebuild.

But he was never under the delusion that either distance or proximity determined intrinsic value. Actually such things were of no importance. The soul recognized its predestined food on sight, and men who had been dead for thousands of years might well mean more to us than those we lived with. It would not have disturbed him to be told that his own perceptions had been influenced not only by the Bible and the Christian tradition upon which he had been reared, but by Oriental seers, medieval and seventeenth-century mystics, and a variety of contemporary and near-contemporary philosophers who emphasized dynamism and organicism, eclecticism and experimental philosophy. He was only seventeen when he learned from Richard Price that our conceptions of good and evil are innate, and Jonathan Edwards himself might have taught him that "inclination" was more determinative than either formulated codes or the conscious will.

Whatever may be suggested to us from without, however, nothing can have any meaning for us until we have felt its truth and reality within ourselves. Moreover, there can be no perception without consanguinity between perceiver and perceived; that is why the existence of a spiritually minded man makes it necessary for us to believe that the universe is spiritual also.

In a way, all this implies, further, the faith that whatever we need, whatever belongs to us, will come to us and abide with us, and that nothing and nobody can take it away. Awareness, readiness, expectancy is all; our best insights involve no effort. We cannot predetermine what we are going to think; this is determined for us by the facts of the case under consideration and our own temperament; what we need to learn is how to stand out of the way and allow forces greater than our own partial personalities to operate through us.

The glorification of spontaneity here involved might well lead an unfriendly critic to object that Emerson's perceptions were all printed on tickets stamped "Good for This Trip and Train Only." Thus his study of Plato has been called inadequate on the ground that he did not submit himself to a Platonic kind of discipline, and it is a little startling to have Charles Lowell Young note that Emerson lays less stress on discipline than even Montaigne. He must have amused the audience to whom he was reading an old sermon when he stopped to announce that the sentence he had just read he no longer believed. Yet the act was in character; to anchor himself permanently to any proposition, whether framed by himself or another, would have been to cut the umbilical cord along which flows the current of the spiritual and intellectual life. Thus, while John Morley may have exaggerated when he said that Emerson "holds [that] our moral nature is vitiated by any interference with our will," it must be admitted that Emerson gave occasion for the exaggeration by placing so much more emphasis upon "impulsive innocence" than upon the strength to resist temptation. Certainly he did believe that the truly good man is good because he lives in harmony with the deepest impulses of his own moral being, and not because he superimposes an alien code upon a nature "naterally wicious." [13]

After the storm precipitated by his Divinity School Address,

Emerson refused to discuss the issues involved with Henry Ware, describing himself as " 'a chartered libertine,' " incapable of methodical writing, "free to worship and to rail," unable to give an account of himself when challenged, and with no intention of defending his thesis against all comers, though no less determined to express his convictions. This is indeed to write "Whim" on the lintel of the doorposts, as "Self-Reliance" advises, yet what else was there for him to say, believing, as he did, that "the children of gods never argue," that Jesus "simply affirmed," and that truth itself ceases to be truth when stated polemically? [14]

Perhaps the most suggestive consideration of spontaneity in Emerson's poetry is in "The Problem," and this is quite as extreme and implicational as the most confirmed Emersonian might ask for. He begins by acknowledging the lure of ecclesiasticism:

> I like a church; I like a cowl;
> I love a prophet of the soul;
> And on my heart monastic aisles
> Fall like sweet strains, or pensive smiles;
> Yet not for all his faith can see
> Would I that cowlèd churchman be.
>
> Why should the vest on him allure,
> Which I could not on me endure?

This is the problem of the poem, but, characteristically, the question posed is never directly answered. Instead, Emerson goes off on what at first seems a complete tangent by discussing Phidias, the Delphic oracle, "the burdens of the Bible," and St. Peter's Cathedral.

> The litanies of nations came,
> Like the volcano's tongue of flame,
> Up from the burning core below,—
> The canticles of love and woe:
> The hand that rounded Peter's dome

> And groined the aisles of Christian Rome
> Wrought in a sad sincerity;
> Himself from God he[15] could not free;
> He builded better than he knew;—
> The conscious stone to beauty grew.

In other words, great achievement, in art and in religion, comes not "from a vain or shallow thought," but from inspiration, love, and passion. But having made this point (if it has been made), Emerson next appears to be carrying us still farther afield by turning to nature—

> Know'st thou what wove yon woodbird's nest
> Of leaves and feathers from her breast?—

after which we are told that "such and so grew these holy piles," that is, the Parthenon, the Pyramids, the English abbeys, and other comparable creations.

> For out of Thought's[16] interior sphere
> These wonders rose to upper air;
> And Nature gladly gave them place,
> Adopted them into her race,
> And granted them an equal date
> With Andes and with Ararat.
>
> These temples grew as grows the grass;
> Art might obey, but not surpass.
> The passive Master lent his hand
> To the vast soul that o'er him planned;
> And the same power that reared the shrine
> Bestrode the tribes that knelt within.

In the last analysis, then, nature, art, and the universe itself are in perfect harmony. The laws by which great art is created are one with those which govern nature herself (the woodbird, the shellfish, and "the sacred pine tree"), and if religion is to have any reality, the same spontaneity must prevail here. "The wind bloweth where it listeth, and thou hearest the sound thereof, but canst not tell whence it cometh, and whither it goeth; so is every one that is born of the Spirit." Hence the seductive appeal of church and cowl, however great or picturesque, must be resisted.

And yet, for all his faith could see,
I would not the good bishop be.

Emerson believed that every man has a vocation and that his talent was his call, but he tends to ignore such dull facts as that even the chosen must test and validate their election, and one wonders whether he was sufficiently aware that, in art specifically, even appreciation needs to be nurtured and guided, since, left to themselves, most people like bad art much better than good and relish the greatest art least of all. Yet we must not forget that he once astonished his wife by stopping a game which she had permitted the children to play when they were kept indoors on a rainy Sunday and that, when he was an old man, he astonished everybody by voting to retain compulsory chapel at Harvard.

Here again, however, the apparent inconsistency is consistent, and Emerson shrank from a too rigid or logical application of his own principles. "Life is a train of moods like a string of beads, and as we pass through them they prove to be many-colored lenses which paint the world with their own hue, and each shows only what lies in its focus." He believed that there is an "optical illusion" about every person we meet and that we have no means of correcting our own distorting lenses. "Perhaps these subject-lenses have a creative power; perhaps there are no objects." But this disturbed him less because he knew it applied not only to intuition, but to purely physical perception (if there is such a thing) as well. "I know that the world I converse with in the city and in the farms, is not the world I *think*." Thus the doctrine of "accommodation" which Calvin developed with reference to theological matters was, in a sense, extended by Emerson to the whole of life.

In the usual sense of the term, Emerson did not believe in what the orthodox Christian calls "revelation." "The secret of heaven is kept from age to age," and there is no drawing back the veil from the other side. "No imprudent, no sociable angel ever dropt an early syllable to answer the longings of saints, the fears of mortals." In a sense, this is no loss. "God never speaks by a third person" because "he is nearer than the nearest." As this works out in practice, however, it is not completely satisfactory, for Emerson never had, nor did he pretend to have had, a deep mystical experience. He was only enough of a mystic to be sure the mystics were right; thus in a sense he was obliged to take mystical awareness on faith, much as other people take the creeds, and he himself remarked that he believed few Christians had never doubted their creed. In 1826 he wrote Aunt Mary of insignificant moments of prescience he had experienced, stirring his wonder and his conscience, experiences of no particular dignity or philosophical weight, but, he thought, carrying conviction for the individual to whom they came. He speaks of Swedenborg's having seen God for "a fluid moment," but his own essay on Swedenborg is one of his least satisfying performances, for he finds so much fault with the seer's claims to special or esoteric knowledge that one wonders why he chose to treat him as the representative mystic. But probably he would not have done much better with another visionary, for he dismisses Socrates, Plotinus, Boehme, Bunyan, Fox, Pascal, and Guyon in this same aspect, all with a slight wave of the hand, and he praises Plato for the very reason that "he never writes in ecstasy, or catches us up into poetic raptures." As for himself, he was always a believer in Unity, and yet, as he says, he beheld two.[17]

VI

"Self-Reliance," "History," and "The Oversoul" are perhaps Emerson's most characteristic essays, outlining his beliefs about man himself and about his relations with other men and with the universe. It would not be too much to call him the prophet of the self, but this is not to consider him an egotist as that term is commonly employed. To be sure, he understood the importance of self-reliance even upon the ordinary, as distinguished from the transcendental, level. He had an important work to do in the world, and he was determined to guard the leisure he needed to do it and to allow nothing and nobody to stand in his way. Once he declared that a man cannot follow his genius if at the same time he is trying to get rich or be a good son or a good husband, which, harsh as it sounds, is, when you think of it, very much what Christ had said before him. Great men fascinated Emerson from childhood, and when he was twenty he felt like crying out to Time an imperious demand to stop in his course and allow him an opportunity to share in human development. As a young pastor, he craved eloquence and the power to move men's souls and dreamed of the possibility of other callings, such as novelist, painter, or scientist. In his old age, he read his own forgotten books and admired them. He admitted too that he forgot and disregarded all the harsh things that had been said about him, but remembered all the praise. I cannot find that in practice he ever made a sacrifice of his family, but it may be worth remembering that when he married Lydia Jackson, he was quite emphatic in his refusal to live in

Plymouth, on the ground that he could not write there. Ink-stand would not budge; therefore there was no help for it but Lydia must desert Plymouth Rock for Concord Bridge! I know of no writer who was guilty of fewer expressions of temper or wounded self-esteem than Emerson, but I should hesitate to say that he had no capacity for these things. He was not considerate of young William Dean Howells when he dismissed Poe as "the jingle man" after Howells had mentioned him. He was pettish too at a later date when Howells, as editor of the *Atlantic*, rejected a poem by another hand which Emerson had recommended, and he compelled him to break up the form and return a contribution of his own when, because of his own delay in making up his mind about it, Howells had been compelled to carry it over for a month.

This much in the way of self-reliance and self-assertion might have been achieved without metaphysic. Nevertheless the metaphysic was there. Emerson's son once said that in moments of weakness his father longed for a master, but all his theory was against this. He believed that individuals must be outgrown and that even great and good men may become dangerous through overinfluence. Religion itself must be indigenous; imitation is suicide. "It seems as if, when the Spirit of God speaks so plainly to each soul, it were an impiety to be listening to one or another saint." In the poem "Sursum Corda," individuality must be maintained against heaven itself, or what seems heaven to the conventionally minded, at any rate. It is true that "our souls are not self-fed," and that culture serves as an important ballast against egotism, yet the whole value of history and biography alike was to increase self-trust. Since Emerson believed in the unity of all life, he could not but believe that all history can be explained—and must be understood—in terms of the individual experience. "The great are our better selves, ourselves with advantages"; in history, as in society, we seek but to find our-

selves in other minds. And since like cannot reveal itself to unlike, no fact can be either credible or intelligible save as it cor-
responds to something within the reader or hearer. What Shakespeare writes of the king is true also of the boy who reads
Shakespeare; otherwise neither Shakespeare nor the king could
have any meaning for him. "The picture waits for my verdict;
it is not to command me, but I am to settle its claims to praise."
Greatness is "the fulfilment of a natural tendency in each man,"
and the first form in which it can appear is self-respect; without
this, without discovering your own bias and obeying it as if it
were a magnetic needle, nothing can be achieved. The uninitiated
often tend to be disappointed upon their first contact with a
great work of art because they had expected to encounter
something radically different from everything that is normal
and universal. But this is not what genius creates. Genius owes
its power to the access it commands to the Universal Mind; because it expresses something greater than the narrow individuality of its possessor, we are able to find ourselves in great artists,
recognizing in them a larger portion of our own humanity than
we ourselves have been able to command. If Emerson had been
given to Irish bulls, he might well have said that a genius is like
other people, only more so.

From all this there follows inevitably the great statement:
"To believe in your own thought, to believe that what is true
for you in your private heart is true for all men—that is genius."
Greatness is "the fulfilment of a natural tendency in each man,"
and the first form in which it must appear is self-respect. Life is
a trial of strength between men and events, but it is also true
that multiplicity is always rushing to be resolved into unity.
Probably the only reason concentration is not fatal, in spite of
its narrowing effect, is that it leads toward knowing a subject
thoroughly, and you cannot do that without knowing it in relation to everything else. This shows even in language, in the ir-

resistible tendency toward tropes. "A happy symbol is a sort of evidence that your thought is just." [18]

Should it be asked at this point why Emerson encourages me to prefer my truth to another's truth—say that of a church or a creed—the answer must be that, in the ordinary sense, this is not what he does at all. In the nature of the case, my truth cannot be superior to another's, for all truth is one. But it *is* the only truth of which I have had, or can have, direct, first-hand experiential knowledge; if I cannot recognize truth here, I shall surely not recognize it elsewhere. Even the Bible asks how a man who does not love his brother, whom he has seen, can possibly love God, whom he has not seen. Emerson always recognized the distorting possibilities of self. He was not arrogant about his own perceptions even in literary matters; when a friend (probably Lowell) undervalued Thoreau, he found it necessary to re-read his old neighbor in order to renew his faith in him. But he was perpetually impressed by the fact that if life is one, it is also infinitely varied; nature never repeats herself. "Every man is a new method and distributes things anew." We did not make ourselves, and even our peculiarities are in a sense a gift. Some distortion or imperfection appears in every standard, and since imitation can never surpass its model, the imitator inevitably limits himself to the second-rate. In this respect it was easier for the ancients than it is for us; they had fewer models to go by. "The soul of God is poured into the world through the thoughts of men," and if I stifle the light that shines from within myself, it will be lost to the world forever, and along with it the service God expected it to perform. I cannot excuse myself by pleading that I have helped preserve the truth perceived and proclaimed by Moses or Buddha or Jesus Christ, which there are many others to understand quite as well as I do. In a sense, this is Emerson's conception of the sin against the Holy Ghost, though I do not recall that he ever calls it that. He does define sin as being untrue to one's own constitution however. For so long as God is thought of as wholly external to the soul, worship involves self-violation and therefore meets with resistance. Vital religion can only begin when a man begins to arrive at his convictions by exploring his own consciousness.

But we have not yet come to the heart of Emersonian self-reliance. As his son says, "the self he refers to is the higher self, man's share of divinity." He believed in the existence of One Mind, whose potentialities were available to all and to which the individual mind aspired to expand. In his view, the self-reliant man lived with God, independent of men's opinions.[19] Once he calls man "God impure"; elsewhere God becomes "the unity of men." But if we cherish our peculiarities because God created them and planned to give the world something precious through them, we must also remember that those actions which proceed from individuality alone are bound to be shallow and awkward. For himself, Emerson hailed the divinity in his heart in the same breath with which he prayed never to lose sight of his own dependence and nothingness. In the poem "Pan" even prophets and heroes are significant only as "pipes through which the breath of Pan doth blow."

He believed that the great man subsumes his times, but he believed more than that. He was convinced that a man can achieve both energy and insight beyond the familiar "by abandonment to the nature of things" and drawing upon the life of the universe itself, for this is the Power "which abides in no man and in no woman but for a moment speaks from this one, and for another moment from that one." More significantly still, he believed that the essential man, like the essential universe, is good, and that evil is a warping, virtually extraneous quality. Thus, to surrender to life means to surrender to goodness, and "a bolder spirit" is "a more surrendered soul, more informed and led by God."

This is not all starry idealism, for Emerson well knew that, as commonly conceived, self might be either God or devil. He once said that he believed not in two classes, but in two moods of men—"Philip drunk and Philip sober"—and no Calvinist ever saw more clearly the presence of a double consciousness in man nor the necessity to choose between "the erring passionate mortal" and the "supreme calm immortal." He varied from time to time in his notion of the means to be employed to bring about the full unfolding of human nature in the "walking monsters" that most men are now, but he was never unaware of the necessity of resisting temptation and obeying the higher self, and he was wholly Kantian when he wrote that the moral discipline of life is based on the perpetual conflict between the universal ideal and the selfish desires of the individual. Thus, self-dependence becomes at last dependence upon God (who alone is self-dependent and self-sufficient), and "only by the supernatural is man strong." [20]

Since Emerson was himself a writer, he could not have avoided applying all these ideas to his writing. In his eyes, the writer was not wholly the creator of his work; it would have less value if he were. The good writer "writes for the love of truth and beauty, and not with ulterior ends." A writer has, indeed, a double dependence: upon the eternal verities whence he draws his inspiration and upon the community which he addresses. "Just as in receiving his first intuition," wrote Vivian C. Hopkins, "so now in imparting the vision, he must not let the will come between the idea and the expression." Man's "privity" echoes the universe, and great men are less "original," in the vulgar sense of the term, than lesser men, who are often off the beam. Great works of art, consequently, share the inevitability of life itself, and nobody ever called the *Apollo Belvedere* "a fancy piece" or speculated about how the *Laocoön* might be improved. Thus, "the saint and the poet seek privacy to ends the most public and universal." Self-abnegation (and self-fulfillment) could hardly go further than Emerson's statement, "That is the best part of each writer which has nothing private in it; that which he does not know; that which flowed out of his constitution and not from his too active invention." The best writing (as in the English Bible) is a kind of communal composition, and it is Shakespeare's greatness that he has no peculiarities, curiosities, egotisms, or importunate topics; "he is wise without emphasis or assertion; he is strong, as nature is strong." Once Emerson reported that there were passages in his old letters that seemed to him quite as inspired as Shakespeare, but he made it clear that the power he felt here was no personal power. When he compared himself with others as an individual, he was humble, but when he remembered that he was an immortal child of God, receiving his endowments from God, and with an immortal destiny, he could perceive no reason why he should bow his head before any man. Similarly, he liked his poems better than his prose, because it seemed to him that in them he had achieved greater universality of utterance.[21] In other words, it was as true for Emerson the writer as it was for the man that the more he lost his life, the more completely he found it.

One final question about Emersonian self-reliance cannot be avoided. Not only have his critics brought it up again and again, but he himself anticipated them. Can his precepts not be used by the unscrupulous to justify selfishness and self-indulgence, or, as Emerson puts it, may we not expect that "the bold sensualist will use the name of philosophy to gild his crimes"?

Some aspects of this question can best be considered later, in other connections. At this point, I think we must recognize frankly that the famous essay has its dangerous aspects. But is not the same thing true of many statements in the New Testament? and have not these too often been made use of by stupid or ill-advised persons, with disastrous results? Can this kind of thing be altogether avoided in any literature which does more than scratch the surface of life?

Emerson was well aware that "ignorant people confound reverence for the intuitions with egotism" and recognized a distinction between will and willfulness. Will must be built on the reason of things, reconciling the individual with the universal, recognizing that "that can never be good for the bee which is bad for the hive." An intelligent man must achieve a certain objectivity even in self-observance. "To be isolated is to be sick, and in so far, dead. The life of the All must stream through us to make the man and the moment great." Men write from aspiration as well as from experience, and they paint the qualities they would like to express. "We perish, and perish gladly," writes Emerson, "if the law remains. I hope it is conceivable that a man may go to ruin gladly, if he see that thereby no shade falls on that he loves and adores." And this is not far from the Calvinistic willingness to be damned for the glory of God.

Emerson does not always spell out these distinctions clearly, or state his implied reservations specifically, and nobody can deny that individual utterances can be found in his writings which it would be quite fair to call wrong-headed or absurd. Nevertheless, everything I have written here was a part of his mind, and what I have said is true of his mind as a whole.

When, in 1924, Richard Loeb and Nathan F. Leopold, Jr., murdered little Bobby Franks for a thrill and attempted vainly to commit the "perfect" crime, there was wide speculation about whether they had been influenced by the glorification of the superman and various immoralities and amoralities in the literature they had been reading. With literate young criminals, it is always difficult to rule out such possibilities entirely. Moreover, even those who do not read often breathe in such ideas "from the air." Emerson's friend Carlyle was a hero in Nazi Germany, where Nietzsche, who had his Emersonian aspects, was also sometimes admired, and writers like Yvor Winters and Quentin Anderson have tried to give Emerson a share of responsibility for the excesses of such later writers as Hart Crane, Robinson Jeffers, Henry Miller, and Allen Ginsberg. But does anybody really believe that the Third Reich would have been different if neither Nietzsche nor Carlyle had ever lived? Life is always much more corrupt than art, and pornography in fiction and drama would simply starve to death if it did not correspond to either the taste or the habits of the people who support it. Corruption may come from without or from within; Emerson admittedly concerned himself much more with the former than the latter danger. I confess I find it difficult to believe that one who could resist the temptations of living in this wicked world would be very likely to be corrupted by the wildest exaggerations in "Self-Reliance," even when taken out of context and misinterpreted.

If intuition was the source of the Emersonian man's spiritual perceptions, and consequently of his self-reliance, this was a natural gift, and nature, by any definition, or his relationship to nature, was a powerful factor in it. Another important source of nourishment was art, and if you were a writer, as Emerson was, then art also became your own medium of expression.

But the artist was a man as well as a writer—not a writer, said Emerson, but a "man writing"—and a man lives with other men and women in society at large and in the world of closer personal relations.

Exploring all these aspects in the course of succeeding chapters will take us pretty far along the road in our study of Emerson's character and personality.

CHAPTER TWO

NATURE

I

In his early days, Emerson once wrote Aunt Mary that he had found enjoyment but not inspiration in the woods. She said, "You should have gone alone," and from that time, says his son, he went almost daily. Once he complained to Margaret Fuller that she went to nature "rather for pleasurable excitement than with a deep poetic feeling."

> The gods talk in the breath of the woods,
> They talk in the shaken pine,
> And fill the long reach of the old seashore
> With dialogue divine;
> And the poet who overhears
> Some random word they say
> Is the fated man of men
> Whom the ages must obey.[1]

Some commentators have played down Emerson's actual enjoyment of nature, but this is ill-advised. It is true that he never achieved quite Thoreau's intimacy. Thoreau, to his way of thinking, spent too much time in the wilderness; if God had meant him to live in a swamp, Emerson told him, He would have made him a frog.[2] Emerson himself cared more for a semi-domesticated nature than he did for the wilds. For all that, he thought a man should live close enough to nature so that he would not need clocks and almanacs to tell him the hour or the season, and he was capable of finding the world so beautiful that he could hardly believe it real. Though he was an "indifferent botanist," he loved flowers—wild flowers especially (he was inclined to complain that his wife's bulbs encroached upon his vegetables!).[3] He loved "yellow days," not "white days" when there was a film over the sun. There is one passage in which he suggests that his enjoyment of nature may have faded as he grew older, but he seems not to have done himself justice in this regard.

He was a good sailor, who enjoyed even his first rough voyage to England,[4] and he was ecstatic in his appreciation of both the sight and the sound of the sea when he stayed alone at Nantasket Beach in 1841, especially enjoying the horizon, which was never visible in Concord. He pitied Dr. Johnson for his blindness to the beauty of mountains, and certainly there can be no question about his relish of his own "camel's hump," his Concord woodlots. John Muir, who met him in the Yosemite, thought him the first visitor who had ever sufficiently admired the pine trees, and his passion for New England's white pine was sufficiently well known so that when the "Concord Edition" was in preparation, Mrs. Alice Stone was employed to draw a picture of this tree which displaced Houghton Mifflin Company's familiar Piper as a printer's device on the title page. Emerson's own praise of the pine in "Woodnotes" is familiar, and there are prose rhapsodies on summer and Indian summer in the Divinity School Address and in "Nature" in Essays, Second Series.

He had an interest in gardening also, to which he credited a cathartic value, though he does not seem to have been very good at it (Waldo was afraid he would "dig his leg" when he was hoeing). As he himself said, he was created "a seeing eye, and not a useful hand." More harshly, he speaks of his "imbecile hands," says that he could split a shingle four ways with a single nail, and compares the garden itself to a dangerous machine which could catch up a workman in an industrial plant and destroy him. Despite his deficiencies, he apparently did not give up gardening entirely, since as late as 1863 he claimed to be as much encumbered with spring planting as any farmer could be. Certainly he loved to see trees planted, and before he had finished, he had increased his two-acre Concord lot to nine acres and become responsible for the production of many apples, pears, and strawberries.[5]

In Emerson's mind, however, our relationship with nature was far too vital a matter to be apprehended wholly in terms of our enjoyment. He did not think of man as the sole object of nature —for that would have made the means seem grossly disproportionate to the end sought—but even as a young clergyman he assumed that the God of the Bible and nature's God were one and cited Saint Paul's testimony to support this view. He lived in a universe in which the same laws govern matter and spirit and, for that matter, even political economy. Man expresses immaterialities by figures drawn from common and even occupational interests, and a spiritually minded man may read the Gospel in chemistry.

> There was never mystery
>   But 't is figured in the flowers;
> Was never secret history
>   But birds tell it in the bowers.[6]

Nature, then, is "a metaphor of the human mind" and "the symbol of spirit," and the universe represents "the externization of the soul." "Particular natural facts are symbols of particular spiritual facts," and every fact carries the sense of the whole. So "nature is as truly beautiful as it is good, or as it is reasonable," and, as "The Problem" makes clear, nature, art, and religion are fundamentally in harmony. We can work effectively only through enlisting her forces, and unless our works are in harmony with her, she will destroy them. Even roads and cities must follow her lines.

"As truly beautiful as it is good." Then, "all high beauty has a moral element in it." What else can you say if, like Emerson, you see the world as "not the product of manifold power, but of one will, of one mind"? You cannot "vote down gravitation of morals," for "the blood" itself is "moral; the blood is anti-slavery." So he wrote in abolition days, for once identifying an immediate cause with the eternal verities. Therefore an immoral law was a perversion of nature; it was upon this basis that he justified disobedience of the Fugitive Slave Law.[7]

In "Woodnotes," nature is faithful to all who trust her, and Emerson's beloved white pine becomes a symbol of nature and of the man who lives in harmony with her. (The "unbound, un-rhymed" man is out of touch with the universe.) Nature cleanses from sin also, in opposition to the orthodox Christian view that this can be accomplished only through Divine Grace, by which man is enabled to rise above nature.

> Come, lay thee in my soothing shade,
> And heal the hurts which sin has made.[8]

Emerson does not leave these views quite unqualified, how-ever. One can follow him without too much difficulty when he writes that "God is the all-fair. Truth, and goodness, and beauty, are different faces of the same All." [9] But when he adds that "beauty in nature is not ultimate," one cannot but note that, though he may call beauty an end in itself, by the time he has finished giving his allegiance to it, it has ceased to be beauty alone, and not all his protestations that he takes an epicure's pleasure in nature, or that he plays with it, not always searching it for a sign, can modify this impression.[10] On the whole, he seems to do better when interpreting his gospel in the large. Hardly anybody will agree with him that both good and evil are instantly requited in this world. "Thefts never enrich; alms never impoverish; murder will speak out of stone walls." Yet one may still well believe with him that "the moral sense is always supported by the permanent interest of the parties," that whatever a man does, he does to himself, and that the ultimate, inescapable penalty of evil lies in being possessed by it and not in anything that may be done to you from the outside on account of it. And if these things are true, then, in a profound sense, we do live, as Emerson believed, in a moral universe.

Sometimes he qualifies by postulating only "a small excess of good" in the nature of things. "Things work to their ends, not to yours," and destiny is stern, sometimes even cruel, while pursuing benevolent ends.

> There are two laws discrete,
> Not reconciled,—
> Law for man, and law for thing.[11]

Sometimes he goes further than this. In "The Method of Nature" he sees phenomena as "discontented and insatiable," clamoring for attention, intruding themselves upon us when our attention should be fixed on higher things. This, presumably, is what he meant when he wrote Margaret Fuller that even nature got between him and the world of the spirit, preventing him from being "alone with the Alone." And in the essay "Nature" he says bluntly that nature does not keep her promises to us. "We live in a system of approximations." There is disappointment in every landscape, and our arts are only suggestive. It cannot be that there is "pure malignity" in nature. To believe that would be atheism. But he is tempted when he asks, "Must we not suppose somewhere in the universe a slight treachery or disillusion"?

The truth is that Emerson refuses to sum up either nature or man's relation to her in a formula. He is attracted by both monism and dualism. Sometimes God is almost identified with nature, but generally nature seems to be the "Not-Me," serving as a kind of medium between God and the soul.[12] She sets man an example, as in the Goethean

> Teach me your mood, O patient stars!
>   Who climb each night the ancient sky,
> Leaving no space, no shade, no scars,
>   No trace of age, no fear to die.[13]

She gives him strength also:

> For Love draws might from terrene force
> And potencies of sky.[14]

Yet in the last analysis he is greater than she is, though he cannot get along without her as his theater.

> Monadnoc is a mountain strong,
> Tall and good my kind among;
> But well I know, no mountain can,
> Zion or Meru, measure with man.[15]

As he is "the compend of time," so also is man nature's correlative, and his imagination can shape even her tragedies and terrors into beauty. In the last analysis, nothing is known of her but what he perceives, and she, presumably, knows nothing of herself at all. "Nature always wears the colors of the spirit."

As "a projection of God in the unconscious," nature is inevitably "a remoter and inferior incarnation" of the Divine than that which has been achieved in man. So Emerson was tempted to pity a tree as some people pity a noble animal for the inescapable limitations of his being. Yet, by the same token, nature holds one advantage over man. In the Bible, and in *Paradise Lost*, nature fell along with man, but not in Emerson, and when Robert Frost wrote that to err was human, and not to, animal, he was a good Emersonian. The projection which divinity has achieved into human consciousness, though higher in itself than what has been achieved in nature, is, for that very reason, flawed by the consideration that human beings possess independent, and therefore often necessarily distracting and obscuring, human wills. Not being subjected to such distortion, the "serene order" of God's self-revelation in nature is "inviolable by us." As far as it goes, it stands therefore as the present, immediate, and infallible "expositor of the divine mind." This is its importance and, for us, its value.

II

Norman Foerster finds that Emerson mentions about twoscore birds in his poems, with the chickadee easily the favorite. Otherwise, animals seem to have contributed less to his enjoyment of nature than is the case with many nature lovers. The Emersons did keep dogs and cats, and at one time a parrot, but we hear little about them. Though he praises the dog as a companion in walking, Emerson seems to have cared more for the grace and beauty of the cat, but apparently he did not care much to handle any animal, and the most detailed descriptions of animal behavior in his journals concern frogs and the parrot. He speaks of snakes with the horror they commonly inspire—"I escape from the writing-desk as from a snake"—and admired insects most when they were flying *away* from his garden.

He was contemptuous of boxing and billiards, and when he was in the Yosemite he saw no sense in the climbing aspirations of younger members of the party. His daughter said he never saw a playing card in his life. He was fascinated by the famous horse-trainer, John S. Rarey, from whom he thought teachers might learn a good deal about proper relations with their pupils. His son has recorded that once when he came home from a horseback ride, his father stopped him, took the horse, and rode off into the twilight, and adds that this was the only time he could remember ever seeing him on horseback. There are references elsewhere to his riding with his daughters however, and he certainly rode in the Yosemite. He skated with his children at Walden when he was fifty; earlier, when he skated with her husband, Mrs. Hawthorne thought Emerson the less graceful skater of the two, but she was not an unprejudiced witness. It is amusing to learn that in San Francisco in 1871, he and a Concord girl skater, doing their stuff in public at the same hour, exchanged tickets, she assuring him that if he came late, she would repeat her performance for him.

He fished, at least on occasion; one day he caught two haddock, a cod, a flounder, a pollock, and a perch! Edward says he could swim strongly and well, but cared for swimming only on very hot days. However, he jumped into the ocean at Nantasket as soon as he got there in 1841, and in 1855 he offered Frank Bellew a dip in an extinct gravel pit during a walk near Walden, and when Bellew objected that they had no towels, he replied, "Oh, that is of no consequence; we can dry ourselves in the sun. I rarely trouble myself about towels."

Late in life, he went with a distinguished party on a camping trip in the Adirondacks. Longfellow, who had been invited to join, did not think it safe to go when he heard that Emerson was to carry a rifle, but he probably would not have gone anyway. Judge Hoar thought Emerson became a creditable woodsman, developing a shagginess worthy of a pirate. He took the discomforts of camping in his stride and apparently had no objection to appearing ridiculous. Nor does he seem to have been proof against the blood lust of some of the other members of the party; though he did not kill a deer, it was ineptitude, not kindness of heart, that prevented him.[16] But Emerson's only real achievements in the world of the outdoors were as a pedestrian. In 1823 he walked from Roxbury, through Newton, Needham, and Natick, arriving at Framingham before noon. By evening he had reached Worcester, and he did not give up until he had arrived at South Brookfield, sixty miles from home. Though such achievements were obviously exceptional, we do hear of his walking from four to eight miles with his children of an afternoon.

III

Emerson's interest in science was not inconsiderable, but like everything else about him, it was a strictly Emersonian kind of interest. He was fond of meeting scientific men, talking with them and inspecting their instruments and apparatus, and he was friendly with Agassiz and other scientists, including his brother-in-law, Dr. Charles T. Jackson, chemist and geologist, who was one of the pioneers in the development of anesthesia.[17] He attended scientific lectures in Paris and a meeting of the Geological Society in London. In his essay on Swedenborg he mentions many scientists and achieves a kind of lay summary of scientific achievement up to his time, and after the Civil War he was almost ecstatic about recent scientific progress. Ecstatic too is his praise of Humboldt ("one of those wonders of the world, like Aristotle, like Julius Caesar, like the Admirable Crichton, who appear from time to time, as if to show us the possibilities of the human mind, the force and range of the faculties") and of Linnaeus, whom he lauds, especially in "Country Life," for his beneficent discoveries.

If there was any one science that interested him more than another, it must have been astronomy—always so unfailing in its appeal to spiritually minded men of imagination—from which he derived considerable poetic imagery. To his way of thinking, a sight of the stars was a sure means of calling men off from vulgar things and inducing "a dignity of mind and an indifference to death." He speculated over the possible astronomical usages of Stonehenge, a subject which others were to pursue after him. The compass fascinated him; it was, he said, like holding "the god in my hand." Late in life he used a small legacy to buy a good telescope.

It could hardly have been expected that a man who read "for lustres" even in his own field would develop anything like what a trained scientist might regard as "method" in his scientific investigations. But one must not take him too literally when he says, for example, that he is repelled by physicists and prefers anecdotes about "men of ideas."

Emerson seems to have done his most diligent reading in the scientific field around the time he was planning to resign from Second Church. The thing that has been discussed most is his attitude toward evolution, to which he was in some sense committed long before Darwin made it popular—and controversial.

> The next into the farthest brings,
> And, striving to be man, the worm
> Mounts through all the spires of form.[18]

He interpreted Lamarck as saying to the caterpillar, "How dost thou, Brother! Please God, you shall yet be a philosopher," and he himself, visiting the Jardin des Plantes in Paris in 1833 was "moved to strange sympathies," feeling an occult relationship between himself and the lowest forms of life.[19] The general view still seems to be that Emerson's science, "largely deductive

in its theoretical base," was "pre-Darwinian and concerned itself more with the classification than with the evolution of
natural phenomena," [20] though Harry Hayden Clark seems to
have accepted Pochmann's argument that Darwin, like Hegel,
became important during Emerson's later years. In Lafayette,
Indiana, for a lecture in 1860, Emerson was waiting eagerly for
access to a copy of *The Origin of Species*, and Frank Sanborn
quotes him as having said that Agassiz himself was really a
Darwinian and that his saying "We are not children of monkeys
but children of God" was petulant and unworthy of him. However Emerson's evolutionism be defined, it apparently comforted
him to think that creation had not yet been completed and that
the world was still "plastic and fluid in the hands of God." From
the beginning he was clear that science, which deals with processes, cannot touch religion, which exists in a world of values;
like John Fiske, Lyman Abbott, and others after him, he therefore perceived the futility of the whole silly "conflict between
science and religion."

In a sense, then, Emerson cared nothing about science for its
own sake; if he wished to learn the law governing the diffraction
of a ray, for example, it was because he hoped this might involve
a moral perception. "Natural History by itself has no value; it
is like a single sex, but marry it to human history and it is
poetry." It must be understood that this statement involves no
positive disparagement of science as such, for if science did not
interest Emerson in isolation, it did not, so far as he was concerned, exist in isolation either. For him the material world was
"emblematic," and man, who is both material and spiritual, stood
between two worlds, knowing that the material mirrors the
immaterial. Taken alone, science was merely sensual and therefore superficial. "The sciences, even the best,—mathematics and
astronomy,—are like sportsmen, who seize whatever prey offers,

even without being able to make any use of it." Viewed in relation to other things, however, its value was greatly enhanced, along with its capacity to explain man to himself. "So the very announcement of the theory of gravitation, of Kepler's three harmonic laws, and even of Dalton's doctrine of definite proportions, finds a sudden response in the mind, which remains a superior evidence to empirical demonstrations." In the last analysis it is the poet who understands, for he alone passes beyond mere phenomena to their significance. For "poet" one must of course read here "poet-prophet-philosopher," the wise man of spiritual insight who possesses a Sense of the Whole.[21]

Whether Emerson was right or wrong about this, it should be understood that what he believed was completely in harmony with his general mode of thought and with the whole bent of his mind and drift of his being. "Man is an analogist," he says; he even admired Alcott's school because he saw him showing children the symbolical character of all things. That the diamond and lampblack are made of the same substance differently arranged interested him not for its own sake but because it suggested the importance of composition.

Since the discovery of Oersted that galvanism and electricity and magnetism are only forms of one and the same force, and convertible each into the other, we have continually suggested to us a larger generalization: that each of the great departments of Nature—chemistry, vegetation, the animal life—exhibits the same laws on a different plane; that the intellectual and moral worlds are analogous to the material.

Edward Waldo Emerson was quite right, then, to speak of his father's using the facts of science "on another plane," with each new fact "a symbol awaiting interpretation." [22] Even mathematics, much as he disliked it, interested him in its use of tropes, and the experiments in "amelioration" made by the Belgian pomologist Van Mons bolstered his faith in compensation. He praised Swedenborg's *The Animal Kingdom* because it reconciled the long estranged worlds of science and the soul. "It was an anatomist's account of the human body in the highest style of poetry," and if Emersonianism has any validity at all, this is the only kind of account that could possibly have any value. Emerson was consistent again when, though he did not believe in alchemy and astrology, nor yet in phrenology and physiognomy, he had a sympathetic feeling for them because, unlike modern materialistic science, they assumed a relationship between the soul of man and the world which he inhabits. That there was such a relationship he was certain, though he had little faith in his own ability or in that of another to spell it out.

Applied science means technology; what Emerson saw of it may not greatly impress us today, but judged by the standards of his time it was considerable. He often refers to its wonders.

By his machines man can dive and remain under water like a shark; can fly like a hawk in the air; can see atoms like a gnat; can see the system of the universe like Uriel, the angel of the sun; can carry whatever loads a ton of coal can lift; can knock down cities with his fist of gunpowder; can recover the history of the race by the medals which the deluge, and every creature, civil or savage or brute, has involuntarily dropped of its existence; and divine the future possibility of the planet and its inhabitants by his perception of the laws of Nature.

And elsewhere:

By new arts the earth is subdued, roaded, tunnelled, telegraphed, gaslighted; vast amounts of old labor disused; the sinews of man being relieved by sinews of steam. We are on the brink of more wonders. The sun paints; presently we shall organize the echo as now we do the shadow. Chemistry is extorting new aids. The genius of this people, it is found, can do anything which can be done by men. These thirty nations are equal to any work, and every moment stronger.

Though his greatest interest is in the intellectual and (if the term be admissible) the spiritual aspects of science, there are times when he seems to relish technological power as much as it can be relished even by those who know nothing higher. "I love results," he says, "and hate abortions. I delight in people who do things." In "History" he lists some of the great inventors along with great scientists; in his paper on Michelangelo, he actually says that he values him because, besides his gifts as an artist, "he possessed an unexpected dexterity in minute mechanical contrivances"! Though Emerson saw an observatory as the most sublime of tools, he was also capable of being stimulated by the McCormick reaper; he, in a way, foresaw the phonograph; and in 1871 he penned a rhapsody on the glories of invention which is worthy to rank with Mark Twain's notorious birthday letter to Whitman.[23] To be sure he tries to spiritualize technology also and, in a measure, even succeeds in doing so. At its best, it represents "new combinations" of man's natural benefactors. No longer need man wait

for favoring gales, but by means of steam, he realizes the fable of Aeolus's bag, and carries the two and thirty winds in the boiler of his boat. To diminish friction, he paves the road with iron bars, and, mounting a coach with a ship-load of men, animals, and merchandise behind him, he darts through the country, from town to town, like an eagle or a swallow through the air.

At one point Emerson makes man's own body the "magazine of inventions" upon whose model everything else is drawn. "All this activity," he says, "has added to the value of life, and to the scope of the intellect." And "when its errands are noble and adequate, a steamboat bridging the Atlantic between Old and New England, arriving at its ports with the actuality of a planet, is a step of man into harmony with nature."

"When"! There must be times then when this is not the case, and the value of technology must therefore be sought beyond technology itself. The conclusion of "Resources" is hurried and unconvincing: "And the resources of America and its future will be immense only to wise and virtuous men." Emerson missed the boat by many miles when he told his readers that American resources were inexhaustible: "The material basis is of such extent that no folly of man can quite subvert it." If he could come back today, he would know that he had seriously underestimated the power of man's folly. The Atlantic cable was wonderful, and wonderful things were happening in medicine, but in a diabolical kind of way, the adulteration of food was wonderful too, and in a sense quite as natural.

Emerson was interested in the act of invention, which was an intellectual step, or series of steps, but the mere mechanical repetition which followed bored him. "I do not wish to do one thing but once," he said. He grasped the truth which some of us did not comprehend even when the United States outraged the moral sense of mankind by giving the supreme demonstration of it in all history, at Hiroshima and Nagasaki, that if man's moral development cannot keep pace with his intellectual and technological development, all his "progress" will prove self-destructive. An advance in art does not necessarily involve an advance in morals. Very great men have lived and died without technological know-how, but they could not have done so without cultivating the spiritual values which technology certainly did not create and toward which it sometimes seems to foster indifference. Moreover, tools can be reagents. "Machinery is aggressive. The weaver becomes a web, the machinist a machine. If you do not use the tools, they use you. All tools are in one sense edge-tools, and dangerous." No, technology creates no values. The best it can do is to provide new means and opportunities through which values can express themselves, and if these ways are not found, then technology becomes not a blessing, but a curse. "I cannot," says Emerson, "accept the railroad and telegraph in exchange for reason and charity." [24]

CHAPTER THREE

ART

I

Emerson's interest in the fine arts probably began with the pictures of cats and rats on the pocket handkerchief of his school chum, William Henry Furness, and was fostered by Furness's own drawings for Emerson's juvenile "Fortus." Furness says he never saw Emerson himself attempt to draw anything, "not even the conventional cat with the triangular face, which almost any boy or girl could do and does do." There are many drawings in his early journals, however, and his son, who credited him with a good sense of form but denied his sensitivity to color,[1] spoke of his drawing heads for his children. In the Boston of his early years, Emerson's contacts with the fine arts were necessarily limited, though he reveled in the Athenaeum collection of plaster casts of classical works of sculpture. His first important exposure to great originals came on his first journey to Europe. In Florence he met Horatio Greenough, with whom he seems to have discussed technical matters, and Greenough was not the only artist with whom he became acquainted.[2]

Raphael's *Transfiguration* seemed to him the greatest of all pictures; he had expected to be overwhelmed by beauty of color and form, but these things, fine as they were, were insignificant compared to the picture's homely reality and spiritual sublimity. Though he was sometimes tempted to consider Michelangelo grandiose, he was still tremendously impressed by him. Titian, handsome as his pictures were, he judged incapable of holding a candle to Raphael on the score of nobility. Later, in London, he was to be "modern" enough to praise Turner as having removed the curse of sterility from English art. Though art galleries always had a certain tendency to overwhelm him, he appreciated the necessity, utility, and significance of museums long before many of his contemporaries did, and when he was a figure of authority, he spoke at the meeting held to organize the Museum of Fine Arts in Boston. The last public address he composed was delivered at the unveiling of French's *Minute Man* at Concord Bridge, which has his famous quatrain about "the shot heard round the world" engraved upon its pedestal.

His standards of evaluation were the same for all the arts. For him art was not imitation, but creation and interpretation, not escape, but prophecy. Not an end in itself, it was a means of approach to something larger—the meaning and significance of life itself. At its best, it was more simple than dazzling, directing its appeal not to technical knowledge, but directly to the human heart. One could not well be more Platonic than to ask the painter of a bunch of grapes to show not those particular grapes alone, but the mind of nature as expressed in them.

He seems to have responded more to sculpture, especially Greek sculpture, than to painting. "Fancy paints," he wrote; "imagination sculptures." [3] He was tremendously impressed by the central figure in the Athenaeum cast of the *Laocoön*—the others, he said, had no value except in relation to it—and the work seemed to come to him like a gift from the Universal Mind. In Europe he found the *Venus de Medici* "the statue that enchants the world"; casts, he thought, gave no adequate idea of its beauty. But he did not want modern sculptors to imitate the Greeks; on this score he disparaged Thorwaldsen, whose *Christ* he did not admire. Michelangelo's *Moses* fascinated him because of its non-classical quality, though he could have done without the horns. Oddly enough, he liked Greenough's half-nude, toga-swathed *Washington*, which many rejected.

In architecture, Emerson valued the simplicity and integrity of the New England meetinghouse because they expressed the faith of the people who built it and the character of those who worshipped in it. Nevertheless, European churches convinced him of the poverty of the American imagination in this area. Greek temples he compared to geometry, while the Gothic style liberated the imagination. York Minster was "beautiful beyond belief," and Amiens Cathedral, in some respects, unmatched in France. He loved St. Peter's, and when the time came to leave Rome, he was sad that he would see it no more; St. Paul's, on the other hand, was a "show building," without moral interest, fit for New York. He admired the exterior of Notre Dame, but inside it was "quite naked and beggarly."

Despite his love for the Gothic, however, Emerson was not bound by it. Vivian C. Hopkins thinks his appreciation of Egyptian art manifested "a flexibility of taste" unusual in his time. In 1879, listing the types of architecture considered in current textbooks—Egyptian, Doric, Ionic, Corinthian, Gothic —he missed the Chinese, Hindoo, Persian, and Saracenic. His basic criterion was organic: the building must grow out of its environment and be adapted to the needs of those whom it was designed to serve. "Hence our taste in building rejects paint and all shifts, and shows the original grain of the wood; refuses pilasters and columns that support nothing, and allows the real supporters of the house honestly to show themselves." He virtually wiped out the distinction between the fine and the practical arts. "The most perfect form to answer an end is so far beautiful." This point of view seems to ally him with such architects as Louis Sullivan and Frank Lloyd Wright, and it is interesting that President Eliot thought "Art" important for the Columbia

University Library, the Harvard Stadium, and other modern edifices.[4]

Emerson's approach to the arts was somewhat wary, however.

I revisited the Tribune this morning [he wrote in 1834] to see the Venus and the Fornarina and the rest of the attractive company. I reserve my admiration as much as I can: I make a continual effort not to be pleased except by that which ought to please me, and I walked coolly round the marble lady, but, when I planted myself at the iron gate which leads into the chamber of Dutch paintings, and looked at the statue, I saw and felt that mankind had had good reason for their preference.

He was always modest in estimating his own credentials as an art connoisseur and grateful to the aids which came to him through friends and independent study. As late as 1864 Rimmer's *Elements of Design* was "a treasure of a book," and even in 1873 he thanked Margaret Foley for attempting to aid his art education. But this does not mean that his self-reliance ever deserted him. He was true to his own reactions, even when they were inconsistent, and he never valued a picture which spoke to him less because its beauty reached him without attestation from the proper authorities. But in 1839 he believed that "ten writers" could "awaken" him for every one artist able to achieve a comparable effect, and it seems unlikely that he ever changed his mind about this. Like Shaw in *Back to Methuselah*, he thought that all art might well be dispensed with when life shall have attained beauty, and he tells us at least once that weather stains on the wall and fantastic shadows sometimes stimulate his imagination more than great paintings.

Emerson once told his daughter that he enjoyed the theater very much, but felt it was not for him. He did not say why. His son conjectures that he went to the theater less than twenty times during his lifetime, but this seems to have been an underestimate.

As a child he was fascinated by the billboards in Boston, but was too poor to see plays. During his years at Harvard, the theater was under an official ban for students, and he himself took the negative side in a debate concerning its moral influence. Yet he was by no means void of dramatic sensitivity; he gave poetry readings as well as lectures and carefully rehearsed even the verses he quoted in his lectures. For himself, he did a good deal of play-reading—Shakespeare, Jonson, Webster, and others— and developed a rather surprising fondness for Beaumont and Fletcher. He included "to sing" and "to amuse" among the gifts worth cultivating and considered recreation important even in the home. He read Shakespeare aloud to his children and apparently took it for granted that they should see good plays. At times he himself experimented with the writing of dialogue.

When he was away from home, his references to the theater were fairly frequent, and I get the impression that he went more often when he was in Europe than he did in America. Among the famous players he saw (and, in some cases, met) were Talma, Mars, Rachel (in *Phèdre*, *Mithradate*, and *Lucréce*), Macready, Helena Faucit, Fanny Kemble, Charles Fechter, Charlotte Cushman, and Edwin Booth. Cushman had sung in his church during her choir-girl period. Rachel impressed him so much that he called her the only good actress he had ever seen and was driven to incoherence in describing her effect. He was extremely critical in the matter of Shakespearean interpretation, and when his imagination was really captured, he could behave much as he did while reading, forgetting the action of the play and pursuing his own line of thought; perhaps this is what he meant by his curious statement that though introversion might be a vice, he was his own comedy and tragedy. In "Inspiration," he speaks of the "great paroxysms" of David Garrick (whom, of course, he never saw), which surprised actor as well as audience. "If this is true on this low plane," he adds in superior tones, "it is true on the higher." I wonder what he would have made of Sarah Bernhardt's statement that when she gave a performance in which she had really surpassed herself, "God was there."

He did not quite scorn the humbler branches of the dramatic art; once he wrote his wife of having seen "shilling shows" in London. He tended to feel that, generally speaking, farce was better done than tragedy because the actors understood it better. There are a number of references to the circus, which was made attractive to him by his relish of physical skill and his preoccupation with the conception of life as a balancing act. On the same basis, he ought to have been attracted to the dance, and, as a matter of fact, he believed in it as a form of social contact and gave it a place in the education of children, though he considered it out of the question for himself. He saw Fanny Ellsler and was impressed by her art, but the story that he turned to Margaret Fuller, exclaiming, "Margaret, this is Poetry!" to which she replied, "Waldo, that is Religion!" is probably apocryphal. Actually he was not quite comfortable about the probable effect of the ballet on young men, though he does speak of Ellsler and the English tenor John Braham together as gifted of God. In later years, his children, like the Alcott children, were interested in amateur theatricals in Concord, and when Emerson visited Salt Lake City, where the theater was valued, he attended a performance of a melodrama called *Marriage By Moonlight, or The Wildcat's Revenge*, whose climactic scene was the rescue, at the sixth stroke, of the hero from a pile-driver which was to have crushed his head at the stroke of seven. Finally, in 1860 he was all ready for the movies, for he was enthralled by a stereopticon show which, he thought, surpassed Cornelius Agrippa, being particularly charmed by the dreamlike way in which one picture blended into the next!

Music skirts the theater and, in the form of opera, identifies with it. Emerson's father took great interest in church music, and his children learned hymns by heart, though Ralph had no musical gifts; he once wrote his wife that she was the only person who had ever heard him sing. He mentions Beethoven in his poem "The Adirondacs," but he begins a sentence in one of his *Dial* papers with the words "The music of Beethoven is said by those who understand it. . . ." He found the great violinist Ole Bull too exhibitionistic; when he heard Chopin's music, he wished that heaven had given him ears for the occasion. Though he knew great composers needed an orchestra, it is hard not to conclude that his own favorite instrument was the Aeolian harp.

Sometimes he tried to comfort himself for the deficiencies of his ear by reference to the keenness of his eyes ("that which others hear, I see"), but he never quite gave up hope of cultivating his musical sensibilities, and on occasion it seemed to him that music had carried him into fairyland. In 1848 he thought he had never heard anything so grand as Handel played on the organ at York Minister, and once he even called music the characteristic modern art, as typical of the age as steam and ship-building.

Among great singers, he speaks of Grisi, Carlotta Patti, Alboni, and Jenny Lind, who fascinated him even before he had heard her sing, as she fascinated his whole generation. Coloratura was evidently not his dish; Alboni in *Cenerentola* pleased him only by "the noble burst" of her voice, her "trills and gurgling" being dismissed as "painful," "surgical," or "functional." He might have liked Wagner better than the old Italian composers; at least he gave him credit for elevating the text to a place of importance beside the score. In any case, the opera so stimulated him that at one time he hoped to achieve freer and fuller expression in his own art because of his exposure to it. Apparently he found the art of the prima donna superior both morally and aesthetically to that of the dramatic actress, and I think it fair to say that what he cared for most in music was a good song

sung by an attractive woman who knew how to project the
words as well as the music. When he heard Bellini's *La Straniera*
in 1833, he was so fascinated by the prima donna that he paid
little attention to the opera itself. It seems odd, therefore, that
he himself should write, "A singer cares little for the words of
the song: he will make any words glorious." This may be true
of singers of hymns and popular ballads, and no doubt it is true
of half-literate singers everywhere, but where a great Lieder
singer is in question, nothing could be more completely beside
the mark. And the Lieder might indeed have moved and delighted Emerson beyond anything else in music if he had only
had the pleasure of being properly exposed to them.

II

On first consideration, Emerson seems inconsistent in his attitude toward reading; on the one hand, he can find nothing too
enthusiastic to say about it; on the other, he insists, at times a
little shrilly, that its place is secondary. Actually, however, there
is no real inconsistency, for his point was never that he loved
reading less, but merely that there were other things in life
that were more important and must take precedence.[5]

He frankly owned himself "the victim of any new page," for
our souls do not feed themselves, and no wise man thinks meanly
of "angels of entertainment, sympathy and provocation." Books
destroy time and space, enable us to move with the speed of
thought, and establish communication with great minds. In his
youth he confessed that a day spent without books was impoverished; in later years he testified that reading was the one
pleasure which did not grow stale with time; when he read a
book which opened up a new field, he said, he wished he might
live 3000 years. In the highest civilization, reading was still the

highest delight, fortifying its devotees against calamity; after Waldo's death, reconciliation with life began to approach him first through reading. It is not surprising, then, that he should have considered some books as important to us as "parents and lovers and passionate experiences," nor that a man's library should be a kind of harem to him (Holmes uses the same figure in *The Autocrat*). He even thought that those who loved the same books would be likely to love one another. And he sums it all up in a pleasant little piece of doggerel:

> When shall I be tired of reading?
> When the moon is tired and waxing and waning,
> When the cloud is tired of raining,
> When the sea of ebbing and flowing,
> When the grass is weary of growing,
> When the planets tire of going,
> And when Death is sick of feeding,
> Then shall I be tired of reading.

Robert Spiller was not the first scholar to remark that Emerson's reading was "completely unsystematic and much of it was in secondary sources, or even in collections of reference works, rather than in the primary English or foreign language texts, or even in translations," but he was able to document this statement more authoritatively than his predecessors. With all his shortcomings, Emerson's voracity as a reader has still been well established, even outside the literary field. He may tell us that he reads only for "lustres," and only when he is in the proper mood for reading the particular kind of thing in hand, but he read science, philosophy, and multitudinous, miscellaneous periodicals; at times (heaven save him!) he even read government reports. On his first visit to Europe, he read Goethe in Naples and Manzoni in Florence and carried Byron in his pocket through the Continent. Wherever he might be, says Kenneth

Cameron, "if he had an hour or part of a day to spare, he sought the nearest reading room for newspapers and journals." And again: "He pursued numbers of foreign and domestic serial publications as they appeared and left few gaps. To do so he had frequent periods of 'hiving' in the vicinity of the Harvard College Library—both in Boston and Cambridge." He valued foreign literature because it helped break subservience to the conventions with which we are familiar. One need not take him too seriously when he tells Margaret Fuller he would like to be a scholar, for, in his more ardent moods, he had a way of wishing himself into various pursuits, even painting; once he startled his wife and mother by telling them that if he could live for a while with people of strong passions he thought he could write tragedies and romances! He may advocate skimming and not becoming absorbed in one's reading. He may quote, often inaccurately, from poor translations or secondary sources, sometimes without knowing much more of the author than what he quotes,[6] but it should not be forgotten that as late as 1868 he was capable of becoming almost rapturous about the privilege of living in a house in which scholarly reference books were available.

Yet the famous Phi Beta Kappa address, "The American Scholar," leaves the impression that Emerson considered reading almost as dangerous as it is useful. "Books are the best of things, well used; abused, among the worst." Their service should be confined to the scholar's "idle hours." "When he can read God directly, the hour is too precious to be wasted in other men's transcripts of their readings." Imitation, even of Shakespeare, is ruinous.

Emerson never changed his mind about these things. He thought Sarah Alden Bradford Ripley choked by her own knowledge, and he was himself "too old" to read the books Charles Lane brought to Concord. He was impatient even of Alcott's praise of Plato and Socrates, bidding his friend find modern equivalents for these masters. "Instead of admiring the Apollo, or the picture, or the victory at Marengo, we ought to be producing what is admirable, and these things should glitter to us as hints and stints merely." Books serve their highest function when they set us free from themselves, and he does not shrink from the thought of outgrowing Montaigne, Shakespeare, Plutarch, and Plotinus, or of seeing Homer and Milton reduced to "tin pans" in time.

Sometimes Emerson commits himself to the proposition that a book means whatever can be read into it. In a way he realizes that to take up this point of view is to open the way to such vagaries as may best be illustrated today by pre- and post-millenarian interpretations of the apocalyptic literature of the Bible. But this did not dismay him.

If a man is inflamed and carried away by his thought, to that degree that he forgets the authors and the public and heeds only this one dream which holds him like an insanity, let me read his paper, and you may have all the arguments and histories and criticism.

He regarded the Swedenborgian interpretation of various passages in the New Testament as wholly false, but since they were in themselves lofty and spiritually minded, and therefore likely to foster spiritual-mindedness in the community, he rejoiced to see them circulated. It seems strange to find a distinguished writer advising readers to ride roughshod over their authors. "I find most pleasure," he says, "in reading a book in a manner least flattering to the author." Actually, he tries to ignore the author, seeking the universal elements in his reading. "I am very much struck in literature, by the appearance that one person wrote all the books." This applies even to his beloved Plutarch: "in reading him, I embrace the particulars, and carry a faint memory of the argument or general design of the chapter." All this, obviously, is ideally calculated to destroy not only scholarship but all considered criticism, and Cabot says frankly of Emerson that "his likings and dislikings were very distinct and persistent, but he never troubled himself to account for them." He had no critical standards and hardly got beyond referring to particular passages he liked. "Commentary and elucidation," he thought, only echoes and weakens the "few great voices of time." Yet he sent out a call for "professors of books," by which I suppose he meant what we now call professors of English or of literature; it would be interesting to know what he expected them to do. Yet, when all allowances have been made, Emerson's methods and standards worked pretty well for Emerson. "His literary obligations . . . are evident," says Stanley T. Williams, "especially in his poetry, but precise relationships, such as that of Spenser's influence on Hawthorne, hardly exist."

In literature Emerson read the Bible, Plato and the Neoplatonists, Catholic mystics, English Renaissance literature, the seventeenth-century mystics and religious writers, and, indeed, English and American literature in general, Hindu and Persian literature, and much besides. Impressive lists have been made of his reading at different periods,[7] and his roll call of the writers he particularly liked in "Books" is fairly standard, as is also his letter of advice about reading to Elizabeth Tucker.[8] He is distinctly more idiosyncratic, however, when, in his essay on Landor, he names "Homer and Aeschylus; Horace, Ovid, and Plutarch; Erasmus, Scaliger, and Montaigne; Ben Jonson and Izaak Walton; Dryden and Pope" (he generally disparages the last two) as taking the reader "out of trivial associations . . . into a region of the purest pleasure accessible to human nature." He was capable of calling Leigh Hunt's "Abou Ben Adhem" the most durable of Victorian poems and of listing Henry Taylor and Mrs. Hemans, and even Garth Wilkinson and Sampson Reed, in the company of writers of much greater reputation.

Once he put Beaumont and Fletcher into the company of Plato, Paul, Plutarch, Augustine, Spinoza, Chapman, Donne, and Sir Thomas Browne, and once, when he mapped out a course for the Concord School of Philosophy, he put himself down for a course embracing them, Percy's *Reliques*, rhetoric, and belles-lettres, while reserving theology, metaphysics, ethics, ecclesiastical history, etc., to his friends and associates.

Emerson was a fairly good, though not an accomplished, linguist. The learned Mrs. Ripley lured him into the study of the classics when he was about eleven, and he seems to have retained enough of his early classical training so that he could use both Greek and Latin when he needed them, though his quotations diminish progressively as he grows older. As to the modern languages, his son quotes him as having said that one could pick up French and German for himself. In the beginning, Margaret Fuller gave him German lessons, apparently rather against his will, and his adventures with that language are somewhat puzzling. We are told that he read through fifty-five volumes of Goethe in the original, which would be a considerable feat, but he also speaks of having carried a volume of Goethe about with him without reading in it, and when Kossuth turned to him, sitting on the platform from which the Hungarian patriot was speaking, to request the English word for "Österreich" (Austria), the flustered Emerson could only think of "ostrich." He seems to have been much given to foreign-language reading while away from home in taverns and on trains. He apparently learned to read German much more easily than he could pronounce it; there is a notebook filled largely with translations from Goethe, and he also translated some Persian poetry from German translations.[9] He was reading a two-volume novel in French as early as 1816 (though he adds that it was easy French). He made some attempt to correspond with his first wife in French, and there are French quotations in the original in his journals. In later years he was keen that his daughter should learn French; apparently it was the only foreign language he ever really tried to speak. He was very fond of Manzoni's novel *I Promessi Sposi*, and since he had a copy of this in the original in his library, he probably read it in Italian. He made a translation of Dante's *La Vita Nuova*, and, oddly enough, he translated a passage from Maria Edgeworth's novel, *Ennui*, into Italian.

Generally speaking, Emerson preferred to do his reading in English. "I should as soon think of swimming across Charles River when I wish to go to Boston, as of reading all my books in originals when I have them rendered for me in my mother tongue." He made an exception of Martial, who "must be read, if read at all," in Latin (he did not say why), and sometimes he even gives the impression of being indifferent to the quality of the translation. Since he read literature mainly for its inspirational power, learning to "read one" in all books and seeking "the one incorruptible text of Truth," this seems consistent enough, but the suggestion of stylistic indifference involved is not quite fair to Emerson. He took great pleasure in figurative language— "language is fossil poetry," he said—and he was often impatient of the kind of awkwardness in other people's poetry that he passed over in his own.

Emerson's views about the Bible may best be considered in connection with his religious convictions.[10] He mentions Homer more often than any other classical poet (generally in connection with the *Iliad*); once he lists Homer, Herodotus, Aeschylus, Plato, and Plutarch as the five Greeks we could not spare. Lucretius gets only a passing nod, but Virgil, Horace, Livy, Cicero, and Caesar are mentioned with reasonable frequency. Though he read Plato mainly in Thomas Taylor's paraphrases, he came closer to being his disciple than he ever did with any other; in Plato's behalf he once committed himself to an exclusivism which even Jesus could not command:

Whenever any skeptic or bigot claims to be heard on the question of intellect and morals, we ask if he is familiar with the books of Plato, where all his pert objections have once for all been disposed of. If not, he has no right to our time. Let him go and find himself answered there.[11]

Yet it may well be that Emerson loved Plutarch even more (in both the *Lives* and the *Morals*), for he could not think of him "without a tingling of the blood." If the books of the world were on fire, he says, he would "as soon fly to rescue [him] as Shakespeare and Plato, or next afterwards." [12] He did not care for Aristophanes, except for his historical value, nor greatly for Seneca. "There is a certain violence in his opinions, and want of sweetness. . . . He is tiresome through perpetual didactics."

Outside of Manzoni, Emerson has nothing much to say about any Italian writer except Dante, concerning whom some of his comments are penetrating ("As a talent Dante's imagination is the nearest to hands and feet that we have seen. He clasps the thought as if it were a tree or a stone, and describes as mathematically") and some quite the opposite. Though he was much interested in John Carlyle's translation of the "Inferno," for which he secured an American publisher, and also in that of T. W. Parsons, it is doubtful that he ever read *The Divine Comedy* through. Yet J. Chesley Mathews, who has studied the matter most carefully, inclined to think that he had rather more understanding of Dante than he has generally been given credit for.[13]

He knew that Cervantes and Rabelais were great comic spirits, but there is no indication that they meant anything to him. Calderón he thought mechanical. His great French genius was Montaigne, surely Emerson's greatest love among writers on what has been called his "johnny cake side." [14] He admired Pascal, and recently Kenneth W. Cameron has argued elaborately[15] that Madame de Staël's *Germany* was a major influence upon Emerson, strengthening his self-reliance, helping to familiarize him with Kant, and affecting his view of the relationship between man and nature. He did some reading in Victor Hugo, Eugène Sue (who was "horrid"), Paul de Kock, and George Sand, to whom, despite some criticisms, he was surprisingly receptive, especially in *Consuelo*, one of his few real favorites among novels.

His greatest German interest was of course in Goethe, but this I prefer to consider elsewhere in another connection. He was chilly toward Schiller, and Jean Paul Richter was too high-keyed for him. He mentions the Schlegels, Platen, and Tieck, and he knew de la Motte Fouqué's *Undine*. But the only German writer besides Goethe who interested him very deeply was Bettina von Arnim, whose genius he rather sentimentally called purer than Goethe's own, and whom he found superior to both Sand and de Staël. In addition to the literary writers, there were also the German philosophers, whose relationship to Emerson has inspired considerable speculation, but this subject cannot be treated in any detail here.[16]

He went furthest afield in his Oriental readings, which have been most discussed in connection with the possible influence upon him of Hindu philosophy.[17] Oriental materials were just beginning to be translated into the Western languages during his youth, and he was one of the first writers to be influenced by them; he was reading them from the age of eighteen, and both the *Bhagavad-Gita* and the *Vishnu Purana* were important to him. But if the Orient interested Emerson as a philosophical thinker, it also interested him as litterateur, most of all the Persians Hafiz and Saadi, who became to him a kind of type of the ideal poet, and J. D. Yohannan has even tried to trace a correspondence of both thought and expression between Emerson and them. "His most characteristic manner, that of a cryptic and often metrically crude expression—giving the effect, in words, of roughly hewn sculpture—is certainly to be found in the plainly rendered German versions of Persian poetry by von Hammer." [18]

George Willis Cooke comments on the contents of Emerson's poetical anthology, *Parnassus*, as reflecting his tastes in English poetry.

Shakespeare is drawn on more largely than any other, no less than eighty-eight selections being made from him. The names of George Herbert, Herrick, Ben Jonson, and Milton frequently appear. Wordsworth appears forty-three times, and stands next to Shakespeare; while Burns, Byron, Scott, Tennyson, and Chaucer make up the list of favorites.[19]

Emerson refers to Chaucer and Boccaccio together in an epigraph to "The Adirondacs," and he printed the passage on Gentilesse in "The Wife of Bath's Tale," which he greatly admired, in *Parnassus*. He also quotes

> Take fire, and bere it to the darkest hous
> Betwix this and the Mount of Caucasus, etc.

as making the point that nature could not be forced, and he is said to have repeated the whole of "Flee from the press" by heart, in a modernized version. Most of Emerson's "facts" about Chaucer, following the scholarship of his day,[20] are wrong, but his understanding and appreciation are generally right. Nothing could be worse, however, than his own modern English version of three verses from the Prologue to *The Canterbury Tales* in his lecture on "Country Life":

> Then long the folk to go on pilgrymages
> And palmers for to seeken stranger strands,
> To serve the saints beknown in sondry lands.

Generally speaking, he seems to have known little about the Middle Ages, which he saw as devoted to fable and tasteless ornamentation. Once he spoke of medieval people as savages; once he lumped antagonists together and referred to "all the barbarous indigestion of Calvin and the Middle Ages." [21] He said that from the *Morte Darthur* he remembered only Merlin's cry from his prison.

Shakespeare, who was undoubtedly more important to Emerson than any other English writer, is considered elsewhere in these pages. Emerson obviously had a temperamental affinity for the seventeenth century, and this applies to both the metaphysical poets and, in the realm of ideas, to the Cambridge Platonists. He thought Vaughan much inferior to Herbert, however, and Donne meant less to him than modern readers might expect.[22] He stressed Platonic influence in English literature and insisted on including Bacon in this tradition.[23] His references to Burton and Browne are not significant. Though he produced an essay on Milton and made a reasonable number of references to him, there is no suggestion that Milton meant as much to him as he did to Lowell and Whittier. Though he judged Milton a "poet by nature," he thought him overburdened by his too great learning, which kept him from being "transcendent, extravagant," as he might otherwise have been. It is a comfort to know that such appreciation as he mustered was not confined to *Paradise Lost* and the prose; on his early, stormy voyage to the Southern states, he passed the time in his berth by repeating "Lycidas" to himself and was pleased to find that he could recall everything except three verses.[24] Robert Herrick's eroticism troubled him somewhat, but he found it difficult to condemn this since it showed the ability of the true poet to employ and transform base materials, as the sunbeam illuminates carrion and violet impartially. Ben Jonson he studied with more care, finding it illuminating to make contact with a mind so fully revealed as his. He did not care for Jonson as a dramatist, but he once called his songs the finest in English, and Hyatt H. Waggoner thinks Jonson the only seventeenth-century poet who was at all like Emerson stylistically.

The eighteenth century got very little attention from Emerson. Pope was disparaged; once Emerson said he had only one good line and got that from Dryden. He perceived some merit in Addison, Burke, and Dr. Johnson. There are some references to the pre-Romantics—he liked Collins's "Ode to Evening," but judged it to have nothing beyond charming melody—but there is little on Blake, whom one might have expected to interest Emerson considerably; evidently he did not know much about him. The surprising utterance is the speech at the Boston celebration of the Burns centenary in 1859, a fervent, heart-warming eulogy, and very nearly the most passionate thing Emerson ever wrote. He is said to have delivered it magnificently; Lowell says that "every word seemed to have just dropped down to him from the clouds."

Among the Romantics, he tried more than once to like Shelley but never succeeded, judging him imitative and lacking in imagination; E. P. Whipple says Emerson disliked Shelley's note of lamentation. Once at least he granted Keats genius (though he dismissed *Endymion*), but he said very little about him. With Byron he had the difficulties one might have expected. He praised Byron's naturalness and lack of pompous formality, and in 1818 he thought the third canto of *Childe Harold's Pilgrimage* the most beautiful poetry he had ever read. But "Beppo" and "Manfred" were purposeless raving, and the indictment he entered in his journal when Byron died was savage. All in all, Emerson was in agreement with Goethe's judgment that Byron's thinking was childish (*"Sobald er reflektiert ist er ein Kind"*); he was essentially a rhetorician. There are some fairly admiring references to Moore (especially *Lalla Rookh*) and Southey. He discussed the *Joan of Arc* in a letter to his brother Edward in 1816, which sounds as if he had then heard of the national heroine of France for the first time. He was admiring in the main, though he seems to have thought Southey exaggerated by making Joan truly inspired.[25]

But of course the great Romantic was Wordsworth. One might have expected Coleridge to mean more, and as a thinker he did, but not as a poet. Emerson does not even seem to have cared much for "The Ancient Mariner." [26] This does not mean that he accepted Wordsworth lightly or easily, nor that the poet gained possession of his heart without storming the bastions. Except for Tennyson, there was no other modern writer whose merits and demerits Emerson so heatedly debated with himself over an extended period. At times, especially during the early years, he entered some extremely severe judgments of Wordsworth, as a poet of pigmies and pismires whose theory of art is radically wrong and as a "deranged archangel" whose genius has epilepsy. When he met him in 1848 he was revolted by Wordsworth's bitter and severe remarks about almost everybody and everything that came up. These judgments were not completely canceled in later years. Wordsworth's poetry was hard and sterile, lacking in grace and variety, and there were torpid places in his mind. Ultimately he succeeded, however, by his honesty and devotion to truth. The most manly poet of his time and "the voice of sanity in a worldly and ambitious age," Wordsworth had always "the merit of just moral perception" if not always that of "deft poetic execution." In his old age, Emerson told Charles J. Woodbury that the author of *The Prelude* was the greatest poet since Milton.

Among the Victorians, Tennyson was praised from the beginning for his ear and his command of language, but for a long time Emerson thought him too elegant and lacking in moral vitality; once he declared that his "musky verses" could only have been inspired by an Old World garden. Tennyson's bread was "pure sugar" and he lacked "rude truth"; he had no subject and climbed no mount of vision, describing Englishmen as they were and proposing nothing better—surely a strange judgment to be entered in the year of *In Memoriam*. It seems even more strange that, having found this poem mere conventional Unitarian moralizing, Emerson should have responded much more warmly to *Maud*, and that when the first four *Idylls* came out, he should have compared Tennyson to Homer, Aristophanes, and Dante (what a combination!), fulfilling the hopes for an Arthurian epic whose roots ran back to Chaucer's time. He liked Tennyson when they met, and in later years his comments upon him were increasingly friendly. Finally, he, Wordsworth, and Carlyle justified modern English literature, and Tennyson himself labored under the single drawback of being alive; if he were not a contemporary, there would be no question about him.

For Browning, on the other hand, Emerson seems to have cared little or nothing. "A wilfully involved style, like Browning's later work," wrote his son, "was odious to him." Of Matthew Arnold he declared that though he was a fine critic, he had written only one good poem, "Thyrsis," and that this was indebted to Milton. Arthur Hugh Clough he seems to have overestimated in comparison to his contemporaries, especially in *The Bothie of Tober-na-Vuolich*, though he did object to the indeterminate ending of *Amours de Voyage*. He thought *The Earthly Paradise* of William Morris good plain-song which allowed skipping, as really great poetry does not. If he did call Swinburne a sodomite in the notorious interview in which he was credited with having done so (he never actually denied it), this incident must be called his worst blunder in taste, tact, and critical discrimination. Swinburne's savage reply, as might have been anticipated, constitutes one of the best examples of foaming at the mouth that English prose has achieved.[27]

About the Victorian prose non-fiction writers there is not a great deal to be said, except for Carlyle, who has appeared, and will continue to appear, from time to time, in these pages. Emerson never got far with Ruskin. He was impressed by Macaulay's learning, vivacity, and prodigious talent, but though his account of William of Orange moved Emerson almost to tears, he could find no originality, moral energy, or elevation of mind in him. Once he compared him to John Banvard, who painted an immense Panorama of the Mississippi, and once he declared that a good greengrocer was spoiled to make him a writer. His loyalty to Carlyle ran all through his adult life, but he was well aware that his friend had a gift for closing his eyes to anything he did not wish to see. This applied to the faults of historical figures like Cromwell and Frederick the Great, and also to contemporary social and political conditions. As a matter of fact, he had known Carlyle was "too self-indulgent" as early as *The French Revolution*, and he complained, interestingly, that philosophical historians had the disadvantage of leaving nothing for him to do in the way of interpretation; they did not stimulate him, like Plutarch and many lesser writers, whose annals were themselves dull and dead in comparison, but who, for that very reason, enabled him to hear the voice of nature through them.[28]

As for fiction, both Victorian and general, Emerson did not deny that he would have liked "to write something which all can read, like *Robinson Crusoe*." He read more fiction than he has generally been given credit for, and he mentions a good many novels from time to time, not all of them by distinguished writers. On the whole, however, his imagination was more at home with myths and folk tales, Norse sagas and Welsh bardic songs. Folklore was just beginning to be studied in his time; though he thought fairy tales and romantic fables less valuable than the ancient myths because they merely entertained instead of interpreting the meaning of life, he knew that they had their place and quoted approvingly Addison's statement that civilization has not quite plucked the old woman out of our hearts. In college days he is said to have toyed with the idea of writing a romance about Richard I; later, under the stimulus of his admiration for *The Bride of Lammermoor*, he thought again about writing fiction, but he never got very far with any of this.

He knew that the universal desire of children to hear stories is a strong testimonial to the naturalness of the human appetite for fiction, and he could criticize Thoreau for railing against it. But his defenses are likely to be somewhat condescending, as when he says that the love of fiction reflects a preference for sentiment over sense, and that most novels, romances, and plays are obviously addressed to grown-up children. He granted novels a certain usefulness "if they teach you the secret that the best of life is conversation, and the greatest success is confidence, or perfect understanding between sincere people"; he thought too that they were improving in his time, being no longer exclusively preoccupied with wooing and attempting more earnestly to penetrate the surface of life.

Yet he had no use for either George Eliot or Jane Austen; the latter he dismissed, apparently after having read *Pride and Prejudice* and *Persuasion*, as vulgar, sterile, conventional, and naïve, without either wit or intelligence, and interested only in marriage! He knew Maria Edgeworth, but he calls *Castle Rackrent* "Castle Radcliffe," and so it stands in his "Literary Ethics" to this day. He was mildly tolerant of Disraeli and his school, and he liked some of Charles Reade, but he could find little good to say about either Thackeray or Bulwer-Lytton. On the credit side, he did have some interest in Charlotte Brontë.

The crucial test case, among the English novelists at least, was that of Charles Dickens, and Emerson could not have asked for a better chance to damn himself as a critic of fiction than he seized when he spoke of "poor Pickwick stuff" and denied dramatic power and the ability to write dialogue to the author of *Oliver Twist*. However, the record as a whole is not quite so bad as that; when Emerson made the remark about *Pickwick* he had only seen a small portion of the book in serial publication. He did recognize Dickens's realism, his generosity of spirit, his resemblance to Hogarth, and the service he performed in exposing social evils, and when his own countrymen were abusing *American Notes*, he defended it as a book which "held bad manners up, so that the churls could see the deformity." There is evidence that the Emersons read *Bleak House* as it was published in parts, and Emerson once described a legal settlement in his wife's family as a Jarndyce vs. Jarndyce case. When he met Dickens, he liked him, thinking him cordial, sensible, and not at all a dandy, as he had feared, and he was tremendously impressed by his reading of "Dr. Marigold" in Boston. Not only did he (according to Mrs. Fields's report) laugh "as if he might crumble to pieces, his face wearing an expression of absolute pain," but he acutely sensed the tremendous tension under which Dickens labored. The novelist, Emerson feared, had "too much talent for his genius; it is a fearful locomotive to which he is bound, and he can never be freed from it nor set at rest." "He daunts me. I have not the key." [30]

His favorite novelist, as all the world knows, was Sir Walter Scott, whose epic note perhaps increased his appeal to Emerson. It is true that there is disparagement even here. At least once he denied him high imagination. Scott's dialogue is "in costume," not "warm with life," like Shakespeare's, nor able to bear the test of repeated reading, though elsewhere we are told that his characters approach Shakespeare's in numbers and variety. He wrote "a rhymed traveller's guide to Scotland," and his poetry is "objective," like Crabbe's. In "The Harp" Emerson spoke of him as "the delight of generous boys," but he undercut the implied disparagement when, in his centenary address before the Massachusetts Historical Society, he added that when we read him, we are all ready to be boys again. When Emerson was in the British Isles, he himself used the "rhymed traveller's guide" as religiously as any pious pilgrim, and his son testifies to his frequent references to Scott and quotations from him to his children. For a long time, we are told, he owned the only set of the "Waverley Novels" in Concord and lent it out all over town. He even thought he saw resemblances between Aunt Mary and Margaret Graeme in *The Abbot*. Emerson came very close to defining the figure in Scott's carpet when he perceived how impossible it was for the novelist to look at a glen or a house or a man in Scotland without perceiving what he looked at in the light of the past as well as the present and as the focus of the historic forces that had made it what it is; this was the power that enabled him to infuse the historical novel with an enduring vitality. And though Emerson got on shaky ground when he interpreted *The Bride of Lammermoor* as an allegory, it is still true that when he tells us of that novel that it "almost goes back to Aeschylus for a counterpart as a painting of Fate,—leaving on every reader the impression of the highest and purest tragedy," he not only pays it the warmest tribute he ever offered a novel, but also bestows one of the most glowing encomia any writer of genius ever offered another.

For Emerson, American literature was largely contemporary literature. He looked back upon Franklin and Edwards to praise them, but he was condescending toward his older contemporaries, Irving and Cooper. Ellen Tucker had been fond of Bryant, and Emerson praised him at the Bryant festival in 1864, but there are no references to him in the collected works.[31] Such a sentence as "The question is often asked, Why no poet appears in America?" was not very complimentary to the "schoolroom poets," nor to himself, and indeed he himself once said, "My reputation, such as it is, will one day be cited to prove the poverty of this time."

Longfellow he seems to have liked as a man (though he thought he lived too luxuriously), but there is no indication that he cared anything about his poetry. He seems to have ranked *Kavanagh* ahead of *Hiawatha*. We are told that when "The Wreck of the Hesperus" was quoted from in his company, he liked the quotation and asked to have it repeated without recognizing the source. He apparently gave more thought to Lowell and made some effort to estimate him fairly. He admired *Among My Books*. At first he thought Lowell's essentially a comic muse, but after the commemoration ode, he was less sure of this. He would not review *The Cathedral* because, though he recognized merit in it, he thought it labored.[32] Even in 1868 he was saying that, though Lowell had gained, especially in technique, he still lacked true poetic flair. There is one quotation from Whittier, in an anti-slavery connection, naturally, and Holmes gets one or two vague compliments.

His failure with Hawthorne was worse. Perhaps his affection for Margaret Fuller might excuse his contemptuous dismissal of *The Blithedale Romance* as "that disagreeable story," but this is not all: *The Scarlet Letter* was "ghastly" and *The Marble Faun* "mere mush." Generally speaking, Hawthorne's stories were steeped in gloom, not about anything in particular, and not worth anything. He also displayed a tendency to show the reader too much of his processes. Once Emerson even expressed the astonishing judgment that Hawthorne was a better critic than writer of fiction. Yet he had been pleased when he heard that Hawthorne was coming to Concord to live, and the two men made a number of attempts to get to know each other, once even taking a walking tour together. Hawthorne talked little, and this caused Emerson, in his own judgment, to talk too much. Of course he disapproved of Hawthorne's politics and his friendship with Franklin Pierce. Once he told Delia Bacon that Hawthorne was not a man like other men, being both more and less; on another occasion, he said that Hawthorne and Alcott together might have constituted a man, which, in view of the admiration he expressed for Alcott elsewhere, is puzzling. In the end he judged Hawthorne to have died of his solitude.[33]

He mentions other American writers from time to time, often in terms of praise. Lydia Maria Child's *Philothea* was a "divine" book. *Uncle Tom's Cabin* impressed him as a publishing phenomenon, but I am not sure he read it. He rejoiced in the success of Louisa May Alcott because it rescued her family from poverty. He instantly recognized the quality of *Two Years Before the Mast*. As editor of *The Dial*, he showed something of the interest in unearthing honest, well-written accounts of experience by hitherto unknown writers which was later to be so valuable a part of the equipment of Ellery Sedgwick as editor of the *Atlantic*. He liked Bret Harte's early stories for Harte's ability to find germs of goodness even in derelicts. In 1870 he was so enthusiastic about the poems of Julia Ward Howe that he wished she had been born in Massachusetts! Unlikely as it seems, even the young Anna Katharine Green, who was later to have an important part in the establishment of the detective novel, was encouraged by him. But the only three young American poets he praises heartily in the Preface to *Parnassus* are Forecythe Willson, a Wisconsin writer whose promise was aborted by early death; "H.H." (Helen Hunt Jackson), whose identity he either did not know or concealed; and, with qualifications, the unnamed author of "Sir Pavon and Saint Pavon."

This is the kind of thing which has led many to call Emerson's swans crows. Few critics have placed Jones Very and Ellery Channing so high as he did; in the 1840's he thought Channing had more "inward music" than anybody else who had written on this side of the water and found it "droll" that W. H. Furness should rate an amateur like Emerson himself higher. But his admiration for Very was shared later by Gamaliel Bradford;[34] on the other hand, Emerson was not unaware of Channing's limitations, and when the poet refused to allow either him or Margaret Fuller to make any changes in his contributions to *The Dial,* he declared testily that he could not see what there was about poetry to sanctify even flies and spiders in the amber nor why the spirit could not learn to parse and spell.[35]

Finally, it must not be forgotten that Emerson did discover and champion two American writers of the first magnitude— Thoreau and Whitman. And the credit he deserves here is all the greater because he was not undiscriminating in his evaluation of either.

His problems with Thoreau were not serious, for, saving the younger man's tendency toward extremism and the plain contrariness he sometimes manifested, there were no barriers of background or temperament to surmount. With Whitman it was different.

He saluted Whitman "at the beginning of a great career," and this was the most brilliant send-off any top-flight American man of letters ever tried to give a top-flight junior. It was natural enough that he should do this, for the first edition of *Leaves of Grass* certainly had its Emersonian aspects, though it has been suggested that the Preface came closer to Emerson's ideas than the poems themselves did.[36] When Whitman printed his letter without permission, Emerson called it "a strange rude thing," which was moderate language indeed. His admiration for Whitman was probably modified by this fact, as it certainly must have been by the increasing sexuality manifested in later editions of *Leaves of Grass* and by what he considered Whitman's rough manners when they met. Rusk was probably right, too, in his conjecture that Emerson may have been somewhat discouraged by the failure of most of his friends to share his high estimate of Whitman's work. Some of the remarks Emerson is reported to have made about Whitman and about *Leaves of Grass* in later years are disparaging: "There are parts of the book where I hold my nose as I read." Once he described the work as a singular blending of the *Bhagavad-Gita* and the New York *Herald*, and once he was sorry that Whitman seemed to have settled for making the catalogues of the nation where he might have made its songs. Even some of his praise was double-edged, as when he compared Whitman's achievement to Brigham Young's or coupled him with one whom he considered a madwoman of genius, Delia Bacon. For all that, Emerson never really took back anything he had said about Whitman. In the letter of recommendation for him which he sent William H. Seward in 1863, he honestly noted Whitman's limitations, but was still cordial in his appreciation.

Among Emerson's eccentricities as a reader perhaps the most startling is the ultra-snobbish attitude he sometimes expressed toward books and authors of the second rank. Thus he spoke of nations as having derived their culture from a single book (as from the Bible) and actually suggested that it might have been better if the work of all English writers except Shakespeare, Milton, and Bacon had been lost! But people who read only the Bible seldom have much understanding of it or of any other book, and the greatness of Shakespeare and Milton could hardly be recognized if there were no other writers to whom they might be compared. Emerson always opposed exclusivism in religion; why did he have to yield to it in culture? He did grant in passing that "now and then, by rarest luck, in some foolish Grub Street, is the gem we want." Surely to uncover such gems is one of the real joys of reading, and the treasures we have unearthed for ourselves are those which generally mean most to us, but if we were to follow Emerson's advice, we should certainly make it harder for ourselves to find them.

> The three practical rules which I have to offer [he once wrote], are 1. Never read any book that is not a year old. 2. Never read any but famed books. 3. Never read any but what you like. . . .

This advice is neither sensible nor consistent. If nobody ever read a book until it was a year old, no book would ever attain that age, and no more books would be published, and to read only "famed" books is as bad as to have no friends who are not in the social register. Finally, as to Number 3: suppose the self-reliant reader does not happen to like one of the "famed" books and does like a book that is not "famed" at all? Fame, after all, must be determined by readers, many of whom are no wiser than he. Why should he throw away the opportunity to cast his vote?

Fortunately, Emerson's practice in this matter was often more sensible and generous than his theory.[37]

III

After reading, writing. For if you are an artist, you do not only enjoy the arts or "react" to them; you practice one. So it was with Emerson the writer.

Not a writer, he said, but a man writing. But he still took his writing very seriously and devoted himself to it as assiduously as any purely "aesthetic" person could have done. He calls writing "the greatest of arts, the subtilest, and of most miraculous effect"; apparently he thought it superior to the others because it employed less material channels of expression. "The man is only half himself," he says, "the other half is his expression," and to his way of thinking all artists are actuated by the single desire "to express themselves symmetrically and abundantly, not dwarfishly and fragmentarily."

> The tongue is prone to lose the way;
> Not so the pen, for in a letter
> We have not better things to say,
> But surely say them better.[38]

Sometimes he seems to have required an absolute concentration from any man who would really accomplish anything in this world; elsewhere he admitted the need for relief and recognized that absolute concentration would be narrowing as well as an intolerable strain. But he entertained no doubts concerning either the value or the dignity of his calling. "The writer, like the priest, must be exempted from secular labor"; he must also "defend" his morning, even against the members of his own household. He told Anna Katharine Green that writing is a calling; it cannot be chosen, but those who are chosen by it have no choice but to obey. It satisfied his need for experience and compensated him for the shortcomings of life. Edward Waldo Emerson said of his father that, to his own mind, his work justified his existence, and that therefore "he must not let slip the gift of each new day." Emerson regarded his ability to work as an index of his health and envied the European scholars he heard of as putting in a twelve- to fifteen-hour day. Five to seven hours was more like what he could manage, but he was very regular in his habits and often continued his writing even while he was on lecture tours. Aside from his loneliness, he once wrote his wife, the greatest disadvantage of absence from home was that his journal ceased to grow, and in reporting his exploration of Mammoth Cave, he lamented that it cost him a day of working time. "Even in college," he says, "I was already content to be 'screwed' in the recitation room if on my return I could accurately paint the fact in my journal." In 1840 he told

Carlyle that he wrote not only because he was convinced of the value of what he produced, but also for the sheer pleasure of "spinning."

All this began in childhood, sometimes with ambitious enterprises that were quite alien from the bent of his genius as later determined. His talent was recognized by his teachers, and he was still a schoolboy when he began collecting materials for writing in his notebooks, as he was to continue to do for the rest of his life. In college he was Class Poet. After he gave up the church, he dreamed of establishing a magazine, but nothing came of this.

He got up early and went to his study, remaining there until the one o'clock dinner which prevailed in those days. Sometimes he would return in the evening; his son says he often worked late but Cabot denies this. "Every artist knows well some favorite retirement. And yet the experience of some good artists has taught them to prefer the smallest and plainest chamber, with one chair and table, and with no outlook, to these picturesque liberties." Apparently he did most of his writing in his rocking chair, on a portfolio which he held on his knees. Sometimes a stroll in the orchard helped to put him in the mood for writing; sometimes he was stimulated by something he had read. There were times when he would take a particularly difficult piece to an inn or a hotel—perhaps the American House in Hanover Street—and once he went alone to Nantasket, where he seems to have missed his family and his familiar surroundings far more than he had been distracted by anything at home. "Desperate of success abroad, I rushed home again; having before found that I could write out of no inkstand but my own." Yet some kind of apartness the writer must secure:

> Trees in groves,
> Kind in droves,

> In ocean sport the scaly herds,
> Wedge-like cleave the air the birds,
> To northern lakes fly wind-borne ducks,
> Browse the mountain sheep in flocks,
> Men consort in camp and town,
> But the poet dwells alone.[39]

Emerson wrote his essays, as everybody knows, by mining the multitudinous notebooks in which he did most of his writing, and many of his journal entries were the direct fruit of inspiration or intuition. "Mr. Emerson's journals," wrote his son, "were mainly records of the oracles which came to his listening in his wood walks, and thoughts which the events and conversation of the day had suggested." Sometimes he even made notes in the woods.

> The gods talk in the breath of the woods,
> They talk in the shaken pine,
> And fill the long reach of the old seashore
> With dialogue divine;
> And the poet who overhears
> Some random word they say
> Is the fated man of men
> Whom the ages must obey.[40]

Emerson knew that if writing is a gift, it is also a knack. He did not believe that the writer is always completely in control of either himself or his craft. "Every writer is a skater, and must go partly where the skates carry him; or a sailor, who can only land where the sails can be blown." Once at least he suggested that writing becomes more difficult with age. His Muse,[41] as he saw it, was feminine, and inspiration ebbed and flowed. He was painfully conscious of the ebb tide, and it produced discouragement, but he stayed on the job. Though he believed that even the thought of an unseen or potential reader might tempt the writer to insincerity, he did not allow this to turn him into the-poet-talking-to-himself, for he knew that until one's intuitions have been communicated, they can accomplish little. Like many writers, he thought it better not to talk about what he was writing; it would be more difficult for him to express his thought fully if he had given it premature and imperfect utterance. But he took little stock in formulating rules for writers or anybody else, and he had few positive do's and don't's about writing. As an essayist he believed in relevance, but defined it in no narrow way. He concerned himself with contemporary subjects, but it was not their temporal aspects which held him. Poetry, he says, is written in "the oldest and simplest words," and he believed the orator might do well to take example by this also, as Lincoln did at Gettysburg and John Brown at Charlestown; there were worse mottoes than "Speak with the vulgar, think with the wise." [42] He also believed that a good writer succeeds by virtue of what he omits as well as by what he includes. After "low style" and compression, what he admired most was probably metonymy, which stimulated his imagination and fitted in with his notion of the symbolic character of the world and of life itself.

His methods of composition being what they were, it is not strange that Emerson should often have been accused of inconsecutiveness. There are no significant paragraphs in Emerson's essays, we have been told again and again, though there are many significant sentences. The end of the composition might just as well be at the beginning, and often what the reader remembers longest has only the vaguest possible connection with the avowed subject of the essay. Emerson himself declared of one composition that when it was finished, he judged it an excellent house, except that he had omitted the stairs, and Lowell wrote of one of his lectures that "it was as if, after vainly trying to get his paragraphs into sequence and order, he had at last tried the desperate expedient of *shuffling* them. It was chaos come again, but it was a chaos full of shooting-stars, a jumble of creative forces." This was what caused Henry James to judge Emerson "a striking exception to the general rule that writings live in the last resort by their form." On the other hand, we have also been assured that since the style is the man, Emerson's style was exactly right for him, a fitting body for his soul, indeed, the inevitable style for a man who believed that matter is significant only as an expression of spirit and that art is not craftsmanship but inspiration, since such a writer must testify to the faith that is in him not only by what he says but by the way he says it.

None of this is entirely wrong; only, unfortunately, it is not entirely right either. Emerson admitted that organization was for him the most difficult part of writing; he certainly did not try for a syllogistic method of presentation, and he deliberately omitted many mechanical connectives which a writer like Macaulay would have included because he wished to goad the reader into figuring out some connections for himself. Such involvement, Emerson believed, was part of what good reading required; sometimes he even thought of himself in this aspect as a sculptor who stopped with "blocking out" his statue. His prose sometimes suggests oral rather than written style,[43] but it makes heavier demands than any but an ideal listener could support. "Emerson's river is all rapids," said Henry van Dyke, and John Burroughs was descriptive, not pejorative, when he called him "abrupt, freaky, unexpected," always "springing" his point. He achieves "an essence, a condensation," and "a preponderance of pure statement" beyond any other writer. "Apparently he does not permit himself a moment's indifference or inattention." [44]

It is amusing to find Emerson saying of the great sailor-preacher, "Father" Edward Taylor, almost exactly what Lowell said about Emerson himself: "The utter want and loss of all method, the bright chaos come again of his bewildering oratory certainly bereaves it of power,—but what splendor, what sweetness, what richness, what depth, what cheer!" Warmly appreciative of the intense poetic temperament of Ellery Channing, he was also well aware of Channing's need to acquire skill in construction, and his analysis of Alcott's compositional faults, in both verse and prose, is both masterly and merciless. Despite his ecstatic appreciation of Carlyle, he made no secret of disliking Carlyle's eccentricities of form, which he regarded as unnecessarily restricting his potential audience, and he wished *The French Revolution* were simpler and "less Gothically efflorescent." Certainly Emerson did not glorify disorganization or inconsecutiveness for its own sake, for he criticized both Wordsworth's poems and Milton's prose for what he considered their defects along this line. Poe disliked long poems because he believed that the intensity required either to write good poetry or to respond to it could not be sustained over a considerable period or through interruptions of reading, but it is clear that when Emerson read a great writer, he kept the structure of the general work in mind and judged individual passages in relation to it.

Neither his high evaluation of spontaneity nor his horror of a mechanical veneer-like "finish" in writing ever led him to scamp his work. Whatever one may feel about the form he *achieved*, he *believed* that writing was analogous to architecture and required comparable attention to win effectiveness. "Let the reader find that he cannot afford to leave out a line of your writing," he says, "because you have omitted every word that you can spare." He is said once to have spent twenty-one hours preparing a lecture and then, having been disappointed in the result, decided to spend sixty on the next one, and Mrs. Fields says it was very difficult for his editor to get a manuscript away from him, as he always wanted to keep it by him so that he could do more work on it. He is known, also, to have corrected four sets of proofs on *English Traits,* and his indexing of his chaotic journals was a remarkable feat. "The published essays," says George Willis Cooke, "are often the result of many lectures, the most pregnant sentences and paragraphs alone being retained." And he adds that the manuscript "is everywhere covered with these evidences of his diligent revision."

Poetry is literature like prose, only more so, and everything Emerson believed about literature he believed about poetry with redoubled force. I have already argued that he was essentially a poet because he had a poetic, intuitive kind of understanding and imagination, and that he manifests this even when he is writing prose. He said, "I do not belong to the poets, but only to a low department of literature, the suburban men," but he also judged himself a born poet, though of a low class and husky voice. In his old age he told Sanborn, "It has been decided that I cannot write poetry. Others have found it out at last, but I could have told them so long ago." He *had* told them. He had even told Carlyle when sending him his poems. He knew only enough about poetry to recognize the faults of his own work; he was only a lover of the Muse, filling in the time until a true poet should appear. On the other hand, he told Elizabeth Peabody that though he was not a great poet, "whatever is of me *is a poet.*" His gift is a poor thing yet his own, for as far as it goes, it has authenticity.

It was natural, then, that if he worked hard on his prose, he should have worked even harder on his verse. As Carl F. Strauch has pointed out, "Few poets have kept such an astonishing mass of manuscripts, and few have exposed so completely in rough drafts the secret of their poetic art." He adds that the first drafts are often "incredibly bad." Emerson even cared about typography, for he knew that the arrangement and appearance of the lines on the page affected the reader's mind and modified the appeal of the poem. Compared to the poems he hoped to write, he thought of his essays as poor, cramped, arid things that he could hardly bear to look at. He was disappointed when he read John Sterling to find no sensitiveness to music in him; he had not expected this of one who admired Carlyle and himself! When James T. Fields praised a new poem in 1866 he was greatly encouraged; he had feared his poetic days were over. And how touching was his statement to J. T. Trowbridge that any indication of familiarity with his poems always moved him. "I feel it a hardship that—with something of a lover's passion for what is to me the most precious thing in life, poetry—I have no gift of fluency in it, only a rude and stammering utterance." But when Trowbridge went on to praise his poems, he smiled and admitted that here and there there might be "a grain among the husks." [45]

Critical evaluation of Emerson's poetry as a whole does not fall within the scope of this book. His theory was that "argument," "thought," or "experience" should determine form, and that ideas should be expressed through symbols, which brings him close to modern symbolists and imagists and all those who hold "organic" theories concerning art and favor implicational and presentational methods. Everybody knows that there is nothing finer in American literature than the best of Emerson's verses, like

> The frolic architecture of the snow

> Music pours on mortals his beautiful disdain

> O tenderly the haughty day
> Fills his blue urn with fire

but though he did manage to turn out a few short poems which might, with at most a pardonable exaggeration, be called perfect (Carpenter chooses "Brahma," "Days"—which Emerson, strangely, could not recall writing—"The Rhodora," "The Snow-Storm," and "Concord Hymn"), he was not noted for his ability to sustain a high poetic tone, and there is nothing worse in our poetry than some of the verses in even so famous a poem as "The Sphinx"; not even Emerson's "jingle-man" Poe explored loftier heights nor lower depths.

The usual explanation of all this is that Emerson's poetic flair, though often inspired by ideas rather than the passions which excite most poets, was authentic, but that he was defective in craftsmanship (Theodore Parker said he was a poet who lacked the accomplishment of verse). To this it is sometimes added that when he fails in the conventional forms, the reason is that he is trying for something else. Unfortunately, however, these pronouncements will not quite cover his case.

One can hardly argue that a man who persuaded his wife to change her first name from Lydia to Lidian because he could not bear to hear New England "hicks" talking about "Lydiar Emerson" lacked ear,[46] and he showed this again, together with his recognition of the importance of craftsmanship, in his comments on the poems sent to him for criticism and even in what he had to say about such masters as Wordsworth and Tennyson. Emerson's poetic interests were by no means confined to what could in any sense be called metaphysical poetry, and the closing "Oracles and Counsels" section in *Parnassus* is surprisingly short. He kept much poetry in his mind and was capable of being haunted by memorable lines. In his early journals and even in childhood, as well as in such early poems as "Indian Superstitions," he demonstrated his ability to write perfectly regular conventional verses (his son went so far as to call Pope and Campbell his early masters), and though these pieces are not valuable, nor in any sense representative of the Emerson we know, it is hard to believe that this power deserted him alto-

gether as he matured. It is true that in "Merlin" he urges the
poet not to encumber his brain "with the coil of rhythm and
number" but rather to "mount to paradise/By the stairway of
surprise." In other moods, he professed to love rime, however,
and we have his own word for it that tunes in various poetic
measures went through his brain in the form of songs without
words or thought content. He himself compared writing bad
verses to going into company with a dirty face, and the truth is
that most of his best poems are fairly regular and that some of
his worst failures are in what we would now call free verse.[47]

In any case, it is difficult to see how anybody could place the
ideal of the poet higher than Emerson does. He is the darling of
the gods, and his achievement has value even for those who do
not understand it.

> His learning should be deep and large,
> And his training should not scant
> The deepest lore of wealth or want:
> His flesh should feel, his eyes should read
> Every maxim of dreadful Need;
> In its fulness he should taste
> Life's honeycomb, but not too fast;
> Full fed, but not intoxicated;
> He should be loved; he should be hated;
> A blooming child to children dear,
> His heart should palpitate to fear.[48]

He must "converse with pure thought" and "demonstrate it almost to the senses." In "weak, unhappy times" he must be silent
and await the

> open hours
> When the God's will sallies free,
> And the dull idiot might see
> The flowing fortunes of a thousand years.[49]

His primary concern is not with the surface of life, but with the soul or meaning or essence of life "as it shines to fancy and feeling." Poetry brings guidance, consolation, and joy to men. It has an advantage over philosophy because "the poet is in the natural attitude; he is believing; the philosopher, after some struggle, having only reasons for believing." Perhaps it even has an advantage over religion, for it allows the imagination "to flow, and not to freeze," while the mystic, the believer shows a tendency to nail "a symbol to one sense, which was a true sense for a moment, but soon becomes old and false." [50]

CHAPTER FOUR

FRIENDSHIP

I

Emerson had "no hostility to nature, but a child's love to it. I expand and live in the warm day like corn and melons." This sympathy extended to those who, as he saw it, lived close to nature, sometimes (Burns-like) even to the rats in the wall and the lizard on the fence, who have worlds of their own that we do not know.

He wanted to explore and to "poetize" "the near, the low, the common," to know the "meaning" of "the meal in the firkin; the milk in the pan; the ballad in the street; the news in the boat; the glance of the eye; the form and gait of the body."

> Give to barrows, trays and pans
> Grace and glimmer of romance,
> Bring the moonlight into noon
> Hid in gleaming piles of stone.[1]

Some will feel, no doubt, that when the low has been "poetized" and its "meaning" extracted, it is no longer "common" at all, but Emerson never ceased to feel that an exclusive devotion to metaphysics was dangerous. "I like a man who likes to see a fine barn," he says, "as well as a good tragedy"—surely as startling a juxtaposition as Carl Sandburg's "hyacinths and biscuits." In "Hamatreya" he got a Concord poem out of the *Vishnu Purana*.

He wanted to share the passions of other men; sometimes he even thought he would have liked to live in revolutionary times. And because he believed that even the writer should do his share of the world's labor, working "with men in their houses, and not with their names in books," there were times when he flirted with the idea that later so much more seriously seduced Tolstoy—that every man ought to do some physical work; in one of his wild lumpings together of totally different things, he lists rambling in the fields, rowing, skating, and hunting as all "moderate and dainty exercise"! Experience, however, proved that this would not work for him. Theoretically, he could also see some sense in the notion that scholars and artists should lead ascetic lives, but there is no indication that he made even a stab at this. "I allow the old circumstance of mother, wife, children, and brother to overpower my wish to right myself with absolute Nature," he said; "and I also consent to hang, a parasite, with all the parasites on this rotten system of property." His horror of extremes saved him in practice from many vagaries, and also, perhaps, from sainthood. It is true that he disliked being waited on—when he went on his lecture tours, he would even insist upon carrying his heavy luggage to the railroad station himself —and once he developed a plan for having the servants eat with the family, but they refused the invitation. At another time, there was thought of setting up a common household with the Alcotts, and now it was Mrs. Alcott's good sense that came to his rescue.

Nevertheless he greatly enjoyed, or thought he enjoyed, the society of the humble. "I much prefer the company of plough-boys and tin-peddlers," he says, "to the silken and perfumed amity which celebrates its days of encounter by a frivolous display, by rides in a curricle and dinners at the best taverns," which is perhaps not quite a fair statement of the choices available. Once, unwontedly writing of himself in the third person, "he confessed he liked low company. He said the fact was incontestable that the society of gypsies was more attractive than that of bishops," thus manifesting, or at least expressing, an inverted form of snobbery which probably gypsies, or their equivalent, share. He pointed out an affinity between slang and poetry long before the same idea had occurred to S. I. Hayakawa, and he was even willing to allow profanity a place; once he speaks daringly of the speech "we listen for in bar-rooms." [2] So he seldom used letters of introduction when away from home, but "preferred . . . taking his chance at a hotel for company," talking to stage drivers and stablemen, as he talked to fishermen and woodchoppers nearer home. He liked boys too, because they were "the masters of the playground and of the street,—boys who have the same liberal ticket of admission to all shops, factories, armories, town-meetings, caucuses, mobs, target-shooting, as flies have." He hoped that when they grew up they would lose their uproar and rudeness but retain their vitality. But he would not overemphasize the importance of manners either, for he thought the vulgarity of selfishness more objectionable than that of speech and habit. Emerson was impressed by the ingenuity of common men also, by their skill in areas where he was helpless and their ability to make use of the resources of nature. He complained of the arrogant contempt learned men feel for the unlearned, a contempt which has certainly not lessened with the years and which has helped to polarize our society so dangerously. He was persuaded that common men were quick to detect flaws in character and even permitted himself to write extravagantly that "the college is not so wise as the mechanic's shop, nor the quarter-deck as the forecastle."

Yet common folk—and human nature in general—are not

idealized. The vein of iron in Emerson's thinking and temperament crops up here as elsewhere; though he was sometimes shocked by Carlyle, there are still times when he talks like him. Human beings are potentially divine, but in their present stage of development, they often look and behave very much like fools. In every age, imbecility predominates in the vast majority. There is a vast number of malefactors, but of benefactors only a handful. All in all, men are still part quadruped, pawing the ground in an effort to shake off their ancient inheritance. Even when he was working against slavery, Emerson declared that survival for either black or white must depend upon fitness to survive. Providence "has given every race its own talent, and ordains that only that race which combines perfectly with the virtues of all shall endure." This conduces to a rather bleak outlook. But perhaps it will not be quite as bad as that, for Emerson also assures us that charity preserves many lives that are not worth preserving.

II

No hermit of the Thebaid ever spoke more disparagingly of sociality than Emerson. He says we "descend to meet," that we need space between ourselves and our neighbors, and that even the walker functions best when he is alone. We are complete when we are alone, but only fractions in society. No man who has fine traits is, in fact, fit for society. Men can work in society only with loss of power; "every brave heart must treat society as a child, and never allow it to dictate." As to courting popularity, "popularity is for dolls." Those with special gifts must live in isolation, only descending into the crowd from time to time as benefactors. Michelangelo "lived alone, and never or very rarely took his meals with any person."

Society is as vulgar as solitude is proud, and it needs to be taken in small doses. People are worth knowing only when they are at their best, and we sink through sympathy as easily as we rise.

> You shall not love me for what daily spends;
> You shall not know me in the noisy street,
> Where I, as others, follow petty ends;
> Nor when in fair saloons we chance to meet;
> Nor when I'm jaded, sick, anxious or mean.
> But love me then and only, when you know
> Me for the channel of the rivers of God
> From deep ideal fontal heavens that flow.[3]

Even conversation is better between two than three, and companions must always be carefully chosen. "Whom God hath put asunder, let no man put together." Ordinary social calls should never exceed ten minutes, unless extension is asked or granted.

> If Love his moment overstay,
> Hatred's swift repulsions play.

The reader of Emerson soon learns, however, that, like most of his extreme statements, these cannot be taken at face value. In practice he always recognized the need for a judicious balance between society and solitude, fearing the excesses of both; you would undo most men, he says, by cooping them up, for society trains the will, always weak in solitude. "We want friendship," he finds, and he puts this desire on a level with our need for knowledge and virtue. "Welfare requires one or two companions of intelligence, probity and grace to wear out life with." Conversation is "the last flower of civilization and the best result which life has to offer us,—a cup for gods, which has no repentance." The most valuable friend is he to whom one can say anything, discussing all topics without fear of offense, and such a friendship doubles the value of life.

And so in groups where debate is earnest, and especially on high questions, the company become aware that the thought rises to an equal level in all bosoms, that all have a spiritual property in what was said, as well as the sayer. They all become wiser than they were. It arches over them like a temple, this unity of thought in which every heart beats with nobler sense of power and duty, and thinks and acts with unusual solemnity. All are conscious of attaining to a higher self-possession.

If this is true, then we do not always "descend to meet." There are people in the world in whose presence we rise with ease above the plane we commonly inhabit. "We are easily great with the loved and honored associate." [4]

Even on a more formal level, society was not wholly rejected. Though Emerson claimed to despise pedigree, he admitted he had been trained to value it, and though he told F. H. Hedge that he classed "good" society with Bacon's Idols of the Cave, it is clear that it was always available to him when he chose to make use of it. His lecture on Chaucer stresses heavily the poet's respect for "gentilesse." He admits that it would be easier to take a meal with a liar than a sloven, and when one eccentric visitor refused to remove his hat in the house, Emerson took him outside to finish his conversation! When he was away from home, he always wanted to go to the best hotels and restaurants available, "for though they cost more, they do not cost much more, and there is good company and the best information." He believed that in some circumstances artificiality itself becomes natural and that fashion is a kind of virtue gone to seed. "Society" does achieve a certain freedom for those who are "in," and good manners, originating in strokes of genius or love but now hardened into usage, has become "a rich varnish with which the routine of life is washed and its details adorned." There is even something to be said for clubs as a refuge against "the vulgarities of the street and the tavern" which Emerson was elsewhere tempted to praise, for there are people whom you cannot cultivate, and the best you can do with these is to keep them "down and quiet" if you can. All in all, I should say that he neither under- nor over-estimated the value of good manners, for though he regarded them as a useful and comforting lubricant, he was always clear that they could not achieve the impossible; the man's own inner inciting force was the final test and determinant. Yet when Anna Barker Ward became a Catholic, he came within hailing distance of both perfect snobbery and perfect bigotry by lamenting to Arthur Hugh Clough that this act would interfere with her social relations! [5]

He regarded himself as singularly lacking in social gifts. "My strength and my doom is to be solitary." So he speaks of his "cloistered and unfriendly manners," his "awkward and porcupine manners," as making him an unpromising candidate for any society. "At the name of a society all my repulsions play, all my quills rise and sharpen." In 1833 he wrote his aunt that he could not get used to men ("they always awaken expectations in me which they always disappoint"), and that same year he informed his brother William that his own study was the best place for him. He found "high thought" lacking in Boston, in London, and in Cambridge, which was only an extension of London, and in later years he was grateful to his residence in Concord for having protected him from many contacts. It is true that though he did not much believe in communities like Brook Farm, which seemed to him only engaged in substituting one prison for another,[6] he did believe in neighborhoods, and there is an 1840 letter to Margaret Fuller in which he flirts with the idea of a "university" built around lectures or conversations with young people in Concord, enlisting himself, Margaret Fuller, and others. Sometimes he even thought he wanted a kind of coffee-house in which writers could meet instead of merely encountering each other as at Munroe's Bookstore, but I am not sure he would have made much use of such a meeting place. He admired —and a little envied—the *savoir faire* of a man like Samuel Gray Ward—handsome, master of the situation and of all themes he cared to discuss—but there is a bit of a sting in his comment that, like Goethe and Madame de Staël, Ward was so well adapted to this world that it seemed a pity he must ever leave it. Even in his own house, Emerson said, he himself viewed other persons across a gulf.[7]

He lamented these tendencies on occasion, but during the early years at least, he did not believe it was in his power to do anything about them. When Horace Greeley accompanied him on a lecture tour, he found him good company but was annoyed by the attention he attracted. It was like traveling with Barnum, he said, and he would take care not to do it again. He once told Lidian that not many persons were as important to him as nature or his books. If he wanted no followers, it was not only because he was on principle opposed to discipleship, but also because he knew they would be a burden to him. "What could I do if they came to me? They would interrupt and encumber me. This is my boast, that I have no school and no followers." He reproached himself for not standing up against conventionally minded people, against the foppish and the impercipient, instead of taking the easiest way by seeming acquiescence. It was humiliating to think that any whippersnapper could embarrass him and put him down in company, even if he had no respect for him.

Emerson seems to have regarded what he described as his deficiency in "animal spirits" as being primarily responsible for his social problems, but this was certainly powerfully reinforced by his childhood residence in a neighborhood where there were no suitable children for him to play with. Because of his poverty he also missed the dancing parties, private theatricals, and other polite amenities with which well-bred children grow up familiar. At thirteen he was asked why all the grown people seemed fond of him while the boys disliked him. He would have been the least likely of all persons to know the answer. In college he was friendly but self-contained. As "president's freshman," he may have disliked the proximity of his room to the president's study, from which he could be called easily to perform his chores, but this probably also provided a certain not uncongenial protection for him.

It does not appear, however, that even Emerson's early solitude was ever carried to extremes. As a schoolboy he sometimes played hooky. He was far from being a grind in college, and he supported his class when, in his sophomore year, some members were expelled after a row with the freshmen. Indeed, then, as later, his whole social record was considerably better than his theory.

It is true that, during his brief pastorate, the sexton was not impressed by him as a conductor of funeral services and that once, when he tried to talk naturally about inconsequent things to a parishioner suffering a terminal illness, he was testily told that if that was the best he could do, he might just as well be on his way. He does not seem to have neglected his pastoral work, however, nor community work outside the church either (we hear, for example, of his making five calls on one day), and although he gave up the ministry, there is no indication that social shyness was a contributing cause. He served his alma mater in various ways and helped raise the money to build Memorial Hall. Later he did not take a leading role in the community life of Concord, but he certainly did not hold himself wholly aloof from it, though he does complain that the only use country people can find for a scholar is to ask him to give a temperance lec-

ture or serve on the school committee. His son says that he
seldom entered Concord shops and that though he would have
liked to join the village worthies at the grocery store, he re-
strained himself, knowing that the presence of a scholar and
clergyman would act as a dampener upon them. As a matter of
fact, the first civic honor for which he was chosen in Concord
was that of hog reeve, whose duty it was to round up stray
hogs, a function traditionally devolving upon the most recently
married man in town! In 1844 he was so much attached to the
Social Circle in Concord, which consisted of twenty-five male
members representing various callings, that he did not like to
be absent from town on the night of their weekly meetings, and,
in later years, he diligently attended the meetings of the Satur-
day Club at the Parker House in Boston. In the course of his
career, he accepted some pretty odd appointments, none queerer
than that of serving on an examining committee at West Point,
but this was during the Civil War, when he, along with a great
many other Americans, was not quite sane on military matters.[8]

The reserve, such as it was, was always there. Though Julian
Hawthorne says that "the grasp of his hand was firm and stout,"
his son makes the interesting if rather obscure comment that
"his look was not too personal to others." It is clear that his
social problems were only partly caused by his love of solitude.
Whether or not it is true that a child lives on in the heart of
every man of genius, it was certainly true in his case. He felt
like a child even in the presence of people who were considerably younger than he was, but unlike the child, he was not satisfied to remain dependent. Men of the world caused him to feel
incompetent and gave him what we now call an inferiority complex, which was no less troublesome because it was occasioned
by people whom he actually did not respect very much. His
position in the photograph of the members of the Adirondack
Club out camping, in which he stands apart from both the

groups included in the picture,[9] may be accidental, but it seems strangely appropriate.

In social intercourse there is no more important element than conversation, and Emerson fully recognized this. Cabot says that

When anything said specially interested him, he would lean towards the speaker with a look never to be forgotten, his head stretched forward, his shoulders raised like the wings of an eagle, and his eye watching the flight of the thought which had attracted his attention, as if it were his prey, to be seized in mid-air and carried up to his eyry.

Perhaps such listening is as good as talking, even though we learn further that Emerson listened much as he read, so that an idea which particularly challenged his attention might send him off on a train of his own musings, the results of which were quite as likely to emerge in a journal entry tomorrow as in his conversation today. We also learn that he "looked his guest kindly and searchingly in the eyes on his arrival, but, in talking with him, he looked fixedly rather beside than at him, while answering his questions not directly, but suggestively." He prided himself on his powers of observation, and there are passages which bear him out in this. "I find out in an instant," he says, "if my companion does not want me, and ropes cannot hold me when my welcome is gone." There is abundant testimony that he sought to draw out those who came to him instead of imposing himself upon them, treating even youngsters as if he had something to learn from them. His evasive or noncommittal way of answering those who came to him with questions and problems was determined in part by his refusal to impose his own ideas upon others and his insistence upon every man discovering the truth for himself, but his natural reserve must also have been involved. And admirable as all this may have been in its way, many persons were troubled by what they thought the hesitancy and inconsecutiveness of his conversation, his omission of links between ideas and disregard of logical sequence, and Holmes says that hearing him talk was like watching somebody cross a brook on stepping-stones.

Yet Emerson had his own brand of social charm. He disliked ridicule and sarcasm and was generally accounted a good-natured man. He himself denied this—he had cats' claws, he said—and he tells us that while he does not envy anybody wealth, he is quite capable of wishing ill to those who have injured him or before whom he has played the fool.[10] Sometimes he worked off frustrations in his garden, permitting nature to restore his self-respect. Sanborn and others indicate that he was capable of severity, but those who felt this most strongly seem to have been moved by their great respect for him and consequent fear of his disapproval. Sometimes, too, they were probably disturbed by Emerson's own lack of ease, for he never became quite the man of the world, and once, when he was told that a young man wished to come to see him in London but was afraid to approach him, he said, in effect, "Let him come. I am afraid of him too." He said he considered truth more important than "fat good nature" and would rather be a nettle than an echo. Yet he had no trouble commanding respect or even admiration from others. Hawthorne, who did not see eye to eye with him, still found comfort in his mingled loftiness and grace, and Fredrika Bremer, who admired him but felt antipathetic toward him because of the inhuman elevation she thought he had achieved, found a "sunbeam" in his face. It was the same with Henry James, Sr., who considered Emerson's philosophical and religious outlook profoundly unsatisfactory: his presence was divine, said James, though he had no more reflective power than an old dame you might come across in a horse car! And though Oliver Wendell Holmes was sure nobody could possibly have thought of taking liberties with Emerson, he also thought no man less abrasive or (in the best sense of a much abused word) sweeter.

> Sunshine was he
> In the winter day;
> And in the midsummer
> Coolness and shade.

Emerson disliked evening "affairs" because he thought they spoiled the next day for him, and he was sometimes tortured at Lidian's "soirées," not feeling at home in his own house, but there is ample evidence that both he and she were extremely hospitable people, and this to house guests as well as dinner guests. Julian Hawthorne says Emerson conducted himself at his own table as the least considerable person present and that his courtesy and deference toward his guests and toward his own wife and children were beautiful. Nobody, surely, could have been more cordial than both the Emersons were to young Moncure D. Conway when he descended upon them with no introduction save a vaguely remembered letter a year or two old; they insisted upon his remaining under their roof for a few days and almost seemed ready to adopt him. If Emerson did not exactly hold himself available to all comers, he was certainly responsive to advances, and when an appointment had been made, he was always on hand to keep it, not on time but ahead of time.[11] He once spent between four and five hours in conversation with John W. Chadwick on the train between Boston and New York, frustrating every attempt Chadwick made to leave him. When he returned from Europe with Norton in 1873, he seems to have been one of the most sociable men on the ship, and on his California journey he delighted everybody by being always accessible, tolerant, understanding, gracious, friendly, interested, and never tired.[12]

Though, as Emerson said, he did not want disciples, he admitted that to meet young men who showed vital interest in his ideas was stimulating and refreshing, and he was responsive to such, even when they sometimes became over-enthusiastic and showered him with burdensome letters. With children he was always charming. Julia Ward Howe once encountered him on a journey, carrying a strange three-year-old on his shoulder, and Edward Everett Hale tells how, as a guest in Philadelphia, Emerson rose in the night to comfort two little boys, fellow guests, who had waked up sick and frightened.[13]

Emerson was skillful and patient in dealing with the innumerable bores and eccentrics whom his fame attracted. One gentleman wished to be advised about his Oriental reading; he also hoped to interest Emerson in studies of the philosophy of crime. A female correspondent complained of his unwillingness to spend an hour a week writing to her, but even she does not seem to have been snubbed as she deserved. Of course he himself was dissatisfied with his performance in this area also; speaking of one of his nuisances, he says, "I am not large man enough to treat him firmly and unsympathetically as a patient, and if treated equally and sympathetically, his disease makes him the worst of bores." He put up with it, however; perhaps, like Longfellow, he remembered that he had been "bored so often." So he fed cranks and listened to them and attempted to take them "by their best handle," and when they did not seem to have any, he tried to think of the time and strength he had spent on them as "a sacrifice to the gods."

III

One special fact must be taken into account in relation to Emerson's sociality or the lack of it, and this is the fact that his business was communication. And because public speaking seems a more direct form of communication than writing, it falls for at least passing consideration here.

Emerson grew up in the great age of American oratory, in the world of Daniel Webster, Wendell Phillips, and Edward Everett. When, in "Spiritual Laws," he describes a "public oration" as "an escapade, a non-committal, an apology, a gag, and not a communication, not a speech, not a man," he is only rejecting formality and insincerity. As a child he spouted poetry from the sugar barrel in Deacon White's store and, for his own amusement, on Boston Common. At Harvard, where, in his time, the Southern boys were generally most adept in the florid oratory the age valued, he carried off the Boylston Prize for speaking, and he is said to have been disgruntled that he was not permitted to read his Class Poem at commencement.

Though he glorified spontaneity in public speaking as in other things, he never really learned to speak extemporaneously; he even says that all good speakers write their speeches. In college he was a member of the Pythologian Club, which was devoted to extemporaneous discussion, and we hear of one debate in which he participated before the Concord Lyceum, but argument was not his forte, and he seldom spoke in town meeting, though he always listened intently. In 1841 he did speak extemporaneously at an antislavery meeting in Worcester, but *The Liberator* reported him as looking up "into the sky and far off into the woods and fields" as if this might help him to get his ideas into order. His one great triumph along this line would seem to have been his famous oration on Burns. He said he re-read Burns's poems before delivering this address, being now much more favorably impressed by them than he had ever been before. "But I had only a few moments to prepare myself for speaking."

Since he started out to be a clergyman, he obviously intended to become a professional speaker, and that is just what he did

become, for in the winter time he often read a lecture nearly
every day, and sometimes twice a day, for weeks at a stretch, and
though this was a matter of economic necessity to him, it is impossible not to believe that he enjoyed it, for he continued it almost to the very end of his life, even after writing itself had become impossible for him.

As a preacher, he knew from the beginning that preaching
involves a meeting of minds, and that where this does not occur,
there is no preaching, however beautiful a composition may be
exhibited. It is true that the wife of one minister with whom he
had exchanged pulpits said that he had preached "with his chin
in the air, in scorn of the whole human race," but there is no
suggestion of anything like this in the sermons that have been
printed, and the safest guess would be that the lady was antipathetic to him; it may even have pleased her to think that he
was inferior to her husband. Emerson himself once criticized a
production by his brother Charles, because he said that though
it was a beautiful work of art, it did not really address the
audience, but left it to them whether they would take it up or
no.

Emerson called oratory a great art and saw a combination of
all the qualities of the artist in the orator; at times he even suggested that he preferred, or might have preferred, it to writing.
He missed preaching as a stated task after he had given it up, and
it is very significant that he seems to have missed it most for the
social contacts it afforded. "I have come almost to depend on
conversations for my prolific hours," he says, and one sometimes
wonders whether he may not even have relished facing mobs as
an abolition speaker! On beginning his divinity studies, he wrote,
"I burn after the *aliquid immensum infinitum que* which Cicero
desired." Speaking involved more action than writing, and thinking on his feet apparently seemed a greater thing to him than

thinking in his study. Indeed, he even perceived an heroic quality in speaking, for the speaker stands before his audience as a challenger and must keep himself a little ahead of them. As late as 1862, Emerson felt aggrieved that not even a small country college had ever offered him a professorship of rhetoric; he thought he might have trained better speakers than he ever became himself, and he told Moncure D. Conway that to be a professor of rhetoric and elocution was a worthy ambition and that communication was the key to peace among men. All this suggests a stronger urge to power in Emerson than one might assume in view of his well-known reluctance to acquire disciples. Perhaps the self-abnegation suggested by this reluctance was a later development, or perhaps it was merely the expression of a different side of his personality. If he accepted the passive, or what we used to call the feminine, aspects of his genius, he also felt their limitations. He would have liked to serve his friends by love and active aid, and not merely by expressing ideas.

But *did* Emerson as a public speaker communicate? There have always been those who insisted that he did not, and David Macrae may speak for many, some of whom were much less respectful than he.

Often his interest seemed more that of one looking at his own thought than of one who has to impress his thought upon others. . . . In so far as he spoke to the audience, he was curt, aphoristic, oracular. There was no arguing, no explaining, no bridging the gaps for little feet or unaccustomed limbs; the giant hurled his stepping-stones into the river-bed and strode across, seldom looking back to see if others could follow.

In England, *The Athenaeum* thought his eye had "a frosty glitter, like that of a basilisk" (an animal with whom the reviewer was evidently quite familiar), while in this country *The Plain-Dealer*, though paying the meaningless tribute of ignorance to Emerson's "massive intellect," would as soon have seen "a perpendicular coffin" behind a lecture desk!

Emerson's idiosyncrasies as a platform artist have furnished commentators with material for a field day time out of mind. Perhaps it is his manuscript which has inspired the most vivid passages—"these ragged, blotted sheets, as if they were hustled together like a pack of cards," says Alcott, "and pasted over in parts, the leaves of different hues." [14] He shuffled them and rummaged through them (and sometimes through his pockets also, as if he expected to find something more there); he lost his place, omitted passages, and skipped inadvertently. Once he is supposed to have stopped in the middle of sentence, searched vainly among his papers, and then left the platform. He twirled his glasses when he had them, but once he came without them and could not see to read until he had borrowed a pair from a member of the audience. Once he upset a vase, descended from the platform, gathered up the scattered flowers, and replaced them, all without any sign of perturbation. When he read the second Phi Beta Kappa Address at Harvard, he kept losing his papers until Edward Everett Hale came to his rescue by putting a cushion under them, and when he read his famous "Boston Hymn," some of his leaves escaped into the audience and had to be retrieved before he could go on. His delivery was, generally speaking, monotonous; he rocked his body and took a hasty backward step after reading a striking passage. His endings were always abrupt, and he left the platform without giving the audience a chance to applaud, inspiring one reporter to quip that "he folded his tent like the Arabs and as silently stole away," which might have seemed more appropriate for Longfellow than for him, except that Longfellow would never have mounted the platform in the first place.

These would be heavy handicaps for anybody to overcome,

and Emerson told Higginson that he was the worst public speaker on record and continually getting worse. At the end, when he had to have Ellen on the platform beside him, to help him over difficult places, he remarked, touchingly, that he was not disturbed by things going wrong because he knew that those who came to hear him now came because they loved him and knew that he was nearly worn out. Yet it is clear that Emerson had his assets as well as his liabilities. He was a leading performer in the Lyceums for many years, and people did not continue to attend his lectures merely to watch him shuffle his manuscripts. He was one of William H. Herndon's favorite lecturers in Springfield, Illinois, and one of Mark Hanna's in Cleveland. In Wisconsin he appeared twenty-three times between 1854 and 1867, contributing importantly, C. E. Schorer believes, to the cultural development of the state.[15] Moreover, he had plenty of reserve power to draw upon when he needed it. He could emphasize a strong point by a direct or penetrating glance at the audience, and after an important passage, delivered forcefully, he would make a pause and begin the next paragraph very quietly. On occasion he could skillfully use the relief of humor, as when he said, "If we could only make up our minds always to tell the truth, the whole truth, and nothing but the truth," and then added, after just the right pause, "to what embarrassing situations it would give rise." At times, too, even his idiosyncrasies had power. An Indianapolis paper remarked that he had a trick "of seeming to forget the last word or two . . . and stumbling upon them unexpectedly with an effect that the most elaborate declamation could not produce."

Finally, it should be noted that, though Emerson gave far fewer public readings than lectures, he was, in his way, an outstanding reader. As Emma Lazarus, who certainly should have been a good judge, wrote,

He indulged in no elocutionary tricks, no studied intonations, but his voice took on an added sonority, the verse seemed to flow from his lips with a mingled force and sweetness which thrilled through the listener's every fibre.

She adds that she found such "subdued organ-tones," such "majesty," such "heroic ring" in his reading of Stedman's "Ossawatomie Brown" that she had never been able to judge the poem dispassionately since hearing him read it. And the Boston *Journal* was in complete agreement:

There is no other man in America who can, by the mere force of what he says, so enthrall and dominate an audience. Breathless attention is given, although now and then the voice falls away so that those seated farthest off have to strain every nerve to catch the words. The grand condensation, the unfaltering and almost cynical brevity of expression, are at first startling and vexatious; but presently one yields to the charm, and finds his mind in the proper assenting mood. The loving tenderness with which Emerson lingers over a fine and thoroughly expressive phrase is beyond description.[16]

IV

Social relations in general are not in themselves friendship, but they certainly condition it importantly. Since friendship rests upon spiritual consanguinity, our friends come to us unsought, like all else that really belongs to us, and "individual character, religion, age, sex, circumstance" mean little or nothing. Harmony can be established between souls in the exchange of a glance, without a word being spoken. "Who hears me, who understands me, becomes mine,—a possession for all time."

The reason why I am curious about you [so Emerson wrote Samuel Ward in 1840], is that with tastes which I also have, you have tastes and powers and corresponding circumstances which I have not and perhaps cannot divine. Certainly we will not quarrel with our companion that he has more roots subterranean or aerial sent out into the great universe to draw his nourishment withal.

And upon re-encountering his old friend W. H. Furness, Emerson wrote, "Those are good companions to whom we have the keys."

Here, as with sociality in general, Emerson's theory is mixed. "Cold as I am," he writes of Alcott and Margaret Fuller, "they are almost dear." It is all very well to believe that "we must have society on our own terms, and admit or exclude it on the slightest cause," but when Emerson says of his friends, "I would have them where I can find them, but I seldom use them," he seems to reveal a rather one-sided conception of friendship. Indeed, he gives the impression of being more austere about friendship than he is about love, and this has led some to suggest that he must have found his own friendships less rewarding than his more intimate emotional life. He once wrote Margaret Fuller that he thought he knew too many people and doubted whether he really needed more than one or two, while Elizabeth Hoar was informed both that he doted upon his friends when they were absent but could not think of anything to say to them when he saw them and that he wished he had a friend in whom he could confide yet doubted that he really had the strength to sustain such a relationship. Here again it is one thing to realize that all human beings are faulty ("friends such as we desire are dreams and fables"), that they can, like books, be outgrown, and that one is not worthy of friendship until he has learned to do without it; perhaps it is even possible to realize that intercourse is likely to mean more when it is somewhat sparing ("we should meet each other each morning as from foreign countries, and, spending the day together, should depart at night, as into foreign countries"); but to draw from this the conclusion that you would just as soon have your friends in

Oregon while you are in Massachusetts is something else again. When John Sterling wrote to Emerson in September, the letter gave him "great joy," but he not only delayed his reply until May but actually cited his devotion to friendship as explaining the delay: "As soon as any man pronounces the words which approve him fit for that great office, I make no haste: he is holy; let me be holy also; our relations are eternal; why should we count days and weeks?" This may be transcendental idealism, but I fancy most people would say it sounded more like great nonsense, and Emerson was capable of even worse than this. When he went to talk with Alcott, he said, it was less to get Alcott's thoughts than to study himself as stimulated by him! He also wanted to outlive both Alcott and Ellery Channing so that he might write about them; if he went first, he thought, two good books would be lost! In fairness to Emerson, however, one must recognize that he did not quite inhabit the material plane. Sanborn says he seldom mentioned his friends by name, and Alcott thought men were too much ideas to him. From a man who believed that true love was never unrequited, that fellowship could endure without contact, and that it was possible to be *en rapport* with a person one had never met, such statements may well seem less icy than they would if coming from a more "normal," probably inferior, human being.

Furthermore, one must remember that this was only one side of the 'scutcheon. If Emerson called his coldness a fault, he also reproached himself for "an excessive desire for sympathy" and told Caroline Sturgis that he comforted himself in solitude by repeating her name and Margaret Fuller's. He could not believe he deserved his friends. Their coming awakened wonder. How many among those who are shocked by Emerson's coldness could say with him: "I carry the keys of my castle in my hand, ready to throw them at the feet of my lord, whenever and in what disguise soever he shall appear"? How many could say, "A new person is to me a great event and will not let me sleep"? How many are loyal to their friends to such an extent that to hear them praised or blamed inspires a passionate reaction, as if they were hearing something about themselves? How many would have cut Wendell Phillips, as Emerson did, after Phillips had spoken harshly and unfairly of Judge Hoar?

Moreover, Emerson's practical relations with others always inclined to accord more with his heart than with his head. Carlyle, Bronson Alcott, Thoreau, Margaret Fuller, Ellery Channing—these were not all the easiest people in the world to get on with, and Emerson's relations with them had their ups and downs, yet he took a vital interest in all of them, and in many more. Also, except for the munificent gift his friends made to him when his house was burned, he was, in all practical matters, far more often on the giving than the receiving end. He went to endless trouble for his literary friends, sometimes bargaining with publishers, far more energetically than in his own behalf, even for people he hardly knew. Once he threatened a lawsuit when he thought Wiley and Putnam had wronged Carlyle. He risked considerable capital to get Carlyle published in America at a time when he himself had little or nothing to spare, even undertaking the, to him, loathsome task of keeping business records. When Arthur Hugh Clough was considering coming to America, he invited him to spend two or three months in Concord while getting his bearings, glossing over his generosity by adding that Clough could help him with his *English Notes*. He showed real kindness toward a former pupil, who had either been refused admission to Harvard or had left during his freshman year, by offering to lend him money if he needed it. He gave Ellery Channing seventy-five dollars toward a trip to Europe in 1846, when that worthy thought his self-development required such an excursion, and solicited further funds in his behalf. He not only attempted to aid Delia Bacon in her Shakespearean researches, but offered to contribute toward her support after she had broken down.[17] But of course the principal recipient of his bounty was Alcott. He financed Alcott's trip to Europe, and he is said also to have helped him buy Orchard House and to have contributed to the Fruitlands venture. It is both amusing and characteristic, however, that when Alcott was soliciting funds for another European jaunt in 1855, Emerson should have opposed the venture and set to work instead to develop a plan to raise a fund which should give Alcott a small income as a "natural Capuchin."

Perhaps Emerson deserves the more credit because he served his friends loyally without idealizing them. We have already seen how Whitman tried him. He was repelled by the hard line Carlyle took toward social questions during his later years, yet, even in 1870, he inscribed a copy of *Society and Solitude*, "To the General in Chief from his Lieutenant." Alcott was godlike, majestic, an American jewel, a towering genius, the most refined and advanced soul in New England, and superior in pure intellect to anybody else Emerson had known. But alas! he was also a "majestic egotist" and "a cold piece of spiritual chemistry." His angles were so generous that the lines did not meet and the apex remained undefined; in addition to this, he was a hopelessly incompetent writer and utterly inept in all practical affairs. He was "a pail without a bottom," and he lived to talk steadily, upon abstract themes, being quite incapable of casual conversation on matters of mere "human" concern; once or twice prolonged exposure to him actually sent Emerson to bed.[18]

With Thoreau, his discovery and, at the outset at least, his disciple, Emerson's reservations were quite different.

There was something military in his nature, not to be subdued, always manly and able, but rarely tender, as if he did not feel himself except in opposition. He wanted a fallacy to expose, a blunder to pillory, I may say required a little sense of victory, a roll of the drum, to call his powers into full exercise. It cost him nothing to say No; indeed he found it much easier than to say Yes. It seemed as if his first instinct on hearing a proposition was to controvert it, so impatient was he of the limitations of our daily thought. This habit, of course, is a little chilling to the social affections; and though the companion would in the end acquit him of any malice or untruth, yet it mars conversation. Hence, no equal companion stood in affectionate relations with one so pure and guileless. "I love Henry," said one of his friends, "but I cannot like him; and as for taking his arm, I should as soon think of taking the arm of an elm-tree."

In other words, Thoreau's self-reliance was perfect, yet he failed in balance and completeness because of his deficiencies on the social side. If all were like him, cooperation between men would be impossible. "Always some weary captious paradox to fight you with, and the time and temper wasted." John Albee thought that Emerson sometimes deliberately tried to draw Thoreau's fire, at once deferring to him and laughing quietly at his "negative and biting criticisms." But Emerson told Daniel Chester French that Thoreau was his own worst enemy, a friend of the farmer and the workingman who felt only contempt for everybody else. It seems clear that if Emerson thought Thoreau too much of a come-outer, the younger man regarded him as too much of a conformist, resenting his refusal to argue and, perhaps, as Frank B. Sanborn suggests, his "*chevaux de frise* of fine manners." [19] And as Thoreau grew older, he also resented standing to Emerson in the old position of discipleship and was unwilling to show him the deference that had seemed natural and fitting at the beginning of their relationship.[20]

Margaret Fuller was much the most important of Emerson's women friends and the one with whom he enjoyed the most complicated relationship, but she was not the one he cared most for. This must have been rather Elizabeth Hoar (who was engaged, until his death, to Charles Emerson) or Caroline Sturgis or Anna Barker, later Anna Barker Ward. Elizabeth's presence was consecration (the word is Emerson's), and Caroline represented, in her loftiness, "the Hope of these modern days." As for Anna, he found the intimacy of her approaches and the relations she established admirable and irresistible, and even after she had disappointed him by turning Catholic, she was "endeared" and "enshrined" to him despite their differences. Of those less intimately associated with him, probably the most important was the young Jewish poet Emma Lazarus, whose verses are engraved on the Statue of Liberty. Emerson encouraged her and invited her to stay at his house, where she seems to have enjoyed herself greatly, though she was apparently surprised that Emerson continued his work as usual during her visit and was not at all times available for conversation, but he nearly broke her heart when he failed to include any of her verses in *Parnassus*.[21] It is true that even with women like these, some of the problems that clouded his relations with Margaret Fuller remained: Emerson could or would give himself only thus far, and from there he retreated into the impregnable fastnesses of his own inner personality.[22] But Margaret furnished the real test case, partly because of the associations they shared, but more because she was herself.

Except with those whom she could dominate comfortably—and Emerson was not dominatable by man or by woman—Margaret's personality was abrasive, and many besides Emerson felt it so. His first impression of her was decidedly unpleasant. "Her extreme plainness,—and a trick of incessantly opening and shutting her eyelids,—the nasal tone of her voice,—all repelled; and I said to myself, we shall never get far." He disliked her intensity and egotism and complained that she brought "profane," amusing gossip into his house, which reminded him of the crackling of thorns under a pot. (She says he rebuked her for her "strong expressions.") Since he looked forward to her visits with a "slight shudder," it may seem odd that she was so often invited to stay with the Emersons, but Lidian seems to have liked her.

Emerson was probably unwise in allowing Margaret Fuller to draw him into prolonged discussions concerning their personalities, their likes and dislikes, and the differences between them; so far as we know, he never did this with anybody else. As time went on, however, he was increasingly impressed by her extraordinary "apprehensiveness, her acquisitions, and her power of conversation." She progressed strikingly, in thought and in character, and he never saw her without observing newly developed power in her. Longfellow and Lowell both disliked her, and Hawthorne hated her; in 1873 Emerson told Charles Eliot Norton that Lowell had not been far wrong about her except that she had another side to her which he did not see, and this, I believe, was an accurate evaluation. Once he compared her to mythological goddesses (which was just what she thought). On the whole he praised her more warmly in his correspondence than in the memoir he wrote of her.[23] In London, in 1848, when he heard that she was ill and in want at Rome, he suggested that she come to Paris to go home with him, and when she died he called her "brave, eloquent, subtle, accomplished, devoted, constant soul" and lamented that with her he had lost his audience. Even then, however, he judged her criticism to be too much colored by personal feelings and considered her writing overrated.

Perhaps the greatest difficulty between Emerson and Margaret Fuller, however, was on Margaret's side. As Emerson says, "She ever seems to crave somewhat I have not, or have not for her." Richard Garnett long ago commented that, in her intercourse with Emerson, Margaret was the ardent wooer and he the proud

beauty, while Harry R. Warfel quotes[24] Caroline Dall: "She and
Mr. Emerson met like Pyramus and Thisbe, a blank wall between them." But Emerson had no desire to be her Pyramus
(nor yet her Ossoli); neither had he any possible obligation to
do so. He endorsed one of her letters, "What shocking familiarity." I am not suggesting that Margaret Fuller tried to
seduce Emerson, but sybil though she was, her subsequent history
shows that she was also a woman whose most imperative need
was to be loved. By 1842 she wrote of her relations with Emerson, "But my expectations are moderate now." Unless he had
wished to break off relations with her altogether, Emerson
probably handled the whole business about as well as anybody
could have done it.

Emerson illustrated his capacity for finding friends in unlikely places most strikingly in his association with Achille
Murat, son of Napoleon's brother-in-law, Joachim, King of
Naples, whom he met on his journey to Florida and South
Carolina in 1827, and who would seem to have been about as
different from him in temperament, background, and convictions
as anybody could be. In the light of the coarse and outrageous
behavior that has been reported of Murat elsewhere, he would
seem to have been at his best with Emerson, but their association
still testifies to considerable capacity for adjustment on the New
Englander's part.[25] Such differences did not exist between Emerson and such New England businessmen as Abel Adams and
George Sampson, yet their interests were very different from
his. He also showed a quick, warm responsiveness to "Indians
who have the spirit," as he called them, people like Mary Rotch
and Rebecca Black who were spiritually sensitive, even if the
mind had not kept pace with the heart. Finally, it may be worth
noting that Emerson was sometimes very appreciative of those
who severely criticized him. Henry James, Sr., for example, was
"true comfort; wise, gentle, polished, with heroic manners, and

a serenity like the sun." Then there was Jones Very, who was attracted to Emerson through his writings, but felt that his "spirit was not quite right" when they met. "It was as if a vein of colder air blew across me," he wrote. Emerson recorded this but took no offense at it. Though he never quite decided whether Very was mad or everybody was mad except Very, he still rated him "a very remarkable person" and "a treasure of a companion." [26]

CHAPTER FIVE

LOVE

College students asked whether Emerson's "Love" deals with sexual love or spiritual love (*eros* or *agape*) are often sufficiently misled by the idealistic tone of the piece so that they reply "spiritual love," but this is an answer which shows more about them and the society in which they live than it does about Emerson. The essay begins with an excellent statement of what "the enchantment of human life" achieves. It

seizes on man . . . and works a revolution in his mind and body; unites him to his race, pledges him to the domestic and civil relations, carries him with new sympathy into nature, enhances the power of the senses, opens the imagination, adds to his character heroic and sacred attributes, establishes marriage and gives permanence to human society.

Love transforms life, character, and the world; through it rude boys and girls learn how to respect personality. Nor is its power wholly confined to the young. All the world loves a lover; Emerson believed that even ordinary men are interesting when they are in love and that only those who have never loved themselves can laugh at such a man. If love leads at last to something beyond itself, so that "one beautiful soul" becomes the door through which "all true and pure souls" may be appre-

hended and cherished, this is not because there is anything
wrong in sexual love itself, but only because the body lacks
the power to fulfill all the promise love holds out. In a true
marriage both the intellect and the heart are refined and puri-
fied year after year.[1]

Emerson certainly showed no undue interest in sex in the
narrower sense, but neither was he ever squeamish about it.
There is an interesting passage in the journals[2] in which the
whole process of generation is called "bifronted," bawdy or
wholly chaste, depending upon the attitude one takes toward
it. He admitted the power of passion frankly and was as impatient of "polite" intercourse as of "prissy" goodness. The
Shakers, he said bluntly, overstressed the value of celibacy to
such an extent that one might suppose them all afflicted with
priapism. He opposed expurgated editions of classics and preferred Plutarch's frankness to what he considered the false
delicacy of modern literature. "The piety of the Hebrew
prophets," he says, "purges their grossness. The circumcision
is an example of the power of poetry to raise the low and
offensive. Small and mean things serve as well as great symbols."
He could write without blinking such a sentence as "Lovers
abstain from caresses and haters from insults while they sit in
the parlor with common friends." In "The Romany Girl" he
composed a dramatic monologue for a gypsy; in "To Rhea" he
proffered advice to a jilted girl. And such a verse as "And kiss,
and couple, and beget" in "Initial, Daemonic, and Celestial
Love," must, one would think, have given many contemporary
readers something of the jolt they experienced from Whitman.
Certainly he never questioned love's power:

> Love on his errand bound to go
> Can swim the flood and wade through snow,
> Where way is none, 't will creep and wind
> And eat through Alps its home to find.

Even the

> Test of the poet is knowledge of love,
> For Eros is older than Saturn or Jove.[3]

He also recognized frankly that without the power to rouse passion, other gifts are of no avail:

> Thy beauty, if it lack the fire
> Which drives me mad with sweet desire,
> What boots it? [4]

He had no question that the nude human body was the prime and supremely appropriate subject for sculpture. But he liked to see flesh and blood bodies as well as marble ones (in Egypt he took them quite in his stride). "We go to the gymnasium and the swimming-school," he said, "to see the power and beauty of the body." A beautiful body was a pledge of wholeness, a symbol of perfection and goodness, and no degradation to which it might be subjected could quite destroy its dignity. Primitive people recognized this when they gave even Deity a human form.

He was very sensitive to beauty in men, women, and children.

We keep a running fire of sarcasm at ignorance and the life of the senses; then goes by, perchance, a fair girl, a piece of life, gay and happy, and making the commonest offices beautiful by the energy and heart with which she does them; and seeing this we admire and love her and them, and say, "Lo! a genuine creature of the fair earth, not dissipated or too early ripened by books, philosophy, religion, society, or care!" insinuating a treachery and contempt for all we had so long loved and wrought in ourselves and others.

Like Meredith, he knew that women are the lawgivers of social life and that without them it would be impossible. Society takes its charm from them. "They are not only wise themselves, they make us wise." And he found support for his faith in the fundamental unity of beauty and goodness in the harmony we all feel in the presence of beauty and our natural tendency to attribute "immaculate innocence" to the women we admire.

Emerson dissented from Plato's view that women are like men, only lesser, believing rather that they have their own strength and weakness. He considered that man's treatment of them had been, generally speaking, barbaric, and he had deep sympathy with them in their economic dependence upon man and the humiliation they must feel in being objects of desire to men who often failed to respond to any other qualities in them. He was thoughtful indeed when he remarked that one pleasant thing about being engaged is that a girl need no longer be concerned to please everybody. He believed that the failure of the Greeks to make women full-fledged human partners aborted the development of their civilization. Emerson gave women greater intuitive power than men (they could, he believed, size up a man's character upon first contact with him) and thought them more inclined to virtue than men are. It was Fourier's failure to understand this latter consideration that helped make his social theories impracticable.

But we must not draw the rash conclusion that if Emerson were with us today he would be marching with the Woman's Libbers. When he says of women, "I think their words are to be weighed; but it is their inconsiderate word,—according to the rule, 'take their first advice, not the second,' " one wonders if he is not disposed to deny them reasoning power. As he saw it, woman's strength was a thing of sentiment, not will. Her will was weak, though often sharply expressed, the overemphasis itself being a sign of weakness. Actually her function was not to do, but to inspire man's doing; he was the rudder, she the sail. "The poet finds her eyes anticipating his ode, the sculptor, his god; the architect, his house." But she herself enters not only trade but also art through necessity, not ambition (only great genius can make a career really agreeable to her), for she always places the affections first. Affection dominates her as intellect does man. He seeks truth, she goodness. Emerson disliked what he called the "Go home and mind your mending" end of Tennyson's *Princess*. He was not willing to allow man either to define woman's "rights" or to prescribe her "duties," and he is on record as having believed that all his own "points" would be carried sooner if women were given the vote, yet he often gives the impression that he would be happier if women did not claim their "rights," and Frank Bellew even quotes him as saying that he admired beautiful women and didn't care about their minds! As he saw it, woman's natural guardian and protector was man; it was only when he failed her that she looked to her own resources; Emerson knew that this often happened, but he regarded it as unnatural and unfortunate for her. There are even a few passages which would give some of our contemporaries a chance to make use of their most recently acquired, dearly cherished, and now sadly worn term of opprobrium: male chauvinism. He complained to his journal of the "feminine vehemence" of Andrews Norton's attack on the Divinity School Address, and there is one scornful reference to "spiritual eunuchs and women" and an opprobrious application to Pusey and others whom he did not admire of the term "female souls." He could even, on occasion, be mildly unchivalrous. In *English Traits* he declares that "England produces under favorable conditions of ease and culture the finest women in the world," but he disliked what he called the "stocky" figures of Englishwomen, and though he achieves nothing so outrageous as Hawthorne did in his description of them in *Our Old Home*, one still winces at his "stunted and thickset persons."

He advises lovers to guard their strangeness and husbands and wives not to expect too much. Yet though marriage even at its best involves a certain measure of disillusionment (no two people could live together on their merits alone, without the addition of good nature and forbearance), there is still some good in even "the worst-assorted connections." We try for complete union with our wives and husbands and, being defeated, we are left alone to fall back upon absorption in the performances going on in our private theaters. But this is no indictment of marriage as such, but merely a part of the human condition, since the same thing is true of all human relations, including those which exist within the families into which we were born. Love may be blind, but so is self, and though the man who possesses what Virginia Woolf was to call "the androgynous mind" (Emerson puts it more coarsely when he calls hermaphroditism "the symbol of the finished soul"), may need a woman less than others do, his need is not therefore canceled out.

Finally, of course, there is the ultimate question of marital fidelity. It was not Emerson's way to evade ultimate questions, and he did not evade this one. In his essay on Montaigne, he called both marriage and the state "open" questions, still on trial obviously, still bound to justify themselves by their utility. Love exists in time, experiencing birth, climax, and decay, like all other living things, and marriage is empirical, not ideal. It would be rash indeed to draw from all this the conclusion that Emerson was a prophet of "open" marriage or any of the other social aberrations with which we are currently blessed, yet "Give All To Love" is one of the most daring poems of the nineteenth century, and though we need to remember that even here romantic love itself is one of the dangerous "half-gods," the quotation of a few stanzas may still make it clear why twentieth-century rebels are still more friendly to Emerson

(those who have heard of him) than they are to some of his
contemporaries.

> Give all to love;
> Obey thy heart;
> Friends, kindred, days,
> Estate, good-fame,
> Plans, credit and the Muse,—
> Nothing refuse.

> 'Tis a brave master;
> Let it have scope;
> Follow it utterly,
> Hope beyond hope:

> Keep thee to-day,
> To-morrow, forever,
> Free as an Arab
> Of thy beloved.

> Cling with life to the maid;
> But when the surprise,
> First vague shadow of surmise
> Flits across her bosom young,
> Of a joy apart from thee,
> Free be she, fancy-free;

> Though thou loved her as thyself,
> As a self of purer clay,
> Though her parting dims the day,
> Stealing grace from all alive;
> Heartily know,
> When half-gods go,
> The gods arrive.

Emerson's discussion of *Jane Eyre*, which is the only thing he has to say of consequence about any Victorian novel, is in similar vein:

The question there answered in regard to a vicious marriage will always be treated according to the habit of the party. A person of commanding individualism will answer it as Rochester does—as Cleopatra, as Milton, as George Sand do,—magnifying the exception into a rule, dwarfing the world into an exception. A person of less courage, that is of less constitution, will answer as the heroine does,—giving way to fate, to conventionalism, to the actual state and doings of men and women.

If Milton between Cleopatra and George Sand seems in curious company, Emerson takes up much the same point of view in his discussion of Swedenborg's *Conjugal Love*, and again in "Initial, Daemonic, and Celestial Love":

> There need no vows to bind
> Whom not each other seek, but find.

That was what Candida thought too.

Yet here, as so often with Emerson, the mind could entertain theoretical possibilities which would not work in practice. And this was not mere timidity on his part, but rather a clear-eyed perception that our minds are far more versatile and hospitable than either our bodies or our hearts. Nature herself may be set on hurrying us out of alliances which have become confining to us, but man in his present state of development cannot be trusted with sexual freedom. It would be dishonest to pretend that a married man can be expected never to gaze longingly at another woman than his wife, but unless he is a fool, and unscrupulously indifferent to producing havoc, he had better content himself with gazing and remember that the same human limitations which have staled his present marriage can be trusted in time to affect any other connection which he may form. That is why Fourier's doctrines, however "delicious" they may be to the imagination, had better not be activated outside of that realm.

For the plain truth of the matter is that indulgence weakens and desensitizes. If we are sensitive enough to delight in pleasure, we ought also to be intelligent enough to understand that pleasure is the cheese in the mousetrap. Sensual ecstasy palls when it becomes merely casual; it is the habitually continent man who is the real epicure. As for Don Juan, sooner or later he must find that the women in whose conquest he has rejoiced have enslaved him. Either he will have tied himself to a "worthless slut" or he will have destroyed his own appetite.

II

A child is born into a family, and a family is born of sex. The child does not, in the beginning, understand this, but it is in the family nevertheless that he first learns the meaning of human affection. Emerson's father, early lost, was, even aside from literary genius, not his son's equal, but he did have some of the same interests Emerson later showed. Not a great deal has been recorded concerning his early relations with his mother, the most striking incident being his ecstasy when she showed feeling after his return home from an all-day absence. "I went to bed in bliss," he says, "at the interest she showed." This hardly seems to testify to an intense degree of habitual intimacy between them. In college days he looked forward to providing a home for her, which he did, and she lived with him and Lidian in Concord until she died in 1853, at the age of eighty-four. Emerson wrote Carlyle that her advanced age did not take away the pain of losing her, and he told his daughter

Ellen that having known her grandmother only in old age, she could not possibly know what a wonderful person she was. Her own religious views were, however, more in agreement with Lidian's than with Emerson's own. During the early years her influence was importantly supplemented by that of his wonderful, eccentric aunt, Mary Moody Emerson, who seems to have been a much more challenging, if also a much more exasperating, personality. Emerson's relations with all his brothers were apparently close and affectionate, though we do not have many details. His brother Edward's death was a great shock to him, for he considered this high-strung young man greatly superior to himself, but he was even more shocked when the super-sensitive Charles died in 1836. What does a wife feel, I wonder, when her husband writes to her in such terms as these after the death of a brother?

And so, Lidian, I can never bring you back my noble friend, who was my ornament, my wisdom, and my pride. . . . I determined to live in Concord, as you know, because he was there; and now that the immense promise of his maturity is destroyed, I feel not only unfastened there and adrift, but in a sort of shame at living at all. I am thankful, dear Lidian, that you have seen and known him to that degree you have. I should not have known how to forgive you an ignorance of him, had he been out of your sight.

III

The facts of Emerson's connection with Ellen Louisa Tucker are painfully simple. He met her late in 1827, when he preached in Concord, New Hampshire, and was apparently attracted to her at once, but seems to have done nothing about it until a year later, when they became engaged. She was still only seventeen. (In one of her letters to Emerson, she says she engaged herself to him after having known him for only two weeks, but she must have been referring only to fairly intimate acquaintance.) As for him, he was lovesick with her beauty, "overthrown by the eye and ear," and considered her as great a rarity as Shakespeare. They were married on September 30, 1829, and her husband said of her that she never once disappointed him except by her death. Unhappily, this followed all too soon. He knew that she was spitting blood before her marriage, and there was much gadding about, ostensibly for health reasons but involving exertion and exposure which must have been of very doubtful medical value. She lived only a year and a half, until February 8, 1831; the poor girl was dead before she was twenty.

She was the love of his life, his "saint," his "enchanting friend," the "angel" who walked beside him in his youth, and he could not have found anybody more worthy to occupy this place. Ellen Tucker was fashionable, spirited, pious, and "incapable of inelegance"—a rare combination. She was well read in the literature of the day, but she read more philosophical and religious works than novels. She slandered herself when she told her husband that she was hardhearted and quick-tempered, but she *was* gay, playful, mercurial, and humorous, ever mindful of the absurd aspects of her own enthusiasms, and never low-spirited for long under any circumstances. One commentator has suggested that Emerson's choice of "this immature and worshipping girl" shows that he needed somebody to look up to him; it is difficult to understand how such a view could survive even a careless reading of her surviving letters.[5] Ellen was terribly in love with Emerson and utterly frank in expressing her love. Young as she was, she also probably understood his gifts better than anybody else did at this time, but she was not in the least in awe of him. She called him "Grandpa" and loved to tease him, making fun of him and of herself, and he was quite aware of all this and delighted in what he considered her feminine wiles. In the verses beginning "When we're angels in heaven," she serves notice on him that earthly memory will not accomplish much there, and that since her wings will be strong, she will not need to keep a carriage. Instead she will "tea out and dine out" as she pleases, not minding him at all, for which she hopes he will not be "raving mad." There is a Dickinsonian touch about this which reminds us that Ellen, like her husband, was a poet, and if we cannot call her his equal or be sure that she would have overtaken him if she had lived, her verses certainly show a mind and a talent in harmony with his own. Moreover, they suggest possibilities for development along the metaphysical line ("To Her Lamb" and "Love scatters oil/On Life's dark Sea") or *vers de société* or both. All in all, he was not wrong when he declared that they had shared one heart and mind between them.

In his heartbroken journal entry, made five days after her death, Emerson wrote that, though he was not worthy of her, he would willingly have died with her. She had promised to be with him after her death; at the end, when she knew she was doomed, she had even tried to comfort him by telling him that she could do him more good by leaving him, and nothing in nineteenth-century fiction is more edifying than her prayer before her death, for him and her assembled family. Until he left for his first trip to Europe, he walked every morning to Roxbury to visit her grave.[6]

What the ultimate relationship between Emerson and Ellen would have been if she had lived, we cannot of course be sure. Inevitably their idyll would have been subjected to the wear and tear of a workaday world, in which marriage is no more perfect than other things. But it seems as safe as any guess can be that she would have been as important to him as Fanny Appleton was to Longfellow or Olivia Langdon to Mark Twain.

Only, she died and became instead one of the most fragrant, winning ghosts in American letters. For Emerson there was, as he himself declared, "one birth, one baptism, one love."

IV

But Emerson would not be Emerson if he could not leave us a chilly word to balance a tender one. Obviously he was talking nonsense when he told Jones Very in 1838 that he had never suffered, and when, two years later, he said that we are consoled for losing the dead by the realization that we no longer need to suffer from their faults, it is not necessary to suppose that he was thinking of Ellen. It *is* true that, as early as 1835, even while declaring that Ellen had completely satisfied him and that he still loved her, he also knew that, since the universe remained for both of them, her death had not spoiled the world for him nor destroyed hope, but this meant merely that he was a balanced soul, whose spiritual life rested upon a secure foundation of faith, and that was quite as Ellen would have had it. The end of "Compensation" raises a question, however, for here he includes the death of a dear wife among the calamities that admit of compensation, on the ground that, among other things, "it permits . . . the formation of new acquaintances and the reception of new influences." Did his second wife, Lydia Jackson of Plymouth, who became Lidian Emerson of Concord, compensate him for Ellen's loss?

Lidian lived with Emerson for many years and mothered all his children, yet the impressions we get of her are much less vivid than those we have of Ellen. She was a descendant of John Cotton and had been reared with some severity on horrendous Calvinism, but she had emancipated herself from this before she met Emerson, and at the beginning her ideas were considered rather wonderfully in harmony with those of her intended husband. Though she did not write poetry like Ellen, she had mystical tendencies, and once she experienced a vision of herself as Emerson's bride. He was thirty-one at the time of their marriage, she about eight months older. Emerson's brother Charles attributed a sybilline wisdom to her but found her in no sense a beauty, and Emerson himself described his joy in her as "very sober" compared to what he had experienced before.

There are many expressions of affection in Emerson's letters to her. She was his Asia, his Palestine, his "angel's heart," his Lydian Queen, and, more familiarly, his Queenie. He called her an incarnation of Christianity and said that if any of the family were saved, it would be through her. But he was not dominated by her. She moved from Plymouth to Concord at his behest and even changed the form of her first name. Emerson's mother was a member of the household until she died; if Charles had lived to marry Elizabeth Hoar, it had been the plan that they should be too. Sanborn described Mrs. Emerson in her later years as "a stately, devoted, independent person, with something the air . . . of a lady abbess, relieved of the care of her cloister, and given up to her garden, her reforms, and her unceasing hospitalities." Many friends and visitors have testified to her hospitality, though Arthur Hugh Clough did complain that she gave him no meat on Sunday, but only cocoa, strawberries, and such.[7] Once when, in a letter, she complained about a neighbor, Emerson replied that he hoped all the quarreling would be on one side; on the other hand, when he himself was irritated, she seems to have taken the larger and more generous view. Finally, it should be noted that it was Lidian who decided that her first daughter should be named Ellen Tucker Emerson, magnanimously making "her gods my gods," as Emerson says. He had recorded, oddly, that "a daughter was born to me," and he added that he could hardly ask more for his child than what this name promised.

As Lidian grew older, she became more conservative in her religious views, and, unlike her husband, she had no objection to arguing about them. Moncure D. Conway recorded [8] her displeasure when Emerson spoke of Goethe in her presence, and how she went on to aver her need of faith. She resented his decision to discontinue family prayers in his home, which, since it was her home also, one can scarcely deny her right to do. She seems to have had a gift for sententious pronouncements, and there is one surprising passage in which her husband credits her with a gift for profanity! She was something of a health fanatic also, putting herself through fads and exercises which might well have killed a stronger person, and she seems to have suffered from "nervous depression" as early as when Waldo was born. Emerson speaks of her "strange selfaccusing spirit" and begs her to omit the apologies with which she begins and ends her letters; once he wrote her from England that he would never dare leave home again if his departure was to signalize the onset of so many woes. And in 1842 he told Margaret Fuller that she had accused him of being a worse egotist than any of whose egotism he had disapproved, and then added, with his customary ability to blink nothing, that she might very well be right about this.

Henry F. Pommer has tentatively suggested that when she named her daughter Ellen Tucker Emerson, Lidian may have "sought to divert some of the father's emotion from a rivaling memory to a shared offspring." If so, fate played a curious trick upon her, for in later years the daughter so named, though not in agreement with all her father's views, became his closest companion and, at last, caretaker, while his wife, apparently, devoted herself to whist with the Alcotts and other social activities. From the 1860's on, Ellen largely replaced her mother even as Emerson's correspondent when he was away from home (he and Lidian had always complained of each other in this aspect), and indeed I get the impression that he had always had to do what he wished to do outside the household pretty much without his wife.

Reports that the Emersons were not very happily married have often been circulated, during their lifetime and since.[9] So far as I know there is nothing to support this view beyond what I have recorded, and it would be a mistake to make too much of it. There was no real mismating; neither was there ever any serious estrangement. They were simply not as close temperamentally as they might have been. Emerson went on paying tribute to Ellen in his journal and in his poems[10] after his second marriage, but he wrote no poems to Lidian. I do not believe that Ellen's ghost ever stood between them; whatever difficulty there was inhered in what they themselves were. It was neither Lidian's fault nor Emerson's that she was only a good, faithful, intelligent wife, and not, like her predecessor, an instrument for the gods to play on.

V

Emerson's sympathy with childhood and youth was one of his most marked characteristics; there are only two casual references to him in Walter de la Mare's encyclopedic study of child lore, *Early One Morning in the Spring*,[11] but nobody would have relished that book more.

The delicious faces of children, the beauty of schoolgirls, "the sweet seriousness of sixteen," the lofty air of well-born, well-bred boys, the passionate histories in the looks and manners of youth and early

manhood and the varied power in all that well-known company
that escort us through life,—we know how these forms thrill, par-
alyze, provoke, inspire and enlarge us.

He believed that what happens in the home is more important
than what takes place in the Senate, and that the helplessness
of a small child serves him better than any power could in
laying a despot's claim upon us. "His ignorance is more charming than all knowledge, and his little sins more bewitching
than any virtue. His flesh is angels' flesh, all alive."

> Youth is (whatever cynic tubs pretend)
> The fault that boys and nations soonest mend.[12]

In his maturity, he seems to have found it easier to establish
social relations with children and young people than with persons of his own age. He used to watch the schoolboys and
girls passing his house each day, not because he was a member
of the Concord School Committee, but simply because he liked
to look at them, and he hesitated to refuse invitations to college
commencements because he always hoped he might be able to
say something that the boys would find helpful. It is true that
he felt the need for contact with mature minds also, and he
showed some sympathy with the old man who declined dan-
dling his twentieth grandchild on the ground that he had said,
"Kitty, kitty" often enough. But he dissented sharply from
Dr. Johnson's ridicule of Milton for rushing home from the
Continent when civil war broke out in England and then de-
voting himself to schoolteaching; to Emerson's mind that was
a very important work and of vital import to the commonwealth. His own maturing had been late, and he always cherished the memories of his childhood. In 1873 he told Norton
that he saw his seventieth birthday as the end of his youth,
but Norton disagreed; Emerson's youth, he thought, would end

only with his life, and he was quite right about this; Emerson lived seventy-nine years, then died illustrating the truth of the Greek saying that the good die young. He had friends much younger than himself; as preacher and lecturer, he made a special appeal to his younger auditors. Children were individuals to him, as much as adults; sometimes, like Martin Luther's schoolmaster, who thought some great man of the future might be under his care, he even contemplated them with awe. "If we look into the eyes of the youngest person we sometimes discover that here is one who knows already what you would go about with much pains to teach him; there is that in him which is the ancestor of all around him." Emerson did not romp with children, but he did put himself to considerable trouble for them, and he sometimes wrote them charming letters. A somewhat surprising element in his intercourse with children was that, for a man whose fingers were all thumbs, he had great delight and competence in handling babies, no matter how young and tender they might be; on his seventy-eighth birthday he took an Alcott child in his arms and carried her about the room, presenting her to the company.[13]

Emerson's relations with his own children were very much what might have been expected of such a man. "Respect the child," he says. "Wait and see the new product of Nature. Nature loves analogies, but not repetitions. Respect the child. Be not too much his parent. Trespass not on his solitude." When Waldo was born, he was a "lovely wonder" who made the universe "look friendly," and the other children were welcomed with comparable affection. Moncure D. Conway's account of his visit shows that the Emerson children were allowed as much freedom as modern children have at home, or at least as much as is good for them. There were picnics and New Year's gifts (often accompanied by father's verses) and parties and charades.

Often piling us into a bedecked hay-cart [says Louisa May Alcott], he took us to berry, bathe, or picnic at Walden, making our day charming and memorable by showing us the places he loved, the wood-people Thoreau had introduced to him, or the wildflowers whose hidden homes he had discovered.

He believed that children can detect falsehood, or evasion, and tried to avoid it altogether in his dealings with them.[14] Often he quoted them, as if he thought their opinions really mattered. It was not that he believed in what is now euphemistically called permissiveness. Promptness was required at meals—only death or mutilation being regarded as adequate excuses—and comeliness and pleasantness at all times were equally important, but it was always the Emersonian ideal not to command the child or forbid him but to analyze the situation, formulate the principles involved, and thus guide him toward making his own decision. No doubt this worked better for him than for some fathers because he was, after all, a man whose presence exhaled considerable authority; as his son says, it was difficult to resist him.

He did not grow cold toward his children as they grew up. In Civil War times, his son Edward's desire to enlist in the army caused him so much anxiety that Edith sought to dissuade her brother by asking him whether he thought that what he accomplished in the army would be important enough to justify putting his father out of commission! He greatly missed Edith after she left home to marry William H. Forbes, and when his first grandchild, Ralph Emerson Forbes, was born, he welcomed him as rapturously as he had welcomed his own children. Edith gave him five grandchildren in all, Edward two.

As the quotation from Miss Alcott shows, the same spirit appeared in Emerson's dealings with other children. Neighborhood children were never refused nuts or apples, but they must ask, not just take. He limited the quantity allowed because this made the gift more precious, and if they made a mess, they must clean it up. When his brother William's son was in trouble at Harvard over hazing, Emerson accepted the melancholy truth that we cannot teach our children much, but must leave them to learn for themselves. It is clear, however, that he has not lost faith in the boy.

VI

Something more must be said of the great sorrow and the great joy among Emerson's children—Waldo, the subject of "Threnody," who died on January 27, 1842, when he was not yet six years old, after only a few days' illness with scarlet fever. Louisa May Alcott never forgot the look on Emerson's face when, upon her coming to the door to inquire how the boy was getting on, he replied, "Child, he is dead."

Waldo was a "wondrous child," a "hyacinthine boy," "a lovely wonder," "a piece of love and sunshine," and "as handsome as Walden Pond at sunset," whom his father regarded with both love and reverence.

> Not mine,—I never called thee mine,
> But Nature's heir.

But when he died and went with such terrible suddenness to "the wastes of Nature," "plight" was broken and the obligations nature had assumed at his birth violated.

> For flattering planets seemed to say
> This child should ills of ages stay,
> By wondrous tongue, and guided pen,
> Bring the flown Muses back to men.[15]

If these judgments seem extravagant, it must be understood that it was not only the Emersons who entertained them. Margaret Fuller said she hoped for more from Waldo than from almost any other living being, and Thoreau feared he was too spiritual to be permitted long to remain upon this earth. But we must not rob Waldo of his humanity, nor forget that he was a real boy. He was quite capable of threatening "I will not love you" when he did not get what he wanted. Even his father called him "the most impish of angels" and found him "abominable" when he was naughty. When he was sick, he was extremely difficult, his fever destroying his morals along with his flesh. According to his own account of the matter, Ellen "*got pushed*" after she put her foot into his sand house, and he would not go to church with Mrs. Mumford because she had red hands and a red face, though the next week he prayed that she might become beautiful and then considered her so. If the Emersons had an angel child, it was neither Waldo nor Ellen, but Edith.

After Waldo died, Emerson's "first outburst of passionate grief," as Cabot calls it, was succeeded by a stunning of the emotions in which he was troubled that he could feel nothing at all. In February he wrote Caroline Sturgis that the experience, like everything else that had happened to him, was dreamlike, touching lightly and passing on, and he repeats this substantially in "Experience," where we are told that something he had supposed was a part of himself, "which could not be torn away without tearing me nor enlarged without enriching me, falls off from me and leaves no scar. It was caducous. I grieve that grief can teach me nothing, nor carry me one step into real nature." Such a statement must not be taken too literally nor permitted to obscure the depth of his very real suffering. The glory of his home had passed with Waldo; he lamented that the whole world would waken next morning, but not his child, and wondered whether he would ever dare to love again. Though he reported that Ellen had symptoms of scarlatina after Waldo's death, he passed this over, almost as if it were of no consequence, so absorbed was he in his grief for the child he had lost, whose death had made the difference between riches and poverty and robbed all his activities of savor, to such an extent that oblivion was now the only hope of consolation he could entertain. Even after two years, he told Margaret Fuller that he had made no progress in adjusting himself.

In 1842 he was able to reach only line 175 of "Threnody": "Born for the future, to the future lost!" Yet even at the beginning he had not suggested that the child had been blotted out; his complaint was rather that wherever Waldo might be, he was now hopelessly separated from his father.

> O, whither tend thy feet?
> I had the right, few days ago,
> Thy steps to watch, thy place to know:
> How have I forfeited the right?
> Hast thou forgot me in a new delight?

But it was not until four more years had passed that he was able to see how, in Platonic terms, the excellent had become the permanent: "Lost in God, in Godhead found." Only in their common relationship to God, and their common inability to fall out of the hands of the Infinite, could father and child— or anything that was human—ever be whole again.

Thus Waldo's death was Ellen's death all over again. The experience failed to touch him only as all experience failed to touch him, which is to say only as all experience is powerless before that inner core of human (or divine) personality which stands above experience and sets up a criterion to evaluate it. Emerson was still Emerson after Ellen's death, and after Waldo's death, because the soul of man, despite all the hideous suffering it can undergo, is still superior to suffering. It remains itself; its relationship to the Universe remains; and God remains. Emerson was a human soul, not a bundle of reflexes, created and destroyed by the exigencies of the passing hour. If this were not so, then, as I argue elsewhere,[16] it would be impossible to write this book about him. But much more important things than this book would vanish, and one of them is the integrity, yes, the very reality of human personality itself.

CHAPTER SIX

POLITICS

I

Emerson lived in the great age of spread-eagle Americanism, and he did not wholly escape its influence. He wanted to extract the "tape-worm of Europe" from the American brain and "cast out the passion for Europe by the passion for America," for he believed that in his time America represented the future of mankind, and he gloried in even her material triumphs.

At times his admiration for American efficiency seems to extend to the kind of trickery celebrated in many folktales; on the other hand, he is always frank in his criticism of American shortcomings. Even when he inclined to find Americans more moral, more intellectual, and more spiritually minded than Englishmen, he did not believe that the grandeur of American character matched its geography. Americans had achieved no "remarkable book of wisdom," made no broad generalization, nor manifested any great power of imagination. Their art was graceful but sterile, "not new but derivative," and they themselves "slight and vain," too easily pleased and depressed. Even in public affairs, they had betrayed the promise of their founding by inclining always to "a selfish verdict" and achieving "no enlarged policy." Their statesmen lacked ideas and served property, not principle, inclining always toward the "selfish verdict."

Of course his America was largely New England, even Massa-

chusetts. Though he had no illusions as to New England's freedom from crime, sin, and disease, he still saw her as comparing
very favorably with the rest of the country and with mankind.
To be sure, her climate gave him pause. "Our climate is a series
of surprises, and among our many prognostics of the weather,
the only trustworthy one that I know is that, when it is warm,
it is a sign that it is going to be cold." Since he himself preferred "solar" to "polar," this was hard on him; it also tended
to discourage the closeness to nature which he valued. On the
whole, however, even the harshness of the climate was an advantage. "I do not know that Charles River or Merrimac water
is more clarifying to the brain than the Savannah or Alabama
rivers, yet the men that drink it get up earlier, and some of the
morning lasts through the day." He inclined to the more than
doubtful view that hot countries do not produce great civili-
zations, and when he was enraged against the South during the
Civil War, the Southerner became "an animal, given to pleasure,
frivolous, irritable, spending his days in hunting and practising
with deadly weapons." Indeed, the only hopeful thing about
the war was that it exposed the Southerners to the superior
culture of the North, embodied in the soldiers who were in-
vading them, and Emerson actually quotes with a straight face
the monstrous egotism of the mercifully unnamed Concord
army captain, to the effect that the conquest must be "a slow
business, for we have to stop and civilize the people as we go
along." Yet when, in other connections, he thought of the early
development of civilization in Egypt and in India, he began to
doubt some of these things.

Here, again, Emerson strove for a balanced view, even if he
did not always achieve it. Even New England, even Boston,
was a complex phenomenon, and what he says about her depends in part upon the situation in hand. About Boston, the
crown of civilization, "folded in the Ocean's arms," he never

published the following lines, but this does not cancel out the
fact that he wrote them:

> O Boston city, lecture-hearing,
> O Unitarian, God-fearing,
> But more, I fear, bad men revering,
> Too civil by half; thine evil guest
> Makes thee his byword and his jest,
> And scorns the men that honeyed the pest,—
> Piso and Atticus with the rest.
> Thy fault is much civility,
> Thy bane respectability,
> And thou hadst been as wise and wiser
> Lacking the Daily Advertiser.
> Ah, gentlemen—for you are gentle—
> And mental maids—not sentimental—

When he was angry at South Carolina, New Englanders were
a mild and intelligent people, but viewed from another angle,
they could also appear overcautious, "calculating," committed
to prosperity, a "debating-society," hypocritical, and weak.
Even the churches and the colleges were subservient to State
Street.

It would not be reasonable to ask entire consistency of
Emerson in what he said of the country outside of New England. He did not care for New York, yet once he threatened
to choose it for his next incarnation. On his early visit to South
Carolina and Florida, he thought the courtesy and grace of the
Southerners far superior to what could be had in New England,
and once he said the same thing about Philadelphians, though
he found no character in their city and thought living there
must be conducive to suicide. His lecture tours gave him more
experience of the West than most of the New England writers
had, but he never went along with Bronson Alcott, who thought
his Western audiences superior to what he encountered on his

native heath. Emerson judged Illinois farmers kindly people, but not more than ten years old in cultivation, and if he saw a Western man reading a good book on a train, he wanted to hug him. He wrote W. H. Furness that Wisconsin, still in the heroic age, was remarkable chiefly for space, and his first absurd judgment of St. Louis was that there was no thinking, nor even reading, man in it. On the other hand, he liked Minneapolis and saw Fond du Lac shining "like a dream." Like Whittier, he was thrilled by the prospect of building a railroad to Puget Sound. "The Kentucky stump-oratory, the exploits of Boone and David Crockett, the journals of western pioneers, agriculturalists, and socialists, and the letters of John Downing" seemed to him to promise vitality to American literature, and when, in his old age, he reached California, he capitulated entirely. Compared to the Golden State, "in its assured felicity," both Chicago and St. Louis were only toys. "If we were all young," he wrote Lidian—"as some of us are not—we might each of us claim a quarter-section of the government, and plant grapes and oranges, and never come back to your east winds and cold summers." [1]

It has been said of Emerson that he cared for little outside America, and in a sense this is true. "A foreign country," he says, "is a point of comparison wherefrom to judge [one's] own." But this had nothing to do with what the unenlightened imagine to be patriotism. "If you have man," he says, "black or white is an insignificance," and his Phi Beta Kappa poem of 1834 makes America an asylum for all races as enthusiastically as Emma Lazarus was to do it. As George Willis Cooke remarked, Emerson had no sympathy with

that boyish egotism, hoarse with cheering for our side, for our State, for our town; the right patriotism consists in the delight which springs from contributing our peculiar and legitimate advantages to the benefit of humanity. Every foot of soil has its proper quality; the grape of the two sides of the same fence has new flavors; and so every acre on the globe, every family of men, every point of climate, has its distinguished virtues.

This is the key. For Emerson self-reliance had a meaning for groups as well as for individuals. Even in art he mistrusted the principle of imitation, though, as Vivian C. Hopkins has observed, he had more sympathy with Aristotle's imitation of things "as they ought to be" than with the imitation of things as they are. It was not that he wished to shed his cultural inheritance, for he thought the first American who read Homer in a farmhouse performed an important service to his country. But if we are ever to have an American culture, Americans must learn to walk proudly even in Rome, and there is no use absorbing other cultures unless you can absorb them creatively and use what you absorb.

England is the only foreign country which he ever afforded anything like careful consideration, and his judgments of it were far from being uniformly generous. But whatever faults he found with England, Scotland and Ireland were much worse. Paris, when he first approached it, was vulgar and commercial, too much like New York, and aesthetically impoverished in comparison to the Italian cities, but it had grace and charm and *politesse*, and ultimately he came to think better of it. There are, however, a number of snap, stock strictures on French morals and religion, and he postponed reading Renan's *Life of Jesus* because he thought it would be too "Frenchy." He was easily seduced by glib generalizations about races, many of which cannot now be taken very seriously or always reconciled with each other. At various times he expressed such ideas as that there is an ethical bias in the English mind which is not to be found in the French, Italian, or Scandinavian; that Celts prefer phenomena to ideas and Teutons the opposite; that the French mind is analytical, not metaphysical, and "the French muse . . . Arithmetic"; that Italians, Frenchmen, Hungarians, and Germans are all sentimental; that the Germans have a genius for order and the English for confusion; that the superiority of German science is due to the German integrity of mind; and that the Germans as a nation have no taste. Even at the end of his life, though he granted Europe's superiority in monuments, Emerson thought nature grander in America and believed that ultimately we would match the European achievement.

Leaving out his patriotic Civil-War-time indignation against England, it may be said that Emerson combined a cordial appreciation of what he considered admirable in English character with as harsh a notation of English shortcomings as any avowed enemy could have achieved. Even after his return home in 1848, he recalled with horror England's "coal-smoke and carpet-smell" and the "iron belt of condition" with which her people were girdled. But this was by no means his only objection.

He acknowledged the great kindness shown him by many individual Englishmen and sometimes admitted that his own "willowy" constitution might have been bettered by "a chip of English oak," but he had no real sympathy with Englishmen, though in a sense he admired them. They were "a rude race, all masculine, with brutish strength," who held women and children cheap. They set up their own standards of manners, however eccentric these might seem to others, and gave little or no attention to the social amenities. They were "rank and aggressive braggarts," using about one-quarter of their minds, cultivating incompatability, and protecting their perceptions by "a savage stupidity." "A sea-shell should be the crest of England, not only because it represents a power built on the waves, but also the hard finish of the men." Though they had humor

and a romantic sense of the past, the English were more concerned with property than with honor, whim, or sentiment.
In their relations with other nations they were "the most vora-
cious people of prey that ever existed." At home, they set up
an artificial social system, saw "bad taste" as the most unfor-
givable offense, and punished most severely such "factitious
crimes" as smuggling, poaching, treason, and nonconformity.
Their public schools were "bear-gardens of brutal strength,"
and their universities existed only to try to galvanize dead languages into some semblance of life. Even their great writers
lacked a distinctive, forward-looking uality which was developing in literature on this side of the water; only the London
Times seemed quite to please Emerson. All in all, it was clear
that their civilization had passed its crest and that the future
lay with America.[2]

There is a story about a Boston lady who, upon being asked
whether she had traveled, replied, "Why should I travel when
I am already here?" The transcendentalists might have questioned her unspoken premise, but they would not have found
her conclusion unreasonable. So it is not surprising to find Emerson describing travel as a "superstition . . . whose idols are
Italy, England, and Egypt" and "a fool's paradise." Italy's
charm, he thought in 1838, was largely a matter of names; one
can "eternize" one's own woodlot, and who can deny that
Thoreau did so? In Naples, Emerson thought an hour there was
worth no more and no less than an hour in Boston, but when he
encountered the wonders of Rome, he was tempted to change
his mind about this. Long journeys were likely to be unreward-
ing in proportion to the expenditure of effort they required.
Generally speaking, it was light characters that were given to
travel, having no task to keep them at home and nobody to
miss them there. Since the world only echoes what we ourselves say, "he who travels to be amused, or to get somewhat

which he does not carry, travels away from himself." Of his own experience he could say that he traveled more to observe resemblances than differences, thus increasing his sense of the basic harmony of all men and of all life.

For he did travel. Here again his love of balance, his horror of extremes, kept him from following his own advice too literally. Travel was necessary of course for certain classes— naturalists, discoverers, missionaries, envoys. Travel might have medicinal value if used discriminatingly and with moderation, and Emerson himself tested out its values along this line. Though its usefulness was severely limited by language barriers, it might still furnish a good shaking-up and help to destroy morbidity, and the transitions between traveling and staying at home might well stimulate creativity.

He called himself a bad traveler. "I was born to stay at home, not to ramble. I was not made for an absentee." When he traveled, the world seemed unreal to him, as if he were detached from common ties and responsibilities; like other men of his temperament, he seems to have enjoyed his travels most in retrospect, when he could assimilate them in his own way—a kind of emotion recollected in tranquillity. But we must not forget that as a lecturer his business was traveling, and he himself once said that the public bet him fifty dollars a night that he could not go through what was required to deliver his lectures and that he replied, "I'll bet I will." He did. He traveled by railroad, canal boat, and steamboat; three times he crossed the frozen Mississippi on foot, once in a rowboat among the ice cakes. Once he arrived at the inn where he was to stay at four o'clock in the morning, with the thermometer at fifty degrees below zero, and once he rode forty-eight miles across the prairies in a buggy to make a train connection. On a canal boat, his bed was a cushion, and he was "crossed at the knees by another tier of sleepers as long-limbed as I, so that the air was

a wreath of legs." At Niagara Falls he was driven out of a
burning hotel; on Lake Erie his steamer caught fire; at St. Louis
he was in the same house with people who were dying of
cholera. Even during his last years, when he could no longer
remember place-names, he traveled alone for several days, with
no help except from the written directions his daughter had
provided for him.[3]

II

Emerson formulated no very elaborate or coherent political
theory. His political affiliations, if he can be said ever to have
had any, shifted from time to time; he considered it degrading
to be subservient to a party. In the 1840's he saw the Whigs
as weak and cowardly and was repelled by the vulgarity and
corruption of the Democrats. Calhoun, Clay, and Webster were
not gentlemen, but underlings who took their cue from society's
dregs. As early as 1825, when Clay was falsely reported to have
been killed in a duel, Emerson wrote an obituary for him in
which he appeared as much a lost soul as Byron. In 1845 he
compared the nativist American Party to a cur which barks
at all strangers. He believed, in theory, that the scholar should
act as a balance wheel on the chariot of state—"let him not
quit his belief that a popgun is a popgun, though the ancient
and honorable of the earth affirm it to be the crack of doom"
—but when his own emotions were involved, notably during
the Civil War crisis, he did not always attain such detachment.
In general, however, he may be said to have grown steadily
more liberal up to the Civil War and to have become somewhat
more conservative afterward.[4]

In Emerson's view, society was fluid, law a memorandum,
and foolish legislation a rope of sand. He realized that many

citizens have conscientious scruples affecting their performance of the so-called duties of citizenship, but this did not disturb him greatly because in his view all states were corrupt and laws should not be obeyed too well; it was not necessary to measure "the ideal right" by reference to the latest act of Congress. As early as 1823, he knew that we shall have a perfect government about the same time we achieve perpetual motion. When he was discouraged, he thought that beasts of prey succeeded best in politics and that even George Washington was tainted, and in 1860, the "ugly Government" was always in the way of whatever good needed to be done, and we should get along better without it.

Though it was the best government for us, democracy was not necessarily the best *per se*, for it is not an end in itself; the end is man and his development. "Man exists for his own sake, and not to add a laborer to the state." Emerson thought aristocracy doomed in England, yet found the greatest English aristocrats the most like cultivated Americans. He knew that out's are no more disinterested than in's and that the poor only envy the rich; himself he once felt that he could live happily under any government administered by gentlemen. Essentially he would seem to have been in agreement with Oliver Wendell Holmes, who was generally so much more conservative in his outlook, that an aristocratic order was legitimate so long as it was organic, that is, so long as it had developed naturally and unforcedly, in obedience to the laws of life, and was supported by merit.

Once at least he felt that the conservatives had the best men and the democrats the best cause. He could be cynical enough about the differences between them to define a democrat as a young conservative and a conservative as an old democrat. His bias, however, was radical, for he also declared that "whatever is old corrupts and the past turns to snakes" [5] and that "all conservatives are such from personal defects. They have been effeminated by position or nature, born halt and blind, through luxury of their parents, and can only, like invalids, act on the defensive," and, again, that "there is always a certain meanness in the argument of conservatism," though he granted that it may be "joined with a certain superiority in its fact." The least government is best, and the real hope lies in the development of individual character, the ultimate goal being a race that is capable of governing itself. The wise man needs no state, army, fort, nor navy; he *is* the state.

This, however, was for the future. For the present, Emerson recognized that people in general cannot live together on their merits or in other than necessary ways. "There must be kindred, or mutual economy, or a common interest in their business, or other external tie." And for the present, again, government must defend the weak against the strong.

Humanity asks that government shall not be ashamed to be tender and paternal, but that democratic institutions shall be more thoughtful for the interests of women, for the training of children, and for the welfare of sick and unable persons, and serious care of criminals, than was ever the best government in the Old World.

It is the duty of the state "to instruct the ignorant, to supply the poor with work and good guidance," and to see that every child has a fair chance for his bread.

He is not wholly consistent about these matters. The speech he made in honor of the Chinese Embassy in 1868, with its openly expressed admiration for China and its championship of Chinese immigration, was remarkable for its time, and he was equally appreciative of Japan at a banquet of 1872. He liked to have gypsies and Indians camp on his lands; he could affirm the basic unity of all mankind and dream of a new and better humanity being formed in America through the intermixture of all races which found an asylum here; "nature loves to cross her stocks," he said. On the other hand, he accepted some rather superficial notions about race, and he could speak without wincing of the possibility of "a rose-water that will wash the negro white." He hailed the coming of the Irish immigrants into New England, but his references to them are not free of condescension. At least he must be given credit for realizing and acknowledging the fact that if immigrants were permitted to come to grief through unhappy living conditions forced upon them here, the native Americans would be forced by the pressure of events to share the cost and pain of their downfall with them. On the other hand, it is difficult to see how the laissez-faire economics to which he seems in general to have been committed could be reconciled with his inclinations toward the welfare state:

The only safe rule is found in the self-adjusting meter of demand and supply. Do not legislate. Meddle, and you snap the sinews with your sumptuary laws. Give no bounties, make equal laws, secure life and property, and you need not give alms. Open the doors of opportunity to talent and virtue and they do themselves justice, and property will not be in bad hands. In a free and just commonwealth, property rushes from the idle and imbecile to the industrious, brave and persevering.

This is not far from the famous railroad president's letter in which workingmen were advised to entrust their interests not to unions, but to the Christian men to whom God had, in His wisdom, entrusted the care of the property interests of the country.[6]

Despite such lapses, Emerson did often perceive, even if he did not ride, the wave of the future. He was no communist, but neither did he have any love for the capitalistic system, nor great faith in it.[7] Like Bernard Shaw, he believed that the worst thing about poverty was the way it demoralized its victims. By 1823 he saw trade as the determining factor in relations between nations. In 1846 capitalists were gobbling up the poor "in all love and peace," just as the nobles used to. In 1848 improvements in machinery had helped everybody except the operatives. In 1859 he copied from Spenser's "Mother Hubberd's Tale": "For now a few have all, and all have nought." In 1868 he declared that gold was not hidden in the Black Hills so that one man should own it all.

As long as our civilization is essentially one of property, of fences, of exclusiveness, it will be mocked by our delusions. Our riches will leave us sick; there will be bitterness in our laughter, and our wine will burn our mouth. Only that good profits which we can taste with all doors open, and which serves all men.

It is true that Emerson gave Malthus less credence than he deserved, but he understood the dignity of labor which the factory system destroys, and he was awake to the adulteration of food and drugs which was already under way. His comment on one group of reformers, that they started out to establish the Kingdom of Heaven on earth but finally settled for unleavened bread and the nourishment of a beard, sounds very much up to date, and he would surely be saddened if he could understand the bitterness with which we today can read his Fourth of July greeting of 1856:

> United States! the ages plead,—
>   Present and Past, in under-song,
> Go put your creed into your deed,
>   Nor speak with double tongue.
>
> For sea and land don't understand,
>   Nor skies without a frown
> See rights for which the one hand fights
>   By the other cloven down.[8]

III

Emerson's optimism has often been arraigned on the ground that it caused him to make insufficient allowance for the power of evil in the world. It is certainly true that he saw evil as a negative, not a positive, thing. Once we get beyond this point, however, I think we must grant that he not only allowed generously for evil but that, for a moralist, he was rather amazingly tolerant in his attitude toward it. I feel it necessary to approach this subject, however, by way of a preliminary consideration of Emerson's moralism and moral idealism in general, and if some of my illustrations seem to the reader to be taking him somewhat far afield, I hope he will remember that there was a high degree of unity in all Emerson's thinking and feeling. His mind was not divided comfortably into compartments.

"For a moralist" I have written. *Was* he, then, that? Santayana called him "the Psyche of Puritanism, 'the latest born and fairest vision far' of all that 'faded hierarchy.' " [9] Did not he himself write:

> Though love repine, and reason chafe,
> There came a voice without reply,—
> " 'Tis man's perdition to be safe,
> When for the truth he ought to die."

and is not this famous quatrain eminently characteristic of both his idealism and the vein of iron running through him? "Wherever the sentiment of right comes in," he says, "it takes precedence of every thing else." Every fact has its ethical sign, being related as much on one side to morals as on the other to sensation. We may try all moods and allow due weight to all objections, but the moral sentiment will never forfeit its superiority, for in it lie the foundations of both culture and character. When his brother Bulkeley died, Emerson rejoiced that, with all his defects, he had lived clean of the vices by which thousands of others were being corrupted. Even as a critic he could permit himself to write, "I think the whole use of literature is the moral."

But it wasn't. And though what I have written in the preceding paragraph is true, it is not the whole truth. Emerson could look askance at the importation into America of European luxuries and refinements—"trifles" like dancers, singers, laces, books of patterns, modes, gloves, cologne, etc.—because they did not make Americans better men, and this is characteristic enough of the New England austerity of his time. But though he did not abuse his Puritan ancestors, he was not enthralled by them either; he praises the achievements of historic Puritanism, but he also notes its shortcomings. He was well aware that liberality in religion and in politics do not always go hand in hand. The Puritans began to turn bigoted and intolerant late in Elizabeth's reign, and they continued along this road until they persecuted Quakers and hanged witches.

Emerson's sensitiveness to beauty was great, and beauty was for him "its own excuse for being," "an ultimate end," and "in its largest and profoundest sense . . . one expression of the universe." With truth and goodness, it made up the triple face of God. Yet from one point of view, Emerson weakened the expression of his allegiance to beauty by going on to assert that perfect beauty and perfect goodness are one and the same. Looking at the *Apollo Belvedere*, he was sure he did not drink port, and he seems to have admired Michelangelo's character quite as much as his art.[10] But those who object to this simply confess their own willingness to settle for a more narrow-minded conception of both art and life than he could live with: they are willing to sacrifice the harmony between the material and the spiritual upon which he insisted. When he proclaimed the moral significance of beauty, he made his point not so much in the interest of morality alone as in his conviction of the unity of life itself; if this were not so, how could he have dared to find even Jesus overdeveloped morally and spiritually, but lacking on the intellectual and aesthetic side? James A. Emanuel has remarked [11] that "when Emerson speaks of virtue the matrix of his thought is as a rule not conventionally moral," and this is quite in harmony with Vivian Hopkins's observation that he was inclined to speak of the "moral sentiment" rather than "the moral Law" and with Stuart Sherman, who had noted, long before either of them, that for Emerson morality inhered "in a right condition and attitude of the whole self, from which particular acts will result with a kind of instinctive and inevitable rightness." For him, unlike some of his readers, "Hitch your wagon to a star" did not mean (or certainly did not merely mean) aiming high in the conventional sense, but rather bringing one's life into harmony with the Central Power of the Universe, which regulates mind and spirit and soul and flesh and is equally at home with truth, goodness, and beauty. [12]

Emerson was capable of summary judgments (sometimes derogatory, sometimes just) on a variety of writers, as when he lumps Scott and Moore as patrician and conventional poets and assigns to Byron and Bulwer the poetry of vice and disease, or finds in Horace Walpole "taste, common sense, love of facts, impatience of humbug, love of history, love of splendor, love of justice, and the sentiment of honor among gentlemen, but no life whatever of the higher faculties, no faith, no hope, no aspiration, no question concerning the secret of Nature." But it was with Goethe and Shakespeare that he faced his real moral-aesthetic conflicts.

The German poet failed in perfect balance, to Emerson's

thinking, both in his work, as in *Wilhelm Meister* and even in *Faust*, and in his life, in being defective on the ethical side. Emerson could tolerate vice, he wrote Carlyle, while "a splendid nature" was "battling with the brute majority in defence of some human principle," but not in a pampered, crowned genius, an egotist of "Olympian self-complacency," who apprehended the spirit, but was not. Emerson was repelled by the Goethe jubilee in 1834; a genius, he thought, had no right to be so comfortable. Thousand-mindedness was not, as he saw it, a virtue; the mind must distinguish between impressions as well as receive them, and when a writer chooses, with Goethe, to paint the actual rather than the ideal world, he becomes a poet "of limitation, not of possibility, of this world and not of religion and hope"; essentially he writes not poetry, but prose. Nevertheless, Emerson could not throw off Goethe's fascination, and he had two statuettes and a picture of him in his study. When the Reverend John Weiss seemed to him to be over-stressing Goethe's failings, his reaction was sufficiently strong to cause him to address a fairly long poem of rebuke to him:

> Life is too short to waste
> In critic peep or cynic bark,
> Quarrel or reprimand;
> 'T will soon be dark;
> Up! mind thine own aim, and
> God speed the mark! [13]

John O. McCormick says that after 1836 Emerson's references to Goethe were mainly laudatory; in that year he wrote his brother William that he was reading practically nothing except Goethe now. After having often criticized *Faust* as representing the unhealthy introversion of its time, he praised Part II in 1843 as the greatest thing since *Paradise Lost*, and in 1852 he defended Goethe against Furness. Yet there are still two fairly severe strictures in an 1840 journal: Goethe lacked moral perception, and nothing that he wrote made the world better.[14]

Emerson's essay on Shakespeare in *Representative Men* is one of the most baffling, contradictory pieces he ever turned out. First invoking the aid of Shakespearean scholarship, and showing a respectable familiarity with it,[15] he then proceeds to throw it all away, making no use of it whatever in his interpretation. Worse still, he sees Shakespeare as a great master, just and sound in his moral values, after which he rejects him as "master of the revels to mankind," a mere "player," who trifled with life, and who, therefore, had no place in a reformed theater and nothing that could really "profit" us.[16] The reader is left helplessly wondering how, then, he could have produced work whose value Emerson has recognized, as it were in spite of himself, or how, if he did, the validity of Emerson's criteria can stand.

None of this means that Emerson does not often praise Shakespeare very warmly and enthusiastically. Vivian Hopkins has noted that, if all Emerson's writings be taken into account, he gives Shakespeare more attention than all the Stuart religious writers put together. Shakespeare was the most robust and potent of all thinkers, a fountain of joy who keeps up the credit of the mind, one who made the real world appear empty by creating such a splendid imagined one to set over against it. Once Emerson denied that Shakespeare was a great *man*, but once too he whittled down his list of supreme geniuses to two —him and Jesus. He was a miracle which cannot be accounted for by material considerations. You read him, go away from him for years, and return to him with all the growth you have since acquired, only to find that he has lost nothing. Though he avoided "pulpiting," he was moral not by formal intent, but, in the Aristotelian fashion, because of the tragic pity and terror he inspired. And perhaps Emerson achieved the ultimate triumph

for a New Englander when he suggested that the Pilgrims might
have been better advised to stay home and read him!

Shakespeare's faults, such as they were, were not peculiar to
him, but were inseparable from all secular poets, including
Homer and (strangely) Milton.[17] Such writers "do not fully
content us. How rarely they offer us the heavenly bread!" This
is essentially what both Tolstoy and Shaw said about Shakespeare, and Emerson would not have dissented from Shaw's
statement that art has never been great except when it was providing the iconography for a live religion. We should not be
surprised, then, by the enthusiastic praise he bestows upon
oracles: "therefore when we speak of the Poet in any high
sense, we are driven to such examples as Zoroaster and Plato,
St. John and Menu, with their moral burdens," or, in other
words, to those who, properly speaking, were not poets at all!

Emerson was quite right when he perceived that Shakespeare
is "secondary" to the Bible in the sense that, while his moral and
religious standards and atmosphere derive from it, it is in no
sense dependent upon him. What is surprising is that a writer
who insisted so uncompromisingly as Emerson did upon the
unity of all life and all experience should permit himself to be
driven into a corner where he differentiates between the sacred
and the secular in literature as sharply as ever the narrowest
sectarian did. "And the holy heart and the old pagan instinct
are at war," he tells us, and then asks, "Shall it be the Bible or
shall it be Shakespeare?" This last quotation is from an early
lecture, but long afterward he could still write that nothing better had come from the human mind than Shakespeare's plays,
barring the single consideration that they *were* plays! For
Emerson all writing must be "by the grace of God" or it was
nothing, and the writer must write "affirmatively" something
that will help somebody. If this is narrowly moralistic, why is
it more so in Emerson than in Whitman ("The true question to

ask respecting a book is has it helped any human soul?") or Katherine Mansfield ("The greatest literature is still only mere literature if it has not a purpose commensurate with its art")? The objection still remains, however, that Shakespeare's was not a "pagan instinct" unless all literature not openly and avowedly devotional is pagan, and this the theologians of Shakespeare's time did not believe. Millions of people still feel that he did write "affirmatively" and "by the grace of God" and that he has "helped" innumerable souls.

IV

But evil is not primarily a literary problem; neither is its first concern with idealistic or puritanical inhibitions. Emerson lost his father in early childhood and grew up in poverty; one brother was mentally defective; two broke down and died young, and his own health was seriously threatened. His adored young wife died after only a year and a half of marriage, and he found himself without a profession before he had fairly got settled in it. Later his first child died with terrible suddenness at the age of five.

He never denies physical evil. To his way of thinking, there was "a crack in everything God has made," and the ideal exists only in thought. There was never a time when life was not hard; even ideal friends are only "dreams and fables." Disease, want, and insecurity cannot be denied, and terror, "which respects not definite evils but indefinite," is perhaps even worse. "He has seen but half the universe who has never been shown the house of Pain." Every man regards man's condition "with a degree of melancholy." To a contemplative eye it may even seem "the prevalent view of things."

"Nature does not cocker us," he wrote; "we are children, not pets; she is not fond; everything is dealt to us without fear or favor, after severe universal laws," in which "famine, typhus, frost, war, suicide," and many other evils have their share. Emerson was no dualist, and he did not believe in demonology, but he well understood why many men have felt compelled to do so. In both "Heroism" and "Fate" he enumerates physical horrors as mercilessly as H. G. Wells was to do it in *The Undying Fire*, perceiving them so clearly indeed as to cause one to wonder how he managed to escape the pessimism which finally engulfed that writer.

We have already seen that Emerson was, in a way, an evolutionist long before that term was in general use. The evolutionary philosophy is not pessimistic in its general outlook, but its processes are pretty strenuous; if you are an evolutionist, then, as Emerson says, even the ways of Providence are a little rude.

> The over-god
> Who marries Right to Might,
> Who peoples, unpeoples,—
> He who exterminates
> Races by stronger races,
> Black by white faces,—
> Knows to bring honey
> Out of the lion;
> Grafts gentlest scion
> On pirate and Turk.[18]

At times, Emerson's evolutionism might even be called Darwinian:

> Cast the bantling on the rocks,
> Suckle him with the she-wolf's teat,
> Wintered with the hawk and fox,
> Power and speed be hands and feet.[19]

Dramatically, as in "Alphonso of Castile," he could go even further:

> Earth, crowded, cries, "Too many men!"
> My counsel is, kill nine in ten,
> And bestow the shares of all
> On the remnant decimal.

In the light of such utterances, it is easy to agree with Firkins's comment: "It is hardly too much to say that he found the sternness of the universe endearing."

But there was evil in man—and in men and in himself—as well as in nature and in society, and this was certainly not endearing. Few Calvinists can have been more conscious of evil than Emerson was, especially during his early life; there are so many expressions of this in his journals that to discuss them all would be impossible. Sometimes he even seems to accept the medieval view that to be in harmony with the world was necessarily to be at enmity with God; indeed, even being prompt and sensible in earthly concerns may indicate too shrewd a capacity for adjustment. In the early days, his expression of these convictions is sometimes extreme. The land "stinks with suicide," and the game is not worth the candle. Growing up means being corrupted, for there are more geese than swans in the world and more fools than wise men. Few, indeed, are really sane. Most men live for their appetites and will embrace even crime if necessary to gratify them. No evil of the imagination can surpass the real evils of life; devils were studied from men. Good is only an island in a sea of evil, and romantic glamour can only attach itself to what we do not know very well.

Unfortunately, the intellectuals were no better than the others. Governors were as evil as the governed, and educated men used their wit and learning in the service of the devil. Physically and morally both, Emerson had a strong stomach. In Florence he inspected a detailed model of a decayed human body killed by plague, and wax models of every organ and process of the human anatomy, and in Padua he attended an anatomical lecture "with a subject." He went through Frascati's, the most famous Parisian gambling hell, and in San Francisco he visited an opium den, achieving one of the masterpieces of understatement on record when he reported that there was not much inspiration or aspiration to be observed there. Perhaps he was fortified against the shock of such sights by what he felt about his own shortcomings. He accused himself of sloth and cowardice and told Caroline Sturgis that he became more ashamed of himself every day. He might be noble and generous inwardly, but these qualities failed to express themselves in action. His talents were small, and he had never been able to achieve anything beyond hoping; as he looked back over his life, many passages in it struck him as blind or mad. He respected himself only when he was alone, and his first consciousness of himself, when awakening to a new, clean day, stained the morning. Once he told his brother William that he had had the sense of being on trial all his life, as if preparing for an examination, and that he never expected to be graduated.[20]

If he did not idealize himself, he did not idealize others either, for though he was sometimes cheered by the purity that appeared in unexpected places, he also knew that the hearts of seemingly good people are often filled with envy, hatred, and lust. He was even capable of exaggerating these things, as when he wrote, absurdly, that "all boys kill cats," which is as great a lie as if he had said all girls are angels. He was clear that nature was no saint, but came drinking and sinning, with her children careless of the commandments. "The natural greatness of health and wild power" attracted him.

I confess that I am much taken by it in boys, and sometimes in people not normal, nor educated, nor presentable, nor church-members, —even in persons open to the suspicion of irregular and immoral living, in Bohemians,—as in more orderly examples.

Though he seems never to have used it, he thought there was something to be said for profanity (he said nothing of obscenity). In the light of what has been discovered since, it is interesting that he should have wondered to Margaret Fuller about the possibility of Wordsworth's having committed some "brave sin"; once he even pondered the possible usefulness of transgression for himself, though he added that he had no immediate intention of committing burglary or arson. He was harder on reformers than on sinners, and seemed inclined to judge Goethe more harshly than Napoleon.

There are suggestions in his journals that Emerson found food a far greater temptation than alcohol.[21] He tippled mildly during his college years and remembered affectionately the delicious Malaga dispensed by a Cambridge grocer.[22] In later years, wine was served at the Emerson table, and sometimes Emerson would take a single glass with a guest, which was a considerable advance upon the clerical household in which he had been reared, where decanters of both wine and spirits were staple features in entertainment. Once he suggested to Bret Harte that they make "a wet night" of it over a glass of sherry, but Harte does not seem to have been impressed. On the other hand, some of Emerson's theoretical remarks about alcohol are not likely to have given much more comfort to the temperance reformers than such silly statements as the slave being as much to blame for slavery as his masters ever gave the abolitionists. He knew that men must have excitement and stimulation and that they will get it by physical means if nothing better is available to them. "Dreams and drunkenness, the use of opium and alcohol are the semblance and counterfeit of . . . oracular genius, and hence their dangerous attraction for men." He knew that alcohol brutalizes the mind. In 1846 he looked forward to an age of bread and water, "sound and grand as nature itself." In 1863 he quoted Edmund Hosmer, with apparent approval, to the effect that saloons do more harm than war itself. On the other hand, he seems to have thought well of Nicholas Longworth's contributions in Ohio to the American wine trade, and once he declared that he abstained from wine only because it cost too much. When one friend gave up wine, he thought it as unfortunate as another's having broken his hip, and he himself once sent a bottle to Thoreau (it is difficult to understand why, since Thoreau would not open it). In France he thought it a luxury that cheap wine should be available to all. In March 1832 he recorded having spent "this year" twenty dollars on wines and liquors, which had now been drunk up, and the drinkers the worse for them; he thought it would have been better to use the money to buy a print, which would have held its beauty for a century, or to pay a debt. Two years later, he wished to discourage the evils of the liquor traffic, but refused to sign a total abstinence pledge because this would be to rob abstinence of spontaneity. But this would be a stronger argument if he had always abstained, which he did not, or if, admitting indulgence to be an evil, he had also felt bound to start from scratch every morning with the consideration of all other evils.

Rusk thought Emerson grew less "spiritual" in his later years. If this is true, it is perhaps manifested in the moderate cigar-smoking which so shocked the elder Henry James. He had, it seems, learned to smoke in college, but did not revive the habit until he was about fifty. He calls tobacco "a rude crowbar . . . with which to pry into the delicate tissues of the brain," and he thought the Turk's addiction to it might help to explain why he had become the "sick man" of Europe, yet he found beauty in the exhalation of smoke, making respiration visible (the natural freezing of the breath in winter air would surely have been a better illustration), and he added that "a man of no conversation should smoke." The problem is to explain why he should have gone to the trouble of acquiring and practicing a habit which evidently meant so little to him as this one did. If he had read as he smoked, he would never have made it out of McGuffey's Readers. Since he sometimes did indulge when alone, even in the face of domestic disapproval, apparently seldom getting through a whole cigar at a time, the suggestion that he used it to overcome social shyness and build a bridge between himself and his associates hardly seems adequate.

Emerson's toleration of evil, however, goes far beyond such matters as the indulgences of the table. "Bruisers" and pirates fascinated him, and he cites an Italian proverb which says that if you wish to succeed, you must not be too good. "I can see nothing at last," he says, "in success or failure, than more or less vital force supplied from the Eternal." He was not shocked by Luther's "when I am angry, I can pray well and preach well," and hardly by Alfieri's statement that the crimes of Italy proved the superiority of her stock or Goethe's "I have never heard of any crime which I might not have committed." But Napoleon is the prime example, and Napoleon fascinated Emerson as Stalin and Mussolini were to fascinate Shaw. Napoleon, he said, "is never weak and literary, but acts with the solidity and the precision of natural agents." Emerson summed up Napoleon's evil, and even his vulgarity, as mercilessly as his worst enemy could have done it, and then went on to declare that he "showed how much may be accomplished by the mere force of such virtues as all men possess in less degrees; namely, by punctuality, by personal attraction, by courage and thoroughness," which seems as vulgar as praising Mussolini, as so many Americans did during the early years of his power, because he had made Italian trains run on time. "To what heaps of cowardly doubts is not that man's life an answer." But vitality alone, independent of the uses to which it is applied, has no meaning, and there were no answers on St. Helena. So Emerson himself had to conclude that Napoleon "was an experiment, under the most favorable conditions, of the powers of intellect without conscience," and that this suicidal attempt "came to no result" but "passed away like the smoke of his artillery, and left no trace."

Emerson's treatment of Napoleon is not entirely anomalous, however. "We permit all things to ourselves," he says, "and that which we call sin in others is experiment for us." At times he seems to have accepted a kind of moral relativity. Everybody who knows anything at all about him is familiar with his reply to one who inquired whether it was not possible that the inner voice to which he listened might not be diabolical rather than angelic. Emerson replied that this did not seem to him to be the case, but that if he was the devil's child, he proposed to live according to the devil. This was clever dialectic; that it had any larger value seems extremely doubtful. And there was no dialectic involved when he wrote, "In the morning I awake and find the old world, wife, babes and mother, Concord and Boston, the dear old spiritual world, and even the dear old devil not far off." His partial acceptance of the "dear old devil" in warfare, partly anticipated in what I have written of his attitude toward Napoleon, must have more extended consideration; here I can only refer in passing to his toleration for the tycoons, which his modern critics have often thrown up against him. Probably this was strengthened in his later years by his daughter's marrying into the Forbes railroad family, but this was not the ultimate source. Ernest Sandeen was quite right when he called Emerson's idea that the moral condition of society at large is improved by having the individuals who compose it strive for their own improvement "the economic principle of *laissez-faire* raised to the moral level," and Daniel Aaron, who considers this problem fairly in his *Men of Good Hope*,[23] is just when he quotes from Henry Adams to the effect that when an age is dominated by the economic mind, "the imaginative mind tends to adopt its form and its faults." Nevertheless Emerson's idea did have a metaphysical basis (the concept of microcosm and macrocosm) which was not invoked by the robber barons themselves, and Aaron also points out that Emerson never intended to justify them. Bronson Alcott was less charitable, however, when he saw his friend permitting the spoilers to "find a refuge from their own duplicity under his broad shield," and the ultimate vulgarization of his toleration was well represented by the blatant tag-line of the old United States Steel Hour radio program: "What is good for United States Steel is good for you." Perhaps, after all, it is not surprising that a man who could be cosmic enough in his outlook to say that if the Russians were to eat up the Poles, it would make no difference in the long run, since the Russians too were men, should also see the railroad, the telegraph, and other technological marvels arriving by a kind of benevolent fatalism, as if in spite of all we could do to prevent it, just when we needed them. Emerson himself enjoyed the excitement involved in the coming of the railroad to Concord, even the explosions and (it seems!) the accidents. For in his time the railroad meant "American power and beauty," and trade, which it serves, was "the principle of liberty" and the correcter of social ills.

V

Emerson's sympathy with Quakerism did not embrace the Quaker position on war and peace, but there were times when it came pretty close. He called war unmanly and soldiers an offensive spectacle. He rejected the widely held view that a gentle-

man must be ready to fight and thought it ridiculous that the
Governor of Massachusetts should sport a military guard. War
is as much man's worst activity as religion is his best. It is a carnal
weapon whose use spells atheism; to kill one's brother is to kill
one's self. His early lecture on Martin Luther makes the great
Reformer virtually a pacifist.

As early as 1838 Emerson suggested a Congress of Nations;
he also anticipated William James in pointing out the need to
establish a moral equivalent for war, that is, a means of releasing
peacefully and constructively the energies which war released
horribly and destructively. He realized that it was better to
suffer injury than to do it, and in one passage he puts the army
on a level with the barroom and the jail. Armies are out of place
in a modern, sensitive, interdependent society, and navies must
go, as piracy, poison, and torture have already gone; to admire
such things now is to confess oneself still in a juvenile state of
development, like the monomaniac who can only talk about
horses. Emerson praises Montaigne for keeping his house un-
fortified, like a Quaker dwelling, during the civil wars which
ravaged France in his time, and, in *English Traits*, he relates how
he shocked Carlyle and Arthur Helps[24] by defending both nonresistance and anarchism:

I said, it is true that I have never seen in any country a man of sufficient valor to stand for this truth, and yet it is plain to me that no
less valor than this can command my respect. I can easily see the
bankruptcy of the vulgar musket-worship,—though great men be
musket-worshippers;—and 't is certain as God liveth, the gun that
does not need another gun, the law of love and justice alone, can
effect a clean revolution.

When fully dressed and in his right mind, Emerson did not
ever really praise war, though at times he suggested that he
preferred it to the corruptions of peace, which is of course a

false antithesis. He read literature like *The Song of Roland* and Southey's *Chronicle of the Cid* to his children, and he said that "man was made for conflict," but he did not think of conflict in essentially military terms. Even during the Civil War, he lauded the heroism of scholars: "For either science and literature is a hypocrisy or it is not."

When Emerson takes the larger and more philosophical view of war and peace, however, he falls into his familiar trick of simultaneously affirming and denying the same proposition to such an extent that he seems to be embracing the evil he hates as warmly as the good he loves. "War civilizes," he writes, "for it forces individuals and tribes to combine, and act with larger views and under the best heads, and keeps the population together, producing the effect of cities; for camps are wandering cities." He is on sure ground when he points out that Alexander's conquest of the East resulted in the dissemination of Hellenic civilization, and he is not without penetration when he writes:

War and peace . . . resolve themselves into a mercury of the state of cultivation. At a certain stage of his progress, the man fights, if he be of a sound body and mind. At a certain higher stage, he makes no offensive demonstration, but is alert to repel injury, and of an unconquerable heart. At a still higher stage, he comes into the region of holiness; passion has passed away from him; his war-like nature is all converted into an active medicinal principle; he sacrifices himself, and accepts with alacrity wearisome tasks of denial and charity; but, being attacked, he bears it and turns the other cheek, as one engaged, throughout his being, no longer to the service of an individual but to the common soul of all men.

He was clear too that

The cause of peace is not the cause of cowardice. If peace is sought to be defended or preserved for the safety of the luxurious and the timid, it is a sham, and the peace will be base. War is better, and the peace will be broken. If peace is to be maintained, it must be by brave men, who have come up to the same height as the hero, namely, the will to carry their life in their hand, and stake it at any instant for their principle, but who have gone a step beyond the hero, and will not seek another man's life;—men who have, by their intellectual insight or else by their moral elevation, attained such a perception of their own intrinsic worth that they do not think property of their own body a sufficient good to be saved by such dereliction of principle as treating a man like a sheep.

Unfortunately Emerson does not stop here. He may write that war now "begins to look like an epidemic insanity, breaking out here and there like the cholera or influenza, infecting men's brains instead of their bowels," but even here he shows a tendency to put it on the same level with the pangs involved in nature. He can tell us that the triumphs of peace are related to the triumphs of war, that war weighs the merits of men and breaks up stagnation, and that though soldiers do not represent the highest force of mankind, they are still needed to defend the highest. Perhaps, after all, war is the natural state of the human race and the nurse of all the virtues; for himself Emerson admires both "Scourges of God" and darlings of the race. "Sword and staff, or talents sword-like or staff-like, carry on the work of the world." Of some men he says, "They are made for war, for the sea, for mining, hunting and clearing; for hair-breadth adventures, high risks and the joy of eventful living," and when Cyrus Bartol asked him whether he approved of war, he replied, "Yes, in one born to fight."

Emerson does not seem quite to have made up his mind about war and the future. He had the fantastic idea that gunpowder had made battles "less frequent and less murderous," and he was sure that nationalism was becoming obsolete and that the elaborate interdevelopments of a complicated civilization were progressively making war less usable. "War is on its last legs; and a universal peace is as sure as is the prevalence of civilization over barbarism, of liberal government over feudal forms." On the other hand, he could declare as early as *English Traits* that the next war would be fought in the air.

When Emerson faced the specific war-and-peace problems of his own time his feet were more mired in the past than beating out a path to the future. Looking back to the Revolutionary War of his grandfather's time, he saw it as inspired by a "devouring thirst for justice," with its soldiers fighting for a "spotless cause," and even in his old age he admired Bismarck, "a statesman of the first class, with a clear head and an inflexible will." "Of course, we are impatient for peace," he wrote Herman Grimm in 1871, "were it only to secure Prussia at this height of well-being." During the War of 1812, he and other schoolboys helped to throw up earthworks in Boston Harbor. The Mexican War furnished no real test of peace principles for him; since it was a war for the extension of slavery, it naturally did not tempt him. For all that, he did not quite set his face against American expansionism, for though he denounced immoral means of effecting it, when he recognized them, he also believed that it was inevitable and that, in the long run, therefore, it would not make much difference how it had been brought about.[25] But the real test came with the Civil War, and Emerson flunked it pretty badly.

He was by no means sure that the war would preserve the Union (nor, it seems, at the outset, was he greatly interested in this aspect). New Englanders never discovered that secession was a wicked doctrine until after the South had taken it up. As early as 1836, Emerson wondered whether the country had not grown too large for patriotism and whether New Englanders might not therefore be more patriotic if they were to go it alone. In 1854 he thought it would have been better not to form a Federal Union than to accept a compromise with slavery, and even as late as 1864, in a public lecture, he considered separation between North and South a conceivable possibility under some circumstances.

He was slow in waking up to Lincoln's greatness, considering him uncouth and even clown-like, though when he met him he found him not so bad as he had feared. Lincoln's stock went up for Emerson when he issued the Emancipation Proclamation, which gave us a clean country and a war worth fighting,[26] but apparently it was only when the President was dead that Emerson was sure he had been so upright and intelligent as not to need to worry about manners or appearance.

When the war began, Emerson wrote Clough that it expressed the madness and mischief of bad boys, and Herman Grimm that he thought it a pity that a nation which had no enemies should commit suicide. He added, contrarily, that the North's advantages were so overwhelming that the conflict must be short. But that same year he was declaring that the war was better than what had preceded, as amputation is better than cancer, and that the "electricity" in the air would exercise a beneficial effect on health to counteract the effects of the killing! And when the son of John Murray Forbes (later Emerson's own son-in-law) enlisted, the sage declared that all wise fathers were coming to see that they had no right to dissuade their sons from this course. (He was not quite so sure of this when his own son wished to go.)

In 1863 he accepted an examiner's appointment at West Point from Secretary Stanton, though when he arrived and found that he was expected to stay sixteen days, he immediately turned his thoughts to cutting his stay short. He was as sentimental as he ever got when he rejoiced in the "innocence" and tenderness of the cadets and thought it well that such as they should be made acquainted with firearms. A letter probably dating from May 1864 favored the horror now known as universal military training; Emerson called it "a wise Militia system" and looked to it to keep boys "sound-hearted"! In 1864 he wrote Carlyle, who must have rejoiced to hear it, that he would always respect war hereafter.

The next year he was rejoicing that the rebels had been pounded, not negotiated, into a peace, and seems to have approved the fascistic sentiments of a fellow townsman who refused to go to town meeting because he did not believe in votes but only in bullets. In the spring, the war had been worth everything it had cost; it had even "moralized" Northern cities and regiments. By November, however, he feared that the energies of the nation had been exhausted by it, leaving us with no strength for other things and as sectional and timorous as ever.

I do not feel called upon to express any opinion here as to whether Emerson ought or ought not to have supported the Civil War, but it is painful to find him glorying in the emotional jag which war provides as shamelessly as any little shopgirl. In his Harvard commemoration address he expressed pleasure in the very sight of a soldier, "the armed defender of the right," and saw even Divine Providence working according to military necessity! The "*morale*" of the war and the way it "gave back integrity to this erring and immoral nation" now showed that it was "a marked benefactor in the hands of the Divine Providence." He quoted approvingly from the mother of Robert Gould Shaw (in whose honor he wrote "Voluntaries"), when her son was offered command of the Fifty-fourth Massachusetts, the first Negro regiment from a free state, though her remark is as bloodthirsty as anything Shakespeare makes Volumnia say: "If he accepts it, I shall be as proud as if I had heard that he was shot." In addition to all this, there was the infatuation with John Brown which Emerson shared with Thoreau and other Concord intellectuals. He is reported to have said that when Brown was hanged, he would make the gallows as glorious (or as venerable) as the cross, to which Hawthorne sharply retorted that no man ever deserved hanging more. There is some question about the exact form of this remark and of the extent to which Emerson would have stood by it in later years (he is also reported to have said, at a later date, that "we have had enough of this dreary business"), but he did list Brown as a great man in a letter to Carlyle written as late as October 15, 1870; the other names in this amazing list are Michelangelo, Machiavelli, Rabelais, Voltaire, and Carlyle's own! [27]

Yet it would be unfair to take leave of these matters without setting them once more against Emerson's general metaphysical assumptions. "Evil, according to old philosophers, is good in the making. That pure malignity can exist is the extreme proposition of unbelief. It is not to be entertained by a rational agent; it is atheism; it is the last profanation." Monsters are only malformations, unions of alien, disparate parts. The surgeon simply restores an order that has been disturbed or interfered with.

Taken by itself, Emerson's idea that pain is superficial, hurting the beholder more than the victim, seems absurd in the extreme. The curious notion that nature always protects the brave is expressed even in the little poem "The Titmouse":

> The Providence that is most large
> Takes hearts like thine in special charge,
> Helps who for their own need are strong,
> And the sky doats on cheerful song.

The hideous facts of life, then, do not disturb a really healthy mind. If wolf, snake, and crocodile have their place in nature, we must learn to deal with wolf-like men also. Completely without supporting evidence, he advances the fantastic idea that great suffering comes only to those who can bear it, as "crucifixions to the obtuse and barbarous, to whom they are not horrid, but only a little worse than the old sufferings." Jesus Christ, for example, and a hundred martyred saints?

To lay hold on such comfort, one must rise above good and evil and human feeling besides, or else sink below it. So Emerson can tell us that the view of saints is partial "because they behold sin . . . from the point of view of the conscience, and not of the intellect; a confusion of thought. Sin, seen from the thought, is a diminution, or *less;* seen from the conscience or will, it is pravity, or *bad*." And there are two disturbing little verses called "Intellect":

> Gravely it broods apart on joy,
> And, truth to tell, amused by pain.

There are people in the world, unfortunately, who are amused by pain. But it is not safe to permit them to roam at large.

None of which means, however, that Emerson's thinking in this area was altogether wrong or lacking in penetration. McGiffert remarks that "it takes a religiously-minded person . . . to perceive that there is no evil without its use." By the same token, it may be said that it takes a religious mind to interpret Emerson's teachings about nature and self and evil as he conceived and intended them. The idea that God can bring good out of evil, making man's wrath to praise Him, is as old as Christianity itself, for it strikes to the heart of the Christian Gospel of redemption, but the first great Christian theologian, Saint Paul, specifically dismissed the mad corollary that therefore he who provides occasion for the exercise of God's Grace by sinning thus serves Him. Does the harshness of nature (which every honest man must admit) represent the mind of the Creator, or does the achievement of consciousness in us as human beings set up within ourselves a standard not derived from nature and with it the obligation to launch a program of amelioration? And is God omnipotent in the sense that everything that He has made perfectly represents His will, or is God the Constructive Power in creation, who still labors to bring recalcitrant materials

under control? Emerson made some of the distinctions suggested here in practice, even though he did not always make
them in theory. "I can think," he said, "of many parts I should
prefer playing to that of the Furies."

Above all, he was determined that "the multitude of the sick
shall not make us deny the existence of health." With somewhat
questionable morality, he once suggested that men's vices be
taxed to lessen the cost of government! "Tobacco and opium
have broad backs, and will cheerfully carry the load of armies,
if you choose to make them pay high for such joy as they give
and such harm as they do." But he went further than this, for,
like Shakespeare, he saw the soul of goodness in things evil.

> But in the darkest, meanest things
> There alway, alway something sings.[28]

The same world which produces the disease also produces the
cure. Good children are born to convict stock in Botany Bay,
and the selfish policies of evil men have been known to result in
unintended good to thousands. Fine art can be made of evil also—

> "For out of woe and out of crime
> Draws the heart a lore sublime"—[29]

and love can redeem it:

> In dens of passion, and pits of Woe,
> He saw strong Eros struggling through,
> To sun the dark and solve the curse,
> And beam to the bounds of the universe.[30]

VI

One final question must be considered before we leave this
phase of our subject: How did Emerson's temperament and

philosophical or metaphysical attitudes affect his attitude toward nineteenth-century reform and his own activity as a reformer?

Reformers as a class he considered "an altogether odious set of people, whom one would shun as the worst of bores and canters." The best he could say for them was that their work was as innocent as that which others were doing around them, and often he would not say even that. They were "narrow, self-pleasing, conceited men" who "affect us as the insane do." Worse still, they went about their work in the same spirit manifested by those whom they opposed, working "profanely, not piously; by management, by tactics and clamor." At their worst they were rebels without a cause. "Don't run amuck against the world," he cries. "Have a good case to try the question on."

But even when the cause could not be questioned, Emerson hesitated to commit himself to it. After Mark Twain had spoken out against Belgian atrocities in the Congo, he was to find it necessary to resist those who would have had him become a full-time propagandist. "My instincts and interests are merely literary," he said; "they rise no higher, and I scatter from one interest to another, lingering nowhere. I am not a bee, I am a lightning-bug." Emerson would have balked at describing his interests as "merely literary" (and certainly Mark Twain's were far from being that), yet he used almost the same figure; compared to the professional reformers, he said, he was a rainbow or a firefly. But he was completely consistent in recognizing and defining the character of his own work and his determination to do it, allowing nothing and nobody to draw him away from it, not even other work which might be very desirable in itself. "My reforms," he says, "include, so will outlast, theirs." And he adds: "I have my own spirits in prison;—spirits in deeper prisons, whom no man visits if I do not." And to disagree with this, one would have to be prepared to maintain that the work Emerson himself did was not worth doing.

But Emerson's philosophical objection cut deeper. His fundamental quarrel with the reformers was that they had lost the sense of the whole and that none of their recommendations went to the heart of the matter. In his view, things went right or wrong together, and no part of society or of life was better than the other parts. He quarreled not with the State of Massachusetts, but with the state of man. Partial reforms were always extravagant. "To interpret Christ it needs Christ in the heart," and even the abolition of war could only be achieved "by private conviction, by private, dear and earnest love." There is no sense, then, in leaving the church every time the minister utters a false sentiment, for the street into which you go will be as false as the church you leave. Even Thoreau's going to jail to avoid paying a war tax was mean and skulking, for this kind of protest against one isolated evil could achieve nothing. Emerson was committed to the harmonious and symmetrical development of all human powers, all aspects of human character, and he wanted progress made not by hating evil, but by the infusion into the soul of a new and larger life.

Thus his basic approach to all social problems is a religious approach. You can redeem society only as you redeem humanity. We must be born again.

If the man were democratized and made kind and faithful in his heart, the whole sequel would flow easily out and instruct us in what should be the new world; nor should we need to be always laying the axe at the root of this or that vicious institution.

In the course of defending this approach, he, almost necessarily, falls into the familiar pattern of what seems to be a defense of evil.

We want to be expressed; yet you take from us War, the great opportunity which allowed the accumulations of electricity to stream off from both poles, the positive and the negative. Well, now you take from us our cup of alcohol, as before you took our cup of wrath. We had become canting moths of peace, our helmet was a skillet, and now we must become temperance milksops. You take away, but what do you give? Mr. Jefts has been preached into tipping up his barrel of rum into the brook; but day after to-morrow, when he wakes up cold and poor, will he feel that he has somewhat for somewhat? If I could lift him up by happy violence into a religious beatitude, or imparadise him in ideas, then should I have greatly more than indemnified him for what I have taken. I should not take away; he would have put away,—or rather, ascend out of this litter and sty in which he had rotted, to get up clothed and in his right mind into the assembly and conversation of men.

It is easy to reply to this that what has been taken away is no more than one of the things which prevent ascension and that Mr. Jefts is certainly not going to be poorer for having the money he spent on rum available for something else. This was essentially the approach of Oliver Wendell Holmes when he remarked that "it would have taken a long while to get rid of slavery if some of Emerson's teachings . . . had been accepted as the true gospel of liberty." The nerve of all reform and social progress would be severed if we should refuse to consider a remedy for any particular evil until the whole has been reformed, as if one should say that there is no use trying to straighten out anything else until the earth's axis itself has been straightened. When his wife agonized over the sufferings of the Negroes in the middle passage, Emerson achieved a kind of Mrs. Gummidge in reverse and at one remove by telling her that they did not feel it as she would, and in 1849 he told an antislavery meeting in Worcester that he thought "the scope left for human exertion, for individual talent to be very small" and rejoiced that "higher laws than any human will" control us. Nobody can blame him for realizing that he himself just did not have the physical strength he would have needed for an active career as

a reformer; he once told William that he was about as well qualified for it as Hamlet. But one can hardly claim that this alone
would justify him in elevating his own temperament to the level
of a universal standard.[31]

This, however, is a much less devastating reply than it might
seem, for in practice Emerson sought and found a golden mean
in the area of reform quite as successfully as elsewhere, and his
record for public protest compares very favorably with that of
many who criticize him. When he did not take a public stand,
it was never fear that motivated him. He opened his Boston pulpit
to abolitionists before he became an abolitionist himself; later he
urged the Concord Lyceum to hear Wendell Phillips; he greeted
Theodore Parker cordially in public at the time when that great
preacher was most in disfavor. His Bowdoin Prize essay of 1821
declared that "the plague spot of slavery must be purged thoroughly"; eleven years later he found that living in a land which
tolerated slavery was too high a price to pay for life. President
Van Buren's crime against the Cherokee Indians darkened the
world for him. He "hated" the letter he wrote the President,
protesting their removal from their homeland, for such "stirring
in the philanthropic mud" was not congenial to him. But he
wrote it nevertheless, and it was one of the bitterest letters any
American President ever received, though certainly not more
so than many have deserved.

You, sir, will bring down that renowned chair in which you sit into
infamy if your seal is set to this instrument of perfidy; and the name
of this nation, hitherto the sweet omen of religion and liberty, will
stink to the world.

Slavery, of course, was the test case. In the early days, he considered this too from a pretty high perch on the abstraction
ladder, declaring, for example, that the degradation of the Negro
did not come "without sin" and that "the negro and the negro-

holders are really of one party." After the murder of Elijah P.
Lovejoy, however, he shocked Boston conservatives by a passing
reference, in a public lecture, to the reformer's having faced a
mob "for the rights of free speech and opinion, and [having]
died when it was better not to live," and after the passage of the
Fugitive Slave Law, he woke up each morning with a feeling of
infamy and ignominy in the Massachusetts air. Shylock said,
"The curse never fell upon our nation till now. I never felt it
till now," and Emerson sounds much the same. "I have lived all
my life in this State and never had any experience of personal
inconvenience from the laws until now." This law, abrogating
Massachusetts law and obliging the citizens to serve as slave
catchers, had "the illuminating power of a sheet of lightning at
midnight," and what it showed was truth. "Our bellies had run
away with our brains." Let Daniel Webster defend it. Webster
was a man of the past, following his own animal nature, without
faith or hope. "All the drops of his blood have eyes that look
downward." There was a hole in his head where the bump of
moral sentiment and perception should be; in his mouth, "liberty"
was as obscene as "love" in that of a harlot. Emerson wrote in his
journal of the Fugitive Slave Law, "I will not obey it, by God!"
and prepared a refuge for slaves in his attic, keeping his wagon
ready to drive them to the railroad station for Canada whenever
they should appear. It is true that none ever came, but that was
not Emerson's fault. He would have been equal to the emergency
if they had appeared.

From then on there was no question where he stood. In 1851
he urged compensated emancipation, not because the planter had
a right to it, but for the sake of the slave and as a practical means
of getting the slaves freed. Later he changed his mind about this,
and on New Year's Day, 1863, he thrilled a Boston audience with
the famous "Boston Hymn"—

> Who is the owner? The slave is owner,
> And ever was. Pay him.

He had been saying that all sane men were abolitionists by the
time of the attack on Senator Sumner. He subscribed for the relief and support of Union men in Texas. By 1861 he was driven
from the platform of an antislavery meeting in Tremont Temple
by an unruly mob. No doubt all this brings Emerson closer to
us and causes us to respect him more. Only one qualification
needs to be entered. Having just gone through the Civil War
with him, we cannot but remember that he did not always see
most clearly when his heart outweighed his head.[32]

CHAPTER SEVEN

THE OVERSOUL

I

Emerson sometimes shows a tendency to narrow religion down to mere morality: "I consider theology to be the rhetoric of morals. The mind of the age has fallen away from theology to morals. I conceive it an advance." Again: "The real religion of the day is reverence for character." And once more: "The progress of religion is steadily to its identity with morals." Once he called Christianity "pure Deism," which must be one of the worst definitions on record, and once he even said that Christianity is individualized and distinguished from other religions only by being moral, a statement which not only quite fails to define the salient qualities of Christianity, but also, by implication, brands all other religions as immoral.

His commanding merit as a reformer [Emerson once wrote of Theodore Parker], is this, that he insisted beyond all [other] men in pulpits . . . that the essence of Christianity is its practical morals; it is there for use, or it is nothing; and if you combine it with sharp trading, or with ordinary city ambitions to gloze over municipal corruptions, or private intemperance, or successful fraud, or immoral politics, or unjust wars, or the cheating of Indians, or the robbery of frontier nations, or leaving your principles at home to follow on the high seas or in Europe a supple complaisance to tyrants,—it is a hypocrisy, and the truth is not in you; and no love of religious music or the dreams of Swedenborg, or praise of John Wesley, or of Jeremy Taylor, can save you from the Satan which you are.

As a rule of thumb for testing the sincerity of religious convictions in the United States of America, this could hardly be bettered, but this consideration does not justify the other cavalier statements I have quoted, and for all Emerson's capacity for snide remarks about theology and metaphysics, he was perfectly aware that where there is no hunger for God, and no attempt to live each day as in His sight, there can be no religion, for he himself spoke of "the gracious motions of the soul,—piety, adoration." "I should say boldly that we should astonish every day by a beam out of eternity; retire a moment to the grand secret we carry in our bosom, of inspiration from heaven." The soul that lives without God in the world, or tries to do so, inhabits a frightful solitude, such as can only "laugh and hiss, pleased with our power in making heaven and earth a howling wilderness."

These views are obviously not out of harmony with New England transcendentalism, but the influence of old New England Calvinism and Puritanism, though not much studied until recent years, had far more importance in this connection than upon Emerson's real or fancied moralism. Something in the austerity of Calvinism appealed to Emerson's temperament; he called it a "dear ghost" and spoke of its "Sabbath peace," appreciated its character-building values, and wondered what would take its place now that it was gone. Even its errors were only exaggerations of truth (the doctrine of Election, though generally presented absurdly, was yet firmly grounded in nature), and Emerson rejected it, insofar as he did, only because its dogmatism barred the way to further light. Jonathan Edwards had called the world "the great apparition" and had found "the shadows of divine things" in it long before Emerson's time, and the two men were in still deeper harmony through the emphasis which both placed upon personal religion. In this sense, Emerson was always evangelical in his outlook; in his pulpit days, he even defended revivals (while deploring their anti-intellectualism) and stressed the need for men to be born again. Even the "rejection of personification" which developed in "the icehouse of Unitarianism" and the partial return to an Hebraic conception of God and of religion had their roots in Puritanism.[1]

Characteristically avoiding extremes, Emerson did not commit himself to the extreme idealistic view—Buddhist or transcendentalist or whatever it may be called—that the external world has only a phenomenal existence. Sane men, he believed, must accept the world more or less at face value, crediting the existence of matter not primarily because of the testimony of our senses, for he knew that, in the scientific sense, we do not see things as they are, but "because it agrees with ourselves, and the universe does not jest with us." "Let us treat the men and women well," he says; "treat them as if they were real; perhaps they are." And there is a delightful story about his excusing himself from his guests upon one occasion to take care of a man who was making a delivery on the ground that "we have to attend to these things just as if they were real."

Nevertheless, he felt very strongly that "the higher use of the material world is to furnish us with types or pictures to express the thoughts of the mind" and achieve the actualizing of thought. "We fetch fire and water, run about all day among the shops and markets, and get our clothes and shoes made and mended, and are the victims of these details; and once in a fortnight we arrive perhaps at a rational moment." Against all appearances, he believed that "the soul generates matter," not matter mind, and it seemed to him that all healthy, wise, manly men must concur in this, for the spiritual force is stronger than any power of matter, and "thoughts rule the world." "I believe," he wrote, "in the existence of the material world as the expression of the spiritual and the real," and again, "I believe the mind is the creator of the world, and is ever creating;—that at last Matter is dead Mind; that mind makes the senses it sees with; that the genius of man is a continuation of the power that made him and that has not done making him."

It is interesting that Emerson should have affirmed the primacy of the spiritual even when he was most keenly aware of material forces. He asked: "How can we not believe in influences of climate and air, when, as true philosophers, we must believe that chemical atoms also have their spiritual cause why they are thus and not other; that carbon, oxygen, alum and iron, each has its origin in spiritual nature?" Again he wrote, "When I stamp through the mud in dirty boots, I hug myself with the feeling of my immortality." All men have stamped through the mud in dirty boots. Many men have hugged themselves with the feeling of their immortality. But very few have performed both actions simultaneously. Emerson did, and this is his hallmark.

Though Emerson gave Bronson Alcott the credit for making the ideal world real to him, Alcott cannot possibly have done anything more than reinforce his natural temperament or water seeds long since planted, for he was still a boy when Berkeley taught him "that there was a Cause behind every stump and clod," so that "fine words" gained the power "to make every old wagon and wood-pile and stone wall oscillate a little and threaten to dance," and even "the selectmen of Concord and the Reverend Pound-me-down himself began to look unstable and vaporous." Throughout his life, he drew inspiration from many sources (without a careful study of the abundant materials which Kenneth W. Cameron has been bringing together of recent years,[2] it is impossible to realize how many they were), and they were not all carefully labeled "transcendentalist." Emerson is obviously not an easy man to categorize in these matters, but Charles Eliot Norton was surely not far wrong when, at the Concord centenary celebration in 1903, he declared:

The essence of his spiritual teaching seems to me to be comprised in three fundamental articles,—first, that of the Unity of Being in God and Man; second, that of the creation of the visible, material world by Mind, and its being the symbol of the spiritual world; and third, that of the identity and universality of moral law in the spiritual and material universe. These truths are for him the basis of life, the substance of religion, and the meaning of the universe.

II

"Oversoul" was a convenient term for Emerson to use for God when he wished to indicate that there was a difference between the ideas he was promulgating and those which his readers had been hearing from a hundred pulpits all their lives, but he never achieved, or hardly attempted, any very clear definition of it.[3] He had, after all, had little or no formal training in philosophy or theology, and J. M. Robertson was not far wrong when he said that Emerson "never took any logical trouble" even to distinguish his theism from pantheism. Sometimes even the great thinkers seemed to him merely web spinners, setting up a kind of screen to veil their ignorance, and there were occasions when he declined to make a clear-cut choice between Unitarianism and Trinitarianism: "I need not nibble for ever at one loaf, but eat it, and thank God for it, and earn another."

Basically the idea of the Oversoul seems to go back to Plotinus and to be conceived of as a kind of "ocean of light" or reservoir of spiritual power, available to all who open themselves to its influence. It is less God in the conventional sense—certainly less God in His Heaven—than the spiritual element in the universe and in man himself, or, better, the universe of which man is a part. This is what Emerson means when he refers approvingly to Abernethy's idea of God as "present and active in all parts of his works," or quotes Pope:

> All are but parts of one stupendous whole,
> Whose body, Nature is, and God, the soul.

In *Nature* he breaks forth into the exuberance which so amused Christopher Pearse Cranch:[4] "I become a transparent eyeball; I am doing nothing; I see all; the currents of the Universal Being circulate through me; I am part or parcel of God."

Did Emerson, then, believe in a Personal God? He seems both to deny it and affirm it. As we have seen, he was fascinated by personality always, and at the same time sharply aware of its limitations. If, on the one hand, he reduced all history to biography, on the other, he reduced persons to thoughts, and if he championed self-reliance in the individual, he limited its value to the expression it achieves of universal validities. Even in nature, he believed that one must not lose the whole in the parts, and in a sense nothing that we see has any value beyond what it suggests of the unseen. To think of God as personality in human terms (or, perhaps better, individuality), would be to make Him only "a great man such as the crowd worships." Once, at least, Emerson said that he preferred to call God "It" rather than "He."

On the other hand, if, when you say you believe in the Personality of God, you mean that God possesses consciousness, then Emerson probably did believe in the Personality of God. He himself declares that when he denies God Personality, it is "because it is too little, not too much," that religion differs from ethics precisely in that it does involve God's Personality, and that it is only in abstract discussion that the Personality of God can be denied. As soon as a devout spirit takes over, God is clothed with shape and color.

There, it seems, we must leave it. It should not trouble us greatly that human personality as we conceive it cannot be postulated of the Infinite, for neither can anything else that is finite. "The human mind seems a lens formed to concentrate the rays of the divine laws to a focus which shall be the personality of God. But that focus falls so far into the infinite that the form or person of God is not within the ken of the mind." Consequently, "personality . . . and impersonality might each be affirmed of Absolute Being."

This position is probably not logically impregnable, but it is far from being Emerson's only paradox. It is worth repeating here that Emerson was an artist by temperament, not a philosopher, and artists of all kinds, from Shakespeare on down, have frequently made contradictory assumptions in the same work and yet found that both made valuable contributions to the end being sought. Emerson's truths are glimpses, intuitions; it is their function to stimulate and foster the life of the spirit, not to contribute to an iron-clad system of belief.

The conception, presented in "Brahma," of what Carpenter calls "a disinterested and impersonal God whose laws lie beyond human good and evil" is not Emerson's own, or at least usual, belief, though he could grasp the idea and express it for its suggestive and imaginative value. But he was quite capable of identifying himself and all men and the universe itself with God and of also maintaining a distinction between Divinity and humanity. "Our compound nature differences us from God, but our reason is not to be distinguished from the Divine Essence." Thus he wished, perhaps contradictorily, to feel God within himself without losing the humility which becomes a man, or giving up his own sense of dependence upon God.[5] Since God is "the last generalization," and since Infinitude is, in the nature of the case, impossible of being contained in finite mind, this again is not really surprising. In the inaccessible depths of His being, God hides Himself from mortal eyes, refusing to be defined or personified, and Emerson cannot speak of Him without faltering or unsaying his words as fast as he utters them.

> In many forms we try
> To utter God's infinity,
> But the boundless hath no form,
> And the Universal Friend
> Doth as far transcend
> An angel as a worm.[6]

The one thing that would be really inconceivable is that either Emerson or anybody else could ever have established a sense of union with a stream of tendency.

III

Emerson called the Christian religion "profoundly true" and permitted himself to speak of "what is peculiar in the Christian ethics, and the precise aid it has brought to man." He did not object to being called Christian or Platonist "or any other affirmative name," for there is no value in negation. But for him Christianity was a rule of life, not a creed, and whatever superiority it possessed over other religions could only be self-attested, all claims of special authority being only a handicap. As early as 1827 he called himself a "Seeker," trying to view Christianity "much as Confucius or Solyman might regard it."

Emerson preached eight sermons on Christ, a total of fifty-one times. He was "the finest character in the world, without doubt" and "the head of all human culture." His was a soul which had no weakness in it and therefore offered no impediments to the

Divine Spirit working through it; unlike other men, he listened only to the voice of God within himself. He understood the soul of man and his true greatness also, perceiving that God incarnated Himself in man, and upon this basis he made a great stand for man's spiritual nature against all sensualism, form, and crime.

Emerson had little or nothing to say about Christ in theological or metaphysical terms. McGiffert identifies his Christology with the Arianism of William Ellery Channing, making Christ "the incarnation of the pre-existent Logos, or Word," though clearly subordinate to the Father. All Emerson's emphasis, however, was on the human side. Deprive Christ of his humanity and you turn his life into "an exhibition, a wonder, an anomaly, "robbing it of its meaning for men. He will be better loved by not being adored, for the place he has occupied in traditional theology is forced, unnatural, and artificial; hence it awakens resistance. When he said, "I and the Father are one," he meant that God spoke and acted through him and would do the same through others if only they gave themselves up to Him. Hence, though Emerson considered himself the "friend" of the Christian revelation and the "child" of Him who sent it, he also felt bound to deny its exclusive or extraordinary claims. Reason was a prior revelation and truth carries its substantiation upon its face. The life and teachings of Jesus were blessed because they were in accord with truth. The tragedy of Christian theology was that it had transferred worship from God to Christ, centering about "the personal, the positive, the *ritual*," and thus introducing a divided mind into religion.[7] Since Christ himself disclaimed finality, we cannot follow his example unless we too attune ourselves to receive and to obey God's message as he did. Both Swedenborg and Jacob Boehme handicapped themselves "by attaching themselves to the Christian symbol, instead of to the moral sentiment, which carries innumerable christianities, humanities, divinities in its bosom."

> Even the Rock of Ages melts
> Into the mineral air,
> To be the quarry whence to build
> Thought and its mansions fair.[8]

Emerson would have liked to include Jesus in his *Representative Men*, but felt he was not equal to the subject. Apparently the readiness never came. There are passages in the early journals particularly which we would now be tempted to call fundamentalistic in contrast to his maturer and more characteristic utterances; there is considerable preoccupation with the Judgment, for example, which he once called a sublime conception. He came pretty close to the idea of the Fall when he said that man, once "permeated and dissolved by spirit," is now a "god in ruins." In one of his sermons, however, he declared that the new astronomy had invalidated the conception of the Atonement. What he was sure of was that Christ must be apprehended spiritually by the individual soul (even the Scriptural testimony is secondary),[9] and that he mediates between God and ourselves only when, as a teacher, he awakens our powers and shows us how to find our own way to the spiritual life. Since God is nearer to every man than his nearest, He does not need to speak by a third person, come from the other side of the planet. Once Emerson spoke of Christ as "one accidental good man that happened to exist somewhere at some time," but this frightened even him, and he veered off, though there is another passage in which he speaks of the history of Jesus as "only the history of every man written large"! The point is that we must "love God without mediatory or veil," and our ability to do this is limited only by the limits of our own capacity to put ourselves aside and let God have his way with us. "That which shows God in me, fortifies me. That which shows God out of me, makes me a wart and a wen." The communication of God's truth which Christianity achieved was of value because it confirmed the intuitions of the soul itself, and if it had not done this, it would have been powerless.[10]

Emerson gave a relatively large amount of attention to Christ's miracles, as recorded in the New Testament.[11] Here the point is not so much that he did not believe in them (once at least he said that Christ probably performed them) as that he himself did not choose to be distracted by them from the more spiritual aspects of Christ's work.

The next age will behold God in the ethical laws—as mankind begins to see them in this age, self-equal, self-executing, instantaneous and self-affirmed; needing no voucher, no prophet and no miracle besides their own irresistibility,—and will regard natural history, private fortunes and politics, not for themselves, as we have done, but as illustrations of those laws, of that beatitude and love. Nature is too thin a screen; the glory of the One breaks in everywhere.

It seemed to him quite as wonderful that a man should be able to see with his eyes as that he should be able to see without them; this, he says, is the difference between the wise and the foolish, that one wonders at the usual and the other only at the unusual, an observation which recalls, by way of contrast, Oscar Wilde's impish remark that Niagara Falls would have been more wonderful if the water had been running the other way. It would not have been from Emerson's point of view, for this would merely have suggested that God was a freak.

Emerson resented the attempts of others to denigrate Jesus: he did not, he said, care to see lilies uprooted to make room for skunk cabbage. Yet he himself objected to a certain lack of balance in the personality: Jesus was not cheerful, and natural science meant nothing to him. But since there was no natural science, in the sense in which we use the term, in his time, this last objection is surely frivolous. Jesus did love and observe nature, as his parables show. That he lacked cheerfulness is at best highly doubtful, and he had enough aesthetic sensibility to be a very gifted story-teller. More could hardly have found expression in his milieu.

In "Song of Nature" Emerson gave offense to many by seeming to place Jesus in the same class with certain other great men:

> One in a Judaean manger,
> And one by Avon stream,
> One over against the mouths of Nile,
> And one in the Academe.[12]

In "The Informing Spirit" we read,

> I am the owner of the sphere,
> Of the seven stars and the solar year.
> Of Caesar's hand, and Plato's brain,
> Of Lord Christ's heart, and Shakespeare's strain.

This is not out of harmony with the "Song of Nature," but most Christians would probably be less offended by it. In the quatrain "Shakespeare" the reference in the last verse is presumably to Christ:

> I see all human wits
> Are measured but a few;
> Unmeasured still my Shakespeare sits,
> Lone as the blessed Jew.

IV

It would be impossible to express more regard for the Bible than Emerson did. He called it the ultimate standard in religion and placed it ahead of Shakespeare. If you throw it out the window, it will come bouncing back in again. He often quoted from it, even in late letters, frequently choosing less familiar passages. He quoted from it to his children also, sometimes making humorous, but never irreverent, applications, as when, having run after the stage to stop it that he might get rid of a guest, he admitted that his running was like that of Ahimaaz, the son of Zadok. Bibliolatry never tempted him, however, for George Fox had taught him, if he needed teaching, that the Scriptures "could not be understood but by the same spirit that gave them forth." The operations of the Holy Spirit are the same in ordinary men as in Isaiah or Milton. If you introduce a man who has nothing in him to a good book, nothing is what he will get out of it, and though the Bible reveals truth, it must be meaningless to one who carries no touchstone for truth in his own spiritual apprehensiveness. If Plato and Plutarch sometimes seemed to have an advantage over the Bible, it was simply because they had not been institutionalized, nor had inadmissible claims been entered in their behalf. Once he thought the Bible would have more vitality without Ruth, Esther, The Song of Solomon, and "excellent, sophistical Pauls," though elsewhere he speaks more highly of Paul. As a preacher, he used scriptural texts as epigraphs for his sermons, rather than as something to be expounded, sometimes even changing the text but leaving the sermon unaltered.

The sacraments meant no more to him than they do to a Quaker, though he recognized their possible value to others. Prayer as a form also troubled him, but prayer as a state of mind, "the contemplation of the facts of life from the highest point of view," was another matter. He tended to feel that prayer which craves a particular commodity is vicious. "As soon as a man is at one with God, he will not beg." God cannot grant unreasonable requests. He who is in accord with the will of God asks only that which God wills, and such prayers are always granted. Without prayer, he felt, the soul could no more live than the child without its mother's milk, and he seems to have valued prayer, or a selection from Plato, as a prelude to writing. Once, on his travels, he so resented the intrusion of another traveler into his chamber that he "turned round to the wall in despair," but when the man knelt down beside his bed to pray earnestly, his feelings toward him changed.

For the Christian Sabbath he had a very warm feeling. It was "the jubilee of the whole world" and "the core of our civilization, dedicated to thought and reverence." In his old age, he once asked his daughter whether today was not the day of heaven. "The Sabbath is my best debt to the Past, and binds me to some gratitude still. It brings me that frankincense out of a sacred antiquity." Hence he was less inconsistent than he has sometimes been considered when he voted to retain compulsory chapel at Harvard. He did not believe that education related to the culture of the mind alone. There ought to be some provision in it for turning the thoughts of young men toward the cultivation of their souls.

Emerson's attitude toward the Christian belief in immortality has occasioned considerable discussion and some disagreement. "Immortality," in *Letters and Social Aims*, is rather disappointing. Emerson thought the rationality of the universe encourages the hope of immortality, but on the actual question of the survival of the individual he was vague. He was right, of course, to emphasize the spiritual significance of "depth of life" over mere "length of life," and he was right when he said, "Jesus explained nothing, but the influence of him took people out of time and they felt eternal," but I think he would have had difficulty in substantiating his statement that Christ "never preaches the personal immortality." To him both space and time were only forms of thought, and he once told Moncure D. Conway that the eternity which really interested him was "the height of every living hour." Perhaps this is why Maeterlinck praised him[13] as having given "an almost acceptable sense to this daily life that has no more than its traditional horizons; he perhaps has been able to show us that it is strange, deep, and grand enough to have need of no other goal than itself."

Nevertheless, Emerson had considerable interest in what the orthodox Christian understands by immortality. McGiffert has shown[14] how important it was to him as a preacher; if he questioned it later, his doubts were not conclusive, since as late as 1855 he declared that the best evidence for immortality was the unsatisfactoriness of any other solution. Early and late, he affirmed immortality again and again. Perhaps his most vivid statement was achieved in Chicago, in reply to a literary lady who asked him point-blank whether he believed—"Madam, are we swill?" [15]—but there are less testy statements which express no less conviction. Emerson *felt* immortal; his soul said to Death, "I don't know you, Sir," [16] and reason, if not understanding, concurred. In 1903 Norton quoted him as measuring a man's intellectual sanity by his faith in immortality. "A wise man's wish for life is in proportion to his wisdom." Since the egg does not foresee the bird, nor the human embryo the man that is to be, he considered our ignorance of the future life no conclusive argument against its possibility. In 1835 he declared that he could go to the grave without fear because he was not going to the grave, and in 1870 he was quoted as believing that since the soul does not age, a man at the point of death might reasonably look forward to "newer existence" with "elasticity and hope." Plutarch's interest in immortality was one of the reasons why Emerson felt drawn to him, and he told Pendleton King that he was impressed by Goethe's references to it.

This is not quite all, however. Emerson was clearly not unmoved by the selfless idealism of such statements as that of Plotinus that he looked for the divine life in him to return to "that divine nature which flourishes throughout the Universe," and as early as 1837 he wrote that he expected to "cease to be an

Individual" and become "Universal," whatever that may mean. But Emerson was a profoundly affirmative spirit, who seldom denied except in the interest of what seemed to him a larger affirmation. He never actually committed himself to denying personal immortality; when he seems to do this, he is only trying to avoid a constricting dogmatism. Like God Himself, immortality seemed too vast a subject to be dogmatic about. His son said that when he asked him about it, he replied merely, "I think we may be sure that, whatever may come after death, no one will be disappointed," which is in harmony with Whittier's account of his having said, "If there is a future life for us, it is well; if there is not, it is well also." This is not doubt, but faith in God and the wisdom of His appointments. According to Fredrika Bremer, Emerson told her that "the resurrection, the continuance of our being, is granted" and that "we carry the pledges of this in our own breast. I maintain merely that we cannot say in what form or in what manner our existence will be continued." Sanborn quotes him as saying that souls can commit suicide, which recalls his suggestion in "Worship" of what theologians have sometimes called conditional immortality, where he says that immortality will come to those who are fit for it and that "he who would be a great soul in future must be a great soul now."

Other things being equal, those who are keen on a future life are likely to be more interested than others in what we generally call occultism. In his essay in *Miscellanies* Emerson oddly[17] called it "Demonology," and his discussion embraced even dreams, in which he showed considerable interest but which he did not treat quite consistently. He was apparently a fairly gifted dreamer, but foolish or undignified dreams seem to have made him angry.

Emerson spoke of *déjà vu*, that "we have been here before" feeling which has interested so many modern writers of fiction, and he recognized what we call charisma, appearing in men "having a force which without a virtue, without shining talent, yet makes them prevailing." If he gagged at spiritualism,[18] astrology, etc., the reason was the "certain want of harmony between the action and the agents. We are used to vaster wonders than those that are alleged." Mesmerism is "high life below stairs," and phrenology is popular only because even unscientific people crave some way of classifying phenomena. He rejected luck because he believed in a universe governed by law, and he rejected these other things for the same reason that he was cold toward miracles, not because they were too wonderful, but because they were not wonderful enough, being much less so than the normal processes of life. Occult phenomena reveal no truth and bring no moral dynamic; they are "physiological," not religious.

There are, however, two qualifications. First, Emerson could not help sympathizing with superstitious persons "because their whole existence is not bounded by their hats and their shoes, but they walk attended by pictures of the imagination, to which they pay homage." So he took an interest in German folklore and praised the use of the supernatural in Scott's novels. Second, he could not help wondering whether the forces now manifesting themselves in "witchcraft and ghostcraft, palmistry and magic and all other scattered superstitions" may not actually correspond to something real and valuable in the universe which may some day be intelligently apprehended and employed. Even of dreams he suggested that "they also shed light on our structure," and once he went beyond this to grant some

insinuation . . . that the known eternal laws of morals and matter are sometimes corrupted or evaded by this gypsy principle, which chooses favorites and works in the dark for their behoof; as if the laws of the Father of the universe were sometimes balked and eluded by a meddlesome Aunt of the universe for her pets.

V

Compared to what it was designed to foster, the church was to Emerson what the tariff was to Theodore Roosevelt—"merely a matter of expediency." His notion that it existed in his time in a state of decay antedates even the Divinity School Address;[19] in the essay he submitted for the Bowdoin Prize in 1821, he accused it of having chosen "darkness rather than light, —a perverse obstinacy of ignorance," and also of bigotry, prescribing "silly and degrading penances, and an offering of whim and delirium in order to propitiate the Deity." Emerson admired Henry Ward Beecher, both in and out of the pulpit, but he did not respond to Charles G. Finney (whom he calls Phinney), judging him all heart and no head, with no sentiment or imagination, but only an elaborate show of logic. He greatly admired the picturesque sailor-preacher of the Boston waterfront, "Father" Edward Taylor, who regarded Emerson as a Christlike man ignorant of Christianity, whom neither God nor the devil would know what to do with, but he was keenly aware of Taylor's intellectual limitations. Emerson had as little use for "know-nothing religions, or churches that proscribe intellect" as for the "scortatory religions; slave-holding and slave-trading religions; and, even in the decent populations, idolatries wherein the whiteness of the ritual covers scarlet indulgence."

As Emerson saw it, Calvinism survived in his time by pride and ignorance, and Unitarianism, which was preferable to Roman Catholicism only in being less committed and therefore closer to the Lyceum.[20] As the perfect socialist expects the state to disappear when men shall have learned to live without it, so Emerson argued that Solomon built his Temple because his own life was not a temple and that churches are filled on Sundays because the worshippers do not keep the commandments on Monday. After 1839 he ceased to attend church, and in the early fifties he took legal action to separate himself not only from the church in Concord, but from the parish. In later years, however, he returned to church-going, often twice on Sunday, and apparently enjoyed it greatly.

Despite all his objections, Emerson's ideal of the Christian minister as expressed in his sermons and elsewhere (he never thought he himself realized it) was very high. During his European tour, he kept the welfare of Second Church on his mind, and the "idolatry" he saw in Italy increased his devotion to the liberal Christianity of New England. When Cyrus Bartol contemplated giving up his ministry, he advised against it, speaking "of his own pain in the rupture of the pastoral tie," and once he remarked sadly to Elizabeth Peabody, "If I had not been cut off untimely in the pulpit, perhaps I might have made something of the sermon."

Though Emerson's mother had been brought up in the Church of England and cherished the Book of Common Prayer,[21] the institution does not get very respectful handling in *English Traits*. Her clergy had become wards and pensioners of the "so-called producing classes" and she herself consequently had lost religious importance. There were still devout souls in England, but they had been driven into the sects and elsewhere. Sometimes one must "cleave to God against the name of God."

The Roman Catholic Church drew more mixed treatment. Her saints and thinkers attracted Emerson, and he agreed with them more than he disagreed. In Baltimore in the early days, and later in Europe, he found in Catholic churches a certain refuge against cold Unitarianism. He felt at home in Santa Croce in Florence; it was a church which belonged to the whole human race. Certainly he was attracted by the Middle Ages,[22] and sometimes he seems to have wished that Catholicism were true, as

Lowell did in "The Cathedral" and as Henry Adams was to do after him. Once he listed fear of the Catholic Church among the superstitions of the age; others include fear of immigration, of radicalism, and of manufacturing interests—again, surely a queer conglomerate! Yet he calls the Church sinister, worldly, and impious, playing upon man's fear of death to get his money and substituting authority for reason, and he puts "the Purgatory, the Indulgences, and the Inquisition of Popery," along with "the vindictive mythology of Calvinism," in the same class with "the Dionysia and Saturnalia of Greece and Rome, the human sacrifice of the Druids, the Sradda of Hindoos." In 1842 he encouraged a Unitarian girl who wished to become a Catholic against the wishes of her parents (though not, perhaps, for reasons which a Catholic would regard very highly), but when Anna Barker Ward became a Catholic, he was displeased and discouraged Father Isaac Hecker, who had converted her, against lecturing in Concord afterward.[23] Part of Martin Luther's appeal to Emerson was due to his emphasis upon "justification by faith," or his conviction that trust in good works, or in the Mass, got in the way of reliance upon God Himself. At the same time, he called Luther's theology Jewish and found more bibliolatry in him than he could approve of.

Emerson's respect for the Society of Friends has been referred to elsewhere in this volume. Though he thought good preaching one of man's great gifts, he once wrote that he valued the silence in the church auditorium before the service began even more. "Silence is a solvent that destroys personality, and gives us leave to be great and universal." His own temperamental sympathy with Quakerism is of course self-evident. "I believe I am more of a Quaker than anything else; I believe in the 'still, small voice.'" Even the Quaker moment of silence before meals seemed valuable and beautiful to him. "It has the effect to stop mirth, and introduce a moment of reflection. After the pause, all resume their usual intercourse from a vantage-ground." Emerson's admiration of the Quakers was not blind, however, nor, perhaps, even without eccentricity. In one odd passage he sees both Fox and Penn as "urgent doers" and therefore men of wrath, and avers that he, contrariwise, sees the world as beauty and God as love, and in his memoir of Margaret Fuller he speaks of Friends as "that once spiritual sect." [24]

Swedenborgianism gets more attention, but the verdict is less single. On the one hand, Swedenborg is hailed as having taken an important forward step in religion and his followers described as the most vital modern Christian sect. There is even a poem, "Solution," in which the founder is put in a class with Homer, Dante, Shakespeare, and Goethe! Yet Emerson also thought Swedenborg slightly insane, and while he was immensely attracted by his conception of the natural world as the symbol of the spiritual world, he had no use for the mythus which Swedenborg developed.[25]

VI

Emerson lived with the "strangers and pilgrims" feeling which is the true hallmark of the religious spirit. Religion, to him, was inexpugnable, God not having left Himself without a witness in any sane mind, and man's soul was not an organ, but the animating force of his entire being. Materialism he identified with quadrupeds (" 'tis of no importance what bats and oxen think"), and he maintained that no materialistic or rationalistic argument can have any weight with one who has ever experienced even a momentary sense of union with the Oversoul. Though he defended the atheist Kneeland again persecution, he considered what he had to say "miserable babbling," and when Harriet Martineau lost her faith, it depressed him. He admitted that

Voltaire did a useful work, but his was a bustard's or tarantula's job, after all. Indeed, Emerson's faith was so strong that he did not fear to give even skepticism its head: "I dip my pen in the blackest ink, because I am not afraid of falling into my inkpot." He agreed with Marcus Aurelius that "it is pleasant to die if there be gods, and sad to live if there be none." For himself, he did not understand how a man can live believing only in chemistry. "Unlovely, nay, frightful, is the solitude of the soul which is without God in the world." Even if the world is evil, it is the spiritual witness within the man which tells him it is evil.

The heart of Emerson's religion was his insistence upon the necessity of a direct and immediate apprehension of spiritual reality. "God is, not was; . . . speaketh, not spake." Our fathers "beheld God and nature face to face"; why should we see them only through their eyes? This is to treat God as if He were dead and to make religion a parrot's talk. Emerson wished to stop putting time between God and himself. To a soul which is alive to God, the world itself is renewed every moment.

It is still possible to understand why the expression of such ideas in the Divinity School Address should have caused Emerson to be called an infidel, but how anybody could have considered him an atheist is beyond the wit of man to explain. It is true, however, that he sometimes carried his demand for spontaneity to fantastic extremes. When one reads, "I am always insincere as always knowing there are other moods," one can make every reasonable allowance for rhetorical exaggeration and emphasis, but he also wrote, "I hate preaching, whether in pulpits or in teachers' meetings. Preaching is a pledge, and I wish to say what I feel and think to-day, with the proviso that to-morrow perhaps I shall contradict it all. Freedom boundless I wish." It is hard to see in this anything but intellectual libertinism. Taken in the large, however, Emerson's insistence upon the integrity of the individual religious experience was certainly wholesome; it was also Puritan and Protestant and evangelical. And though he may not have been much of a mystic himself, it certainly allies him with all modern mystics, as opposed to authoritarians, in religion. One must still wonder, however, whether he made sufficient allowance for religious tradition and training. God never leaves Himself without witnesses, but would Emerson have been the same spiritual being he was if he had been born a Comanche or a Hottentot? Though we cannot be sure of the answer, I think it very doubtful. But the essential point to make here is that he never really faced the question.[26]

WHAT EMERSON IS

Hardly anybody who has ever written about Emerson at any length has been able to resist quoting Matthew Arnold: "He is the friend and aider of those who live in the spirit." Lowell added: "Emerson awakened us, saved us from the body of this death."

These statements do not have quite the precise or exact scientific ring which modern literary scholarship values. But it may be that there is something in Emerson which will not yield comfortably to exact scientific definition. And if we ask what Arnold and Lowell meant, the only answer that can reasonably be given is that if you need to ask, no answer is possible.

He had perhaps the most seminal mind we have ever produced in this country. He believed that the development of the human soul was an ultimate end; that whatever stood in the way of the development and expression of that soul is vicious, however venerable or even sacred it may appear; and that unless life can be lived spontaneously and fully and gladly, there is no hope for the future of the world. It is not enough that God spoke to Moses; He must speak to me and to you. It is not enough that Shakespeare and Michelangelo created great art; you and I must create it also, and if we cannot do this ourselves, we must recognize its value in those of our contemporaries who can. It is not enough that we shall have pie in the sky by and by; life must be triumphant here and now. And what do you want with immortality, he asks you, if you are bored every time you are left alone for half an hour here?

But Lowell also called Emerson "a Plotinus-Montaigne," with "a Greek head on right Yankee shoulders," and found his writing, which was the expression of himself and the fruit of this combination in him, "home-spun cloth-of-gold." Emerson thought of the Greeks in general as having carried physical development as far as it could go; they were both perfect in kind and extremely limited, but he found in Plato a balance of the active West and the contemplative East. When he was still a very young man, Henry Ware criticized him for using such homely illustrations in his sermons. His reply was both deferential and independent; he would use more Scripture, he promised, but he did not promise to give up the homely illustrations. Later he praised Goethe because he combined genius and common sense, thus reconciling the ideal with the actual world. Good writing, he believed, must deal with common things and meet the needs of common men. He blamed savants for being out of touch with actuality and philosophers for failing to see the beauty of common life.

He was a spiritual man, not because he despised the senses but because he wished to live a complete life. To his way of thinking, asceticism was not a satisfactory alternative to indulgence; both were bad. Any single fact, taken by itself, misleads; the libertine and St. Simeon Stylites were equally revolting to him. We were not made to breathe pure oxygen or talk in blank verse or even to be always wise. The perfect man knew both poetry and mathematics, joined a hunger for beauty with a high devotional spirit, loved justice and possessed beautiful manners. Our daily prayer should be to accord just measure to all that the universe contains. Washington Gladden once preached a famous sermon called "Where Does the Sky Begin?" His answer was that the sky begins where the atmosphere begins and that therefore man lives in it. Emerson would have enjoyed that sermon, and he would have felt quite at home with Rufus Jones's homely figure when he saw man as an amphibian, who must, even now, inhabit two different worlds or elements. Hence Emerson's ideal man was not pure spirit, but a balance between spirit and matter, reason and understanding.

The dancer, the skater, and the equestrian furnished important figures to him. The dance of life is a balancing act. The art of living is the art of learning to skate on surfaces, and the equestrian in the circus, throwing himself from horse to horse, and balancing first on one foot and then on the other, achieves what we must all achieve in other ways. We should not be surprised, then, when "Merlin" informs us that

> Balance-loving Nature
> Made all things in pairs,

nor yet that

> Like the dancers' ordered band,
> Thoughts come also hand in hand;
> In equal couples mated,
> Or else alternated.

And "Uriel" adds that there are no straight lines in the universe and that everything moves by indirection:

> Unit and Universe are round;
> In vain produced, all rays return.

Man is his own balancing point, "whereof everything may be affirmed and denied with equal reason." As the health of the body depends upon circulation, and sanity of mind upon variety and facility of association, so we need the whole society to achieve symmetry, accepting "the clangor and jangle of contrary tendencies." Every act, be it only the writing of a sentence, imposes limitations and commits to choice. Through excess of wisdom the wise man becomes a fool; if he fasten his attention upon one idea and neglect the others, the truth will turn to falsehood. Both rationalists and mystics have their place; one brings us closer to experience, the other to God. True skepticism is not unbelief, denial, scoffing, nor profligate jeering, for the doubter must always doubt his own doubts; so Emerson praised Montaigne for occupying a middle ground between the abstractionist and the materialist, finding "both wrong by being in extremes" and striving to take up his own stand on "the beam of the balance." Perry Miller remarked wittily of Emerson, Thoreau, and Theodore Parker that "they were but transcendental north-north-west; when the wind was southerly they knew the difference between Beacon Hill and South Boston." Alcott could not achieve such variety; he cared nothing for the pleasant side of things and could not be amused; in the end, therefore, Emerson found him monotonous.

In the course of this book we have seen Emerson's stubborn determination to maintain his balance emerging in various connections on both the theoretical and the practical level. He balanced solitude, which is "impractical," against society, which is "fatal"; "our safety is in the skill with which we keep the diagonal line." He balanced freedom against fate, trying to determine what was foreordained and what was not, reaching the eminently pragmatic conclusion that "it is wholesome to look not at Fate but the other way," and at last attempting to "build altars to the Beautiful Necessity" and making even the limitations of our freedom part of the unity of all life. His philosophy was, in some aspects, that of a supra-personalist, but who was ever more enthralled by personality than he was? He believed implicitly in the individual and the importance of the individual vision, but when he discovered that his most private thoughts had been anticipated by the ancients, he was not disturbed, for this simply meant that he had tapped the universal, normal insight of mankind. He admitted political paternalism for the sake of those who needed special protection now, but this was an emergency measure; he would have preferred not to meddle with the spontaneous, inevitable operation of the laws of life, and his ideal was a world in which just that would be possible.

The most frequently quoted of the extreme statements which Emerson sometimes enjoyed making was that "a foolish consistency is the hobgoblin of little minds." It is true that his own inconsistencies of statement are sometimes glaring, occasionally even grotesque, but in the long run they are not very important. He was like the heretic who offered to sign all the creeds, and H. D. Gray was quite right when, long ago, he attributed this inclination to Emerson's conviction that "the perfect truth lay deeper than any actual expression of it" and his consequent determination to keep his mind open to the reception of new truth. Basically, Emerson's consistency was that of his own temperament; he chose from every system what he could use and ignored the rest. He accepted himself basically because he accepted the God that had made him, and he knew that consistency can be spelled *reductio ad absurdum*. Whatever contradictions may lie on the surface, Emerson was always Emerson; in the sense of addressing mankind with a single voice, few writers have ever been more consistent than he.

G. K. Chesterton once pertinently reminded us that our time is only a time, not the Day of Judgment, and if we are tempted to reply that it *is* the Day of Judgment for us, we might do well to remember that it is also we who are being judged. Emerson is not necessarily right because he tends to agree with us on a number of subjects. We may be wrong, and he may even have helped to lead us astray. Consequently we do not get far by reminding ourselves that he is in harmony with all the non-materialistic aspects of contemporary scientific thinking, that his emphasis on self-expression allies him with a whole host of modern thinkers and artists all the way from Freud to the stream-of-consciousness novelists, and that several aspects of his aesthetic theory—his stress upon the psychological aspects of the aesthetic experience, his commitment to the organic principle, his anticipation of John Dewey's protest against the separation between the "fine" and the "useful" arts, etc.—are very close to what we believe ourselves. Nobody, whatever he may have thought about Emerson's thinking, has ever doubted that he was a good man, but it is more important here to realize that he exemplifies the *kind* of good man we must breed in increasing numbers if democracy, whose long-run success in this world is still far from being assured, is to survive. Norman Foerster has remarked that though Emerson does speak of the poet as trusting to the horse's instinct to guide him aright, he also speaks of uniting freedom with precision. He cites the Hindu conception of God as the "Internal Check" and sees the Quaker "Inner Light" not so much as inciting action, but rather as barring unfit action. His glorification of ecstasy gave him an intellectual understanding of those who have made the orgy an expression of holiness, but he was never in the slightest danger of being seduced by any of them. Many modern non-orgiastic creeds and cults have also found themselves in various Emersonian texts, but here again he kept himself free of extremes. The Emersonian ideal is that of the man who is free to do as he likes but who chooses to do what is right and in harmony with the Will of God. Since this is the only true freedom or morality that man has ever achieved, it does not represent a distinctively or exclusively modern ideal. Saint Augustine expressed it in his "Love and do as you like." But democracy has given it a new imperative and a new importance, however "Will of God" may be defined and whatever theological or non-theological assumptions may prevail. Unless we can achieve it, we must either forfeit our freedom on the one hand or be content to turn our cities into jungles on the other. Until we have overtaken him upon this point, Emerson will, therefore, still have considerable relevance for us, whether we have the wit to recognize it or not.[1]

A NOTE ON EMERSON SCHOLARSHIP AND ON THE AIM AND METHOD OF THIS BOOK

This book is concerned with the character and personality of Ralph Waldo Emerson rather than with either his ideas or his writings as literature, but it has not always been possible to differentiate clearly between the various elements. Where other poets were inspired by emotions, Emerson was often inspired by ideas, and sometimes we have found that if we wish to understand what manner of man he was, we must make our approach through studying what he believed. Even here, however, I have tried to keep the focus not upon the ideas themselves, but upon what they show concerning the man who held them. Obviously it has not, in every instance, proved possible to dismiss the ideas without some evaluation of their validity, but this is apart from the main purpose of the book. I should not care to be labeled either Emersonian or anti-Emersonian, and I am not concerned either to parade my views or to conceal them.

Since Emerson was not unfamiliar with the writings of Sainte-Beuve, who first coined the terms psychograph and psychography (though Gamaliel Bradford later coined them again independently), he may possibly have known these words, but I do not recall that he ever used them. He did find himself, in spite of all the supra-personal aspects of his philosophy, "a devout student and admirer of persons." He added: "I cannot get used to them: they daunt and dazzle me still." He believed that the man and the writer are, or should be, one, and he quoted approvingly from George Fox: "What I am in words, I am the same in life." He found "biographies which record conversations" (Plutarch, Xenophon, Coleridge, Haydon, etc.) "fascinating, and so far as true, better and more interesting than formal biographies." He himself had no psychographic method; neither, for that matter, had Sainte-Beuve; the method awaited Bradford. But he came as close to composing psychographs as one can come without method in *Representative Men* and his other biographical papers, and he spoke for all psychographers when he declared: "I would draw characters, not write lives. I would evoke the spirit of each, and their relics might rot." Certainly the importance of Emerson's own character as a factor in his work has long been recognized. Henry James, Sr., wrote that "the influence exerted by Mr. Emerson over the minds of his contemporaries is not in the least of a dogmatic or intellectual, but of a purely personal quality. And personality—character—as it seems to me, is the distinctive badge of Mr. Emerson's genius." Later, John Jay Chapman added: "It is solely as character that he is important. . . . We must regard him and deal with him simply as a man."

It has been objected that the psychographic method does not make adequate allowance for developments and changes in the life of its subject. The essential differences between psychography and conventional biography are that the former concentrates upon character and personality rather than events and arranges its material not chronologically but topically. I think it must be admitted that since it adheres to the same time order as life experience itself, the narrative method does have an advantage in the presentation of all matters directly tied up with chronological development. By the same token, I am obliged to add that it loses in its presentation of the total personality and, except in the most skillful hands, I believe it encourages much tiresome repetition and tends to create a scattered effect. If, for ex-

ample, Emerson did something which revealed his idealistic aspiration in the year 1822, and said something on the same subject
in 1865, and if reasonable inferences concerning his motivations
in this area may be inferred from something which happened
in 1876, then the orthodox biographer will be compelled to
consider Emerson's idealism in all three places without achieving
a unified, over-all consideration of this quality in any one place.
He *can* stop to summarize, to be sure, and, by the same token,
the psychographer *can* indicate changes and developments under any one of the particular topics he considers in his attempt
to build up a developed picture of the whole personality. But the
respective advantages and disadvantages of the two methods
remain.

For the student of Emerson all these considerations now have
a special and particular interest. Ever since 1953, when Stephen
E. Whicher published *Freedom and Fate*,[1] there has been a
tendency to stress the idea of a changing, if not contradictory,
Emerson. Whicher's own statement of his views was submitted
to so many qualifications that it is difficult to summarize briefly,
but its essence seems to be that around 1840 Emerson underwent
a spiritual crisis which ultimately resulted in his abandonment
of the pure transcendentalism of *Nature* for the more disil-
lusioned attitudes of "Experience." This is a coarse and inadequate statement concerning a very subtle book, for Whicher
did not commit himself to extreme positions, and *Freedom and
Fate* is one of the most sensitive studies we have, not only of
Emerson but of any major American writer. Whicher misrepre-
sented himself when he wrote that the change marked "the
end of any belief on Emerson's part in the rationality of life,"
and that, "once he had accepted the defeat of his first hopes, he
regularly took for granted the inherent absurdity of the human
situation." This is, indeed, as exaggerated as Emerson's own
writing "Whim" on his doorposts and asking, "Are they *my*

poor?" Indeed, Whicher himself immediately qualified: "But the defeat of his early dreams of victory must not be overstated. The promise of the Soul remained, though all experience told against it." Neither did he wish to suggest that Emerson "did not find the secret of a serene and affirmative life. The evidence is overwhelming that he did." Perhaps, indeed, "sense of limitation" might more accurately indicate what he developed than "tragic sense." His faith, as well as his doubt, was the fruit of experience and an expression "of the God within" which was not to be shaken. Almost more than any other writer, he "believed in the dignity of human life. . . . To reject Emerson utterly is to reject mankind."

Whicher's views and those of the scholars who share his general outlook and approach have been accepted uncritically in some quarters and carefully scrutinized elsewhere. For one thing, the publication of the first nine volumes of the Belknap-Harvard edition of the *Journals* has shown conclusively that Emerson faced doubt long before the period selected by Whicher as crucial.[2] This kind of thing was edited out of the old Houghton Mifflin edition; as Alvan S. Ryan says, "Had the dialogue we find in the early journals been conducted in public, Emerson's impact would have been far different."[3] Sheldon W. Liebman,[4] though admitting a "very profound metamorphosis," could find no evidence of either a particular crisis in Emerson's life or any special influence to bring it about, and John Lydenberg, who tried to find in Emerson "the shudder, the feeling of nightmare, the note of horror that characterizes the dark tradition of Poe and Melville, Hemingway and Faulkner," still concluded by leaving the Concord sage "a leader of the party of hope, one of the major spokesmen for the American dream."[5]

It should also be remembered, however, that, though they were not in possession of all the materials we have to work with now, older writers were not wholly unaware of the presence of conflict and change in Emerson. Benjamin De Casseres' discussion, in "Emerson: Sceptic and Pessimist," [6] was absurdly one-sided, but this does not prevent it from illustrating my point, and Henry James, in *Partial Portraits*, saw Emerson going through "movement, experiment and selection" and this through "effort . . . and painful probation." Finally, the St. Louis Hegelian Denton J. Snider[7] interpreted Emerson's life in terms of not one but a series of crises, though he was far indeed from believing that his subject was a chaos; his last chapter is called "The Reconciled Emerson." Whether these writers were right or wrong, their existence does underline the dangers of reading only recent criticism.

Psychography, however, is more concerned with being than with becoming, with what the man was rather than how he got that way. Without minimizing the importance of other things, the psychographer chooses as his particular task the attempt to bring into focus the whole personality of the man who has achieved a certain maturity and a reasonable degree of equilibrium. Of course this does not mean that he has no interest in the child who became the father of the man, but he can no more deal with that child directly than could a painter who should execute a portrait of the adult, nor than, say, the author of a critical study of one of Shakespeare's plays could afford to concentrate on source study.

All this rests upon the assumption that there is such a thing as character, a certain element of stability in a human being, which, however it may be affected by circumstances, can never be fundamentally altered. If this is not true, there can be no psychography, but since there can be nothing else that makes life worth living either, we need not concentrate upon this aspect. This book, at least, assumes that Ralph Waldo Emerson was a man, not a syndrome whose constituent elements changed from year to year or from day to day, and this much, I believe, must be granted by every human being who has himself achieved any greater degree of awareness and self-consciousness than a fieldmouse.

Emerson, we know, granted it, and those who knew him found their own convictions along this line strengthened by their contacts with him. Even his critics were aware of it, as when Whitman complained that he still held the same ideas he had adhered to a generation before. Emerson would not have objected to this charge, for he did not seem to himself to have altered essentially since boyhood. In later years, when rumors were circulating that he had become more orthodox, he always said that what he believed had been expressed in his books and that his beliefs had undergone no changes in many years, and he once told Moncure D. Conway that the only change he could see in himself was that he had become more optimistic than he had been twenty years before. This is quite in harmony with what Perry Miller called the basic transcendental belief "which declared truth to be forever and everywhere one and the same, and all ideas to be one idea, all religions the same religion, all poets singers of the same music of the same spheres, chanting eternally the recurrent theme." Emerson scorned "this wild, savage, and preposterous There or Then," and told Samuel G. Ward that he hated to acknowledge times as much as Dr. Johnson did the weather.

At the beginning of Part III of his *Emerson and the Soul,* Jonathan Bishop admits that he has hitherto concerned himself with "the essence of the Emersonian achievement" as "abstracted from the whole body of his work, . . . without regard to the changes Emerson's ideas underwent during his lifetime." There were such changes, he asserts, and he proceeds to describe what he considers two distinct crises, yet he still declares that the "illusion" of a unified Emerson "nevertheless contains a predominance of basic truth. The soul does act from eternity, as

Emerson would have been quick to maintain, and it would not be hard to imagine him defending a method of displaying his ideas about the soul that he used himself when he dealt as a critic with the work of other thinkers." That, essentially, is what I have tried to do in these pages, and if it be objected that I have considered a great many things which seem to have no connection with the soul, I can only reply that for Emerson there were no such things.

EMERSON'S PREFACE
TO *PARNASSUS*

NOTE: Emerson's Preface to his poetic anthology, *Parnassus*, is an important statement of his beliefs about literature, and it is not easily available. It has therefore been reprinted here exactly as it appeared in 1874.

THIS volume took its origin from an old habit of copying any poem or lines that interested me into a blank book. In many years, my selections filled the volume, and required another; and still the convenience of commanding all my favorites in one album, instead of searching my own and other libraries for a desired song or verse, and the belief that what charmed me probably might charm others, suggested the printing of my enlarged selection. I know the convenience and merits of the existing anthologies, and the necessity of printing in every collection many masterpieces which all English-speaking men have agreed in admiring. Each has its merits; but I have found that the best of these collections do not contain certain gems of pure lustre, whilst they admit many of questionable claim. The voluminous octavos of Anderson and Chalmers have the same fault of too much mass and too little genius; and even the more select "Golden Treasury" of Mr. Palgrave omits too much that I cannot spare. I am aware that no two readers would make the same selection. Of course, I shall gladly hail with the public a better collection than mine.

Poetry teaches the enormous force of a few words, and, in proportion to the inspiration, checks loquacity. It requires that splendor of expression which carries with it the proof of great thoughts. Great thoughts insure musical expressions. Every word should be the right word. The poets are they who see that spiritual is greater than any material force, that thoughts rule the world. The great poets are judged by the frame of mind they induce; and to them, of all men, the severest criticism is due.

Some poems I have inserted for their historical importance; some, for their weight of sense; some, for single couplets or lines, perhaps even for a word; some, for magic of style; and I have admitted verses, which, in their structure, betray a defect of poetic ear, but have a wealth of truth which ought to have created melody. I know the peril of didactics to kill poetry, and that Wordsworth runs fearful risks to save his mental experiences. Some poems are external, like Moore's, and have only a superficial melody: others, like Chaucer's, have such internal music as to forgive a roughness to the modern ear, which, in the mouth of the bard, his contemporaries probably did not detect. To Chaucer may be well applied the word of Heraclitus, that "Harmony latent is of greater value than that which is patent."

There are two classes of poets,—the poets by education and practice, these we respect; and poets by nature, these we love. Pope is the best type of the one class: he had all the advantage that taste and wit could give him, but never rose to grandeur or to pathos. Milton had all its advantages, but was also poet born. Chaucer, Shakspeare, Jonson (despite all the pedantic lumber he dragged with him), Herbert, Herrick, Collins, Burns,—of the other. Then there are poets who rose slowly, and wrote badly, and had yet a true calling, and, after a hundred failures, arrived at pure power; as Wordsworth, encumbered for years with childish whims, but at last, by his religious insight, lifted to genius.

Scott was a man of genius, but only an accomplished rhymer (poet on the same terms as the Norse bards and minstrels), admirable chronicler, and master of the ballad, but never crossing the threshold of the epic, where Homer, Dante, Shakspeare, and Milton dwell.

The task of selection is easiest in poetry. What a signal convenience is fame! Do we read all authors to grope our way to the best? No; but the world selects for us the best, and we select from these our best.

Chaucer fulfils the part of the poet, possesses the advantage of being the most cultivated man of his time, and so speaks always sovereignly and cheerfully. Often the poetic nature, being too susceptible, is over-acted on by others. The religious sentiment teaching the immensity of every moment, the indifference of magnitude, the present is all, the soul is God;—this lesson is great and greatest. Yet this, also, has limits for humanity. One must not seek to dwell in ethereal contemplation: so should the man decline into a monk, and stop short of his possible enlargement. The intellect is cheerful.

Chaucer's antiquity ought not to take him out of the hands of intelligent readers. No lover of poetry can spare him, or should grudge the short study required to command the archaisms of his English, and the skill to read the melody of his verse. His matter is excellent, his story told with vivacity, and with equal skill in the pathos and in triumph. I think he has lines of more force than any English writer, except Shakspeare. If delivered by an experienced reader, the verses will be found musical as well as wise, and fertile in invention. He is always strong, facile, and pertinent, and with what vivacity of style through all the range of his pictures, comic or tragic! He knows the language of joy and of despair.

Of Shakspeare what can we say, but that he is and remains an exceptional mind in the world; that a universal poetry began and ended with him; and that mankind have required the three hundred and ten years since his birth to familiarize themselves with his supreme genius? I should like to have the Academy of Letters propose a prize for an essay on Shakspeare's poem, "*Let the bird of loudest lay*," and the "*Threnos*" with which it closes; the aim of the essay being to explain, by a historical research into the poetic myths and tendencies of the age in which it was written, the frame and allusions of the poem. I have not seen Chester's "*Love's Martyr*," and "the Additional Poems" (1601), in which it appeared. Perhaps that book will suggest all the explanation this poem requires. To unassisted readers, it would appear to be a lament on the death of a poet, and of his poetic mistress. But the poem is so quaint, and charming in diction, tone, and allusions, and in its perfect metre and harmony, that I would gladly have the fullest illustration yet attainable. I consider this piece a good example of the rule, that there is a poetry for bards proper, as well as a poetry for the world of readers. This poem, if published for the first time, and without a known author's name, would find no general reception. Only the poets would save it.

To the modern reader, Ben Jonson's plays have lost their old attraction; but his occasional poems are full of heroic thought, and his songs are among the best in the language. His life interests us from the wonderful circle of companions with whom he lived,—

with Camden, Shakspeare, Beaumont, Fletcher, Bacon, Chapman, Herbert, Herrick, Cowley, Suckling, Drayton, Donne, Carew, Selden,—and by whom he was honored. Cowley tells us, "I must not forget Ben's reading: it was delicious: never was poetry married to more exquisite music:" and the Duchess of Newcastle relates, that her husband, himself a good reader, said he "never heard any man read well but Ben Jonson."

Spence reports, that Pope said to him, "Crashaw is a worse sort of Cowley: Herbert is lower than Crashaw,"—an opinion which no reader of their books at this time will justify. Crashaw, if he be the translator of the 'Sospetto d'Herode,' has written masterly verses never learned from Cowley, some of which I have transcribed; and Herbert is the psalmist dear to all who love religious poetry with exquisite refinement of thought. So much piety was never married to so much wit. Herbert identifies himself with Jewish genius, as Michael Angelo did when carving or painting prophets and patriarchs, not merely old men in robes and beards, but with the sanctity and the character of the Pentateuch and the prophecy conspicuous in them. His wit and his piety are genuine, and are sure to make a lifelong friend of a good reader.

Herrick is the lyric poet, ostentatiously choosing petty subjects, petty names for each piece, and disposing of his theme in a few lines, or in a couplet; is never dull, and is the master of miniature painting. On graver themes, in his "Sacred Numbers," he is equally successful.

Milton's "Paradise Lost" goes so surely with the Bible on to every book-shelf, that I have not cited a line; but I could not resist the insertion of the "Comus," and the "Lycidas," which are made of pure poetry, and have contented myself with extracts from the grander scenes of "Samson Agonistes."

The public sentiment of the reading world was long divided on the merits of Wordsworth. His early poems were written on a false theory of poetry; and the critics denounced them as childish. He persisted long to write after his own whim; and, though he arrived at unexpected power, his readers were never safe from a childish return upon himself and an unskilful putting-forward of it. How different from the absolute concealment of Shakspeare in all his miraculous dramas, and even in his love-poems, in which, of course, the lover must be perpetually present, but always by thought, and never by his buttons or pitifulness! Montaigne is delightful in his egotism. Byron is always egotistic, but interesting thereby, through the taste and genius of his confession or his defiance.

Wordsworth has the merit of just moral perception, but not that of deft poetic execution. How would Milton curl his lip at such slipshod newspaper style! Many of his poems, as, for example, "The Rylstone Doe," might be all improvised: nothing of Milton, nothing of Marvell, of Herbert, of Dryden, could be. These are verses such as many country gentlemen could write; but few would think of claiming the poet's laurel on their merit. Pindar, Dante, Shakspeare, whilst they have the just and open soul, have also the eye to see the dimmest star, the serratures of every leaf, the test objects of the microscope, and then the tongue to utter the same things in words that engrave them on the ears of all mankind.

The poet demands all gifts, and not one or two only. Like the electric rod, he must reach from a point nearer to the sky than all surrounding objects, down to the earth, and into the wet soil, or neither is of use. The poet must not only converse with pure thought, but he must demonstrate it almost to the senses. His words must be pictures: his verses must be spheres and cubes, to be seen and handled. His fable must be a good story, and its meaning must hold as pure truth. In the debates on the Copyright Bill, in the English parliament, Mr. Sergeant Wakley, the coroner, quoted Wordsworth's poetry in derision, and asked the roaring House of Commons, "what that meant, and whether a man should have a public reward for writing such stuff?"—Homer, Horace, Milton, and Chaucer would defy the coroner. Whilst they have wisdom to the wise, he would see that to the external they have external meaning. Coleridge rightly said that "poetry must first be good sense, as a palace might well be magnificent, but first if must be a house." Wordsworth is open to ridicule of this kind; and yet, though satisfied if he can suggest to a sympathetic mind his own mood, and though setting a private and exaggerated value on his compositions, and taking the public to task for not admiring his poetry, he is really a master of the English language; and his best poems evince a power of diction that is no more rivalled by his contemporaries than is his poetic insight. But his capital merit is, that he has done more for the sanity of his generation than any other writer.

"Laodamia" is almost entitled to that eminence in his literary performance which Landor gave it when he said, that "Wordsworth had now written a poem which might be fitly read in Elysium, and the gods and heroes might gather round to listen." I count that and the "Ode on Immortality" as the best.

Wordsworth has a religious value for his thoughts; but his inspirations are casual and insufficient, and he persists in writing after they are gone. No great poet needs so much a severely critical selection of the noble numbers from the puerile into which he often falls. Leigh Hunt said of him, that "he was a fine lettuce with too many outer leaves."

Byron's rare talent is conspicuously partial. He has not sweetness, nor solid knowledge, nor lofty aim. He had a rare skill for rhythm, unmatched facility of expression, a firm, ductile thread of gold. His rhymes do not suggest any restraint, but the utmost freedom, as the rules of the dance do not fetter the good dancer, but exhibit his natural grace. In his isolation he is starved for a purpose; and finding no material except of romance,—first, of corsairs, and Oriental robbers and harems, and, lastly, of satire,—he revenges himself on society for its supposed distrust of him, by cursing it, and throwing himself on the side of its destroyers. His life was wasted; and its only result was this brilliant gift of song with which he soothed his chosen exile. I do not know that it can retain for another generation the charm it had for his contemporaries; but the security with which he pours these perfectly modulated verses to any extent, without any sacrifice of sense for the sake of metre, surprises the reader. In contrast with Wordsworth, Byron interests by his egoism, through the taste and genius of his confession or his defiance.

Tennyson has incomparable felicity in all poetic forms, surpassing in melody also, and is a brave, thoughtful Englishman, unmatched in rhythmic power and variety. The thoroughness with which the fable has been thought out, as in the account of the supreme influence of Arthur on his knights, is only one of his triumphs. The passion of love in his "Maud" found a new celebration, which woke delight wherever the English language is known; the "Dirge of Wellington" was a more magnificent monument than any or all of the histories that record that commander's life. Then the variety of his poems discloses the wealth and the health of his mind. Nay, some of his words are poems.

The selections from American writers are necessarily confined to the present century; but some of them have secured a wide fame. Some of them are recent, and have yet to earn their laurels. I have inserted only one of the remarkable poems of Forceythe Willson, a young Wisconsin poet of extraordinary promise, who died very soon after this was written. The poems of a lady who contents herself with the initials H. H. in her book published in Boston (1874) have rare merit of thought and expression, and will reward the reader for the careful attention which they require. The poem of "Sir Pavon and Saint Pavon," by another hand, has a dangerous freedom of style, but carries in it rare power and pathos.

The imagination wakened brings its own language, and that is always musical. It may or may not have rhyme or a fixed metre; but it will always have its special music or tone. Whatever language the bard uses, the secret of tone is at the heart of the poem. Every great master is such by this power,—Chaucer and Shakspeare and Raleigh and Milton and Collins and Burns and Byron and Tennyson and Wolfe. The true inspiration always brings it. Perhaps it cannot be analyzed; but we all yield to it. It is the life of the good ballads; it is in the German hymns which Wesley translated; it is in the "Marseillaise" of Rouget de Lisle; it gave their value to the chants of the old Romish and of the English Church; and it is the only account we can give of their wonderful power on the people. Poems may please by their talent and ingenuity; but, when they charm us, it is because they have this quality, for this is the union of nature with thought.

R. W. E.

The following abbreviations are employed, both in the Notes and in the Bibliography:

ABC	American Book Company	DUP	Duke University Press
AL	*American Literature*	E	Emerson
AQ	*American Quarterly*	ESQ	*Emerson Society Quarterly*
AS	*American Scholar*	H	Harper & Brothers
ASp	*American Speech*	HB	Harcourt, Brace & Company
Atl	*Atlantic Monthly*	HLB	*Harvard Library Bulletin*
ATQ	*American Transcendental Quarterly*	HTR	*Harvard Theological Review*
AUA	American Unitarian Association	HUP	Harvard University Press
BNYPL	*Bulletin of the New York Public Library*	Iowa	*University of Iowa Humanistic Studies*
BP	Beacon Press	JHI	*Journal of the History of Ideas*
BPLQ	*Boston Public Library Quarterly*	JMN	*Journals and Miscellaneous Notebooks of Ralph Waldo Emerson*
Ce	*Century Magazine*		
CE	*College English*		
ColUP	Columbia University Press		
CUC	Cupples, Upham & Co.	K	Alfred A. Knopf, Inc.
D	Doubleday and Company	LB	Little, Brown and Company
DM	Dodd, Mead & Co.	LiM	*Lippincott's Magazine*

LG	Longmans, Green & Co.	PS	Pacific Spectator
M	The Macmillan Company	RB	Roberts Brothers
		RWE	Ralph Waldo Emerson
MHM	Michigan History Magazine	S	Charles Scribner's Sons
Miami	University of Miami Press	SAQ	South Atlantic Quarterly
Mich	University of Michigan Press	SeR	Sewanee Review
		SP	Studies in Philology
MLN	Modern Language Notes	SR	Studies in Romanticism
MLQ	Modern Language Quarterly	TSL	Tennessee Studies in Literature
MP	Modern Philology	UCP	University of Chicago Press
MR	Massachusetts Review		
N	W. W. Norton & Company	UFP	University of Florida Press
NEM	New England Magazine	UNCP	University of North Carolina Press
NEQ	New England Quarterly	UOP	University of Oklahoma Press
OUP	Oxford University Press	VQR	Virginia Quarterly Review
P	G. P. Putnam's Sons	WF	Western Folklore
PMLA	Publications of the Modern Language Association	WHR	Western Humanities Review
		YUP	Yale University Press
PQ	Philological Quarterly		

Books not otherwise assigned are all published by Houghton Mifflin Company or inherited by them from their predecessors. The Houghton Mifflin edition of Emerson's *Journals* is tagged "*Journals*, HM edition" to distinguish it from the later Harvard edition, which is cited as "*JMN*."

WHAT EMERSON WAS NOT

1 Clara Barrus, *The Life and Letters of John Burrough* (1925), II, 379.

2 *RWE: Representative Selections* (ABC, 1934), p. xxxviii.

3 *Essays Before a Sonata and Other Writings*, ed. by Howard Boatright (N, 1962).

4 *Literary Reviews and Criticisms* (P, 1908), p. 298.

BIOGRAPHY

1 "THE BOSTON ATHENAEUM,—on whose sunny roof and beautiful chambers may the benediction of centuries of students rest with mine!" Thus wrote Emerson in the *Memoirs of Margaret Fuller* (I, 265), and there much of the reading for this book was done.

2 See E's own paper about her in *Lectures and Biographical Studies*; also George Tolman, *Mary Moody Emerson* (privately printed, 1929), and Rosalie Feltenstein, "Mary Moody Emerson: The Gadfly of Concord," *AQ*, V (1953), 231–46.

3 Charles W. Eliot, *Four American Leaders* (AUA, 1906).

CHAPTER ONE: SELF-RELIANCE

1 Edward Wagenknecht, ed., *Mrs. Longfellow: Selected Letters and Journals of Fanny Appleton Longfellow (1817–1861)* (LG, 1956).

2 "E's Personality," *Ce*, N.S. II (1882), 545–56.

3 Besides a bust of Emerson, French created the fine, seated figure, now in the Concord Public Library, which has been reproduced in O. W. Firkins's *RWE* and elsewhere. French's first impression was of a "very tall, spare, loosely hung figure with small head and rather large hands and feet, with clothes worn for use and

without thought of them." He speaks of "the deep, full, beautiful voice with its matchless enunciation and perfect diction," "the clear, piercing eyes," "the courtesy towards man or child, high or lowly, which was unfailing." Of the bust E told French that "the trouble is that the more it resembles me the worse it looks" and remarked of the effort of another sculptor that it made him look as harmless as a parsnip. See Daniel Chester French, "A Sculptor's Reminiscence of E," *The Art World,* Oct. 1916, pp. 44–47, and cf. Frank B. Sanborn, "The Portraits of E," *NEM,* n.s. XV (1896), 449–68, reprinted *ESQ,* No. 59 (1970), pp. 67–86.

4   Edith Garrigues Hawthorne, ed., *The Memoirs of Julian Hawthorne* (M, 1938), pp. 94–95.

5   Emerson's letter writing was declining in quantity and quality by the sixties, and at the end Ellen seems virtually to have taken it over. Along with his inability to remember words came the loss of his power to spell; some of the letters printed toward the end of Rusk's collection contain blunders which would have been quite impossible for any literate person in possession of his powers. For a vivid picture of E in his old age, see *The Americanization of Edward Bok* (S, 1922), pp. 53–59.

6   See *AL,* XXVII (1955–56), 28.

7   In "The Influence of E," in *Shelburne Essays,* First Series (1904), to which, when it was first published in *The Independent,* Mrs. Eddy replied. See Daniel Aaron, ed., *Paul Elmer More's Shelburne Essays on American Literature* (HB, 1963), pp. 189–98.

8   Sara Norton and M. A. DeWolfe Howe, eds., *Letters of Charles Eliot Norton . . .* (1913), I, 504.

9   Mrs. Eddy seems to have made an effort to interest all the prominent New England writers in *Science and Health,* but apparently the only one who gave her any encouragement was Alcott; see Odell Shepard, ed., *The Journals of Bronson Alcott* (LB, 1938).

10   A number of E's friends attribute considerable humor to him. James B. Thayer speaks of his laughing with a "quiet groundswell" of a laugh, and Albee says he was an excellent mimic and once imitated Carlyle for him. There is a good deal of fooling in early letters, some of it ponderous, self-conscious, and inclined to humorous self-vaunting. Later he used more subtle humor in his lectures, and showed his appreciation of his audences' enjoyment of it with what Mrs. Fields calls "a kind of squirrel-like shyness and

swiftness." He could enjoy a laugh at his own expense, as when his lecture audience was described as composed of the "effete" of Boston, or "Brahma" was parodied. The two most careful studies are Arthur M. Cory, "Humor in E's *Journals*," *University of Texas Studies in English*, XXXIV (1955), 114–24, and Reginald L. Cook, "E and the American Joke," *ESQ*, No. 54 (1969), pp. 22–27. Cf. also Lawrence F. Abbott, *Twelve Great Modernists* (D, 1927). Abbott should have known; he discovered E's humor while reading him during an attack of lumbago!

11   Silver's book was published in 1967. Constance Greiff has produced *Lost America from the Atlantic to the Mississippi* and *Lost America from the Mississippi to the Pacific* (The Pyne Press, 1971, 1972).

12   See Henry F. Pommer, "The Contents and Basis of E's Belief in Compensation," *PMLA*, LXXVII (1962), 248–53; Roland F. Lee, "E's 'Compensation' as Argument and as Art," *NEQ*, XXXVII (1964), 303–5.

13   J. M. Robertson, *Modern Humanists* (Swan Sonnenschein, 1891), pp. 120–21, was certainly correct in pointing out that those who use the analytic method use intuition also, but, having done so, they test the validity of their perceptions by critical examination. The rationalist "knows that while the test of reasoning, the test of universal consistency, verifies some of his inspirations, it discredits many more; and he knows better than to bow before a notion merely because it came into his head. . . ."

14   It would not be correct to say that E *never* argued. He seems to have argued with Burroughs about Thoreau, and once he allowed himself to be drawn into an argument about predestination with an orthodox clergyman on a ferryboat. But he was not at his best in such encounters. He was more in character when he told a man who tried to argue with him about a point in a lecture that if he had said anything helpful to his auditor he was glad and that there was no use carrying consideration of the matter beyond that point. More significantly, he once received a statement of dissent, brought to him in fear and trembling by young Charles J. Woodbury, with a smiling, "Very well. I do not wish disciples."

15   There is no antecedent for "he," but the architect is implied.

16   Having rejected "thought" in line 9 of "The Problem," E embraces "Thought" in line 39. The first is the ordinary, common-

sensical, garden variety of reasoning power, which depends upon logic and functions in the ordinary, everyday affairs of life. The second is philosophical insight, religious sensitivity, intuitive under-standing, "the highest faculty of the soul." E somewhere speaks of "My England of the Understanding, my Germany of the Reason."

17 E tells a touching story about his New Bedford Quaker friend Mary Rotch who, when asked by her little girl for permission to do something, asked the child in turn what the little voice said. The girl went off to think it over and, returning, replied, "Mother, the little voice says no." But he is not impressive in his account (*JMN*, IV, 263–64) of how this same Mary Rotch refused to go to England with her sister and brother-in-law, Professor John Farrar, of Cambridge, because, having made all her plans, she felt a reluctance to leave. No reason appears, there or thereafter, why she should have changed her plans nor any evidence that she was doing other than indulging a whim.

18 Cf. E's discussion of parallels to time as illustrating the unity of life in "Poetry and Imagination" (*Letters and Social Aims*), especially the passage beginning on p. 46 in "Concord Edition," Vol. VIII. This becomes almost comic in the poem "To Eva," where the speaker loves the girl because she looks like him!

> And let me blameless gaze upon
> Features that seem at heart my own.

19 In addition to the essay "Self-Reliance," see the poem of the same title.

20 In "The Poet," E (rather oddly for a Unitarian) calls "the Father, the Spirit and the Son" "the Knower, the Doer, and the Sayer." It is a little hard to match them up, but when he adds that "these stand respectively for the love of truth, for the love of good, and for the love of beauty," he seems to equate doing with doing good. For a strong statement of the view that "E's theory is almost the obverse of what is generally meant by 'self-expression,' " see Stuart Gerry Brown, "E's Platonism," *NEQ*, XVIII (1945), 325–45. Cf. Stuart C. Woodruff, "E's 'Self-Reliance' and 'Experience': A Comparison," *ESQ*, No. 47 (1960), pp. 48–50.

21 Harriet Beecher Stowe has often been ridiculed for her declaration that not she but God had written *Uncle Tom's Cabin*.

Her expression may have been naïve, but if her point of view was ridiculous, then E is tarred with the same brush. He applied some of the ideas that have been expressed here even to criticism. It has been said of him that he listened "hungrily" to the opinions of others, and he objected to Margaret Fuller's criticism as too "idiosyncratic." The good critic, he believed, must measure himself against a work of art, showing here something of the same kind of passivity he manifests toward nature or God. It is worth remembering at this point that Bronson Alcott, always enamored of personality, thought the absence of idiosyncrasy from E's writing and conversation a serious drawback.

CHAPTER TWO: NATURE

1 "The Poet."

2 Paul O. Williams, "E Guided: Walks with Thoreau and Channing," *ESQ*, No. 35 (1964), pp. 66–67, shows how both men were useful and important to E in connection with his observation of nature, but each in his own way.

3 On E's references to flora, especially roses, see Norman Foerster's excellent chapter on him in *Nature in American Literature* (M, 1923).

4 On his way home from England in 1848 he called the sea voyage "one long disgust," but this seems to have been prompted by the discomforts of the vessel and his dislike of being shut up with people from whom he could not get away. In England, however, the "nakedness" of the sea-line along the coast had made him uncomfortable, like the sight of a naked human body.

5 E was flattered when the Massachusetts Horticultural Society sent a committee to inspect his orchard, but alas! they had only come to see the soil which had produced such poor specimens of such fine varieties! When he was told that it cost him more to raise pears than he would have had to spend to buy them, he replied, "Yes, they are costly, but we all have expensive vices. You play at billiards, I at pear-trees."

6 "The Apology."

7 H. D. Gray believed that E showed his Unitarian back-

ground by his belief that "to the well-born child all the virtues are natural and not painfully acquired." In his Bowdoin Prize essay of 1821, "The Present State of Ethical Philosophy" (*Unpublished Essays*), E opposed the view of Hobbes that nature is committed to "the character and circumstances of bears and tigers." This essay is more or less in harmony with the later view of John Fiske in his famous essay, "The Cosmic Roots of Love and Self Sacrifice" in *Through Nature to God* (1899). William L. Hedges, "A Short Way Around E's Nature," *Transactions of the Wisconsin Academy of Sciences, Arts and Letters*, XLII (1953), 21–27, approaches E's conception of nature from a neo-classical rather than the usual Romantic point of view.

8 "Woodnotes." This poem also contains Wordsworthian anti-intellectual passages, like

> Leave all thy pedant lore apart;
> God hid the whole world in thy heart.

It is only fair to note that popular forms of Christianity have also often been anti-intellectual, but E junks the churches along with the schools:

> Behind thee leave thy merchandise,
> Thy churches and thy charities.

Equally anti-intellectual is such a passage as this in "Waldeinsamkeit":

> See thou bring not to field or stone
> The fancies found in books;
> Leave authors' eyes, and fetch your own,
> To brave the landscapes' looks.

In "April" we read that

> Goodfellow, Puck and goblins,
> Know more than any book

and that

> The masters quite omitted
> The lore we care to know.

And in "The Walk" nature can teach her son more

> In one wood walk, than learned men
> Can find with glass in ten times ten.

On the other hand, E expresses the Christian point of view in "Grace"; see G. R. Elliott's interesting discussion, "On E's 'Grace' and 'Self-Reliance,'" *NEQ*, II (1929), 93–204, reprinted in his *Humanism and Imagination* (UNCP, 1938).

9   This is also the point of "The Rhodora":

> Tell them, dear, that if eyes were made for seeing,

(that is, setting one axiom over against another),

> Then Beauty is its own excuse for being.

10   See, in this connection, two important and suggestive articles: Joel Porte, "Nature as Symbol: E's Noble Doubt," *NEQ*, XXXVII (1964), 453–76, and Norman Miller, "E's 'Each and All' Concept: A Reexamination," *NEQ*, XLI (1968), 381–92. Lawrence Willson, "The Gods of New England," *PS*, IX (1955), 141–53, reminds us that Jonathan Edwards had seen the world as an emanation of God's "infinite fullness, created to express his glory."

11   "Ode Inscribed to W. H. Channing."

12   See Stanley T. Williams, "E: An Affirmation," *TSL*, II (1957), 41–50.

13   "Fragments on Nature and Life."

14   "The Waterfall."

15   "Monadnoc."

16   William J. Stillman, who was a member of the party, described these expeditions in *The Autobiography of a Journalist* (1901) and in two papers in *The Old Rome and the New* (1898), but the best account is in Paul F. Jamieson's article, "E in the Adirondacks," *New York History*, XXXIX (1958), 215–37. When Stillman returned to the area, twenty-five years later, he was sickened by the devastation wrought by the loggers. E's favorite tree, the white pine, commercially the most valuable, was the first to go. Says Jamieson:

"If the Adirondack Club had survived the Civil War, its members would have made an early stand for conservation and because of their renown might have been instrumental in checking some of the devastation. The forest amendment to the State Constitution in 1894, with its 'forever-wild' principle, came too late to save all but a few parcels of virgin timber."

17   When controversy developed as to whether Dr. Jackson or Dr. T. G. Morton deserved the credit for having first applied ether in surgery (the inveterate punster, Oliver Wendell Holmes, suggested that the monument in Boston's Public Garden be erected "to ether," which was done), E characteristically felt the matter not worth arguing about, the important thing being to have done the job and kept on working, but when Dr. Jackson's claims were, as he saw it, cavalierly and maliciously disregarded, he felt it necessary to make a stand. Once, however, E confided to his journal that he had learned nothing of value from his contacts with Jackson. On E's views concerning the teaching of natural science at Harvard, see his interchange with Agassiz in Elizabeth Cary Agassiz, *Louis Agassiz, His Life and Correspondence* (London, M, 1885), II, 619–21.

18   "May-Day."

19   Bliss Perry makes much of a comparison between E's revelation in the Jardin des Plantes and Balzac's discovery of his scheme for his *Human Comedy*, both in the summer of 1833. "Congratulate me, my dear, I am about to become famous," said Balzac to his sister, and E declared "I like my book about Nature" before he had written a line of it.

20   See *Early Lectures*, I, 1–4. After the four scientific discourses included in this volume, E composed only one more—"The Humanity of Science" (1836)—which he never published. "The Relation of Man to the Globe" sees all creation preparing for man, who appeared just when the world was ready for him, not later and not before. This is essentially a more sophisticated presentation of the testimony of the pious old lady who cited as evidence of God's goodness and care for man her observation that wherever He had set a large city, He had placed a large body of water close to it. In "The Naturalist" man is interested only in man, but man is related to the whole creation; hence human interests become, in a sense, universal. I think few will agree with E that man, alone among the animals, feels quite at home in his own body. In general, however, these

lectures, simple as they are, seem just about what a popular audience in E's time needed and could accept. Harry Hayden Clark's "E and Science," *PQ*, X (1931), 225–60, is an important study. Joseph Warren Beach, "E and Evolution," *University of Toronto Quarterly*, III (1934), 474–97, though useful, is biased by the author's distress over E's failure to become a thoroughgoing naturalist under the influence of evolutionary ideas. See, further, Frederick William Conner, *Cosmic Optimism: A Study of the Interpretation of Evolution by American Poets from E to Robinson* (UFP, 1949).

21 It is interesting to note how close Emerson comes here to a writer for whom he had no regard—Edgar Allan Poe (in *Eureka*). Poe wrote:

What I here propound is true:—therefore it cannot die:—or if by any means it be now trodden down so that it die, it will rise again to the Live Everlasting.

Nevertheless it is as a Poem only that I wish this work to be judged after I am dead.

For further consideration of E and Poe, see Patrick F. Quinn, "Poe's *Eureka* and E's *Nature*," *ESQ*, No. 31 (1963), pp. 4–7; Arnold Smithline, "Poe as Transcendentalist," *ESQ*, No. 39 (1965), pp. 25–27; Ottavio M. Casale, "Poe on Transcendentalism," *ESQ*, No. 50, Supplement (1968), pp. 85–97; James E. Mulqueen, "The Poetics of E and Poe," *ESQ*, No. 55 (1969), pp. 5–11.

22 Cf. the following extracts from "Intellect": "Every substance is negatively electric to that which stands above it in the chemical tables, positively to that which stands below it. Water dissolves wood and iron and salt; air dissolves water; electric fire dissolves air, but the intellect dissolves fire, gravity, laws, method, and the subtlest unnamed relations of nature in its resistless menstrum." "Truth is our element of life, yet if man fasten his attention on a single aspect of truth and apply himself to that alone for a long time, the truth becomes distorted and not itself but falsehood; herein resembling the air, which is our natural element and the breath of our nostrils, but if a stream of the same be directed on the body for a time, it causes cold, fever, and even death."

23 See *Journals*, HM edition, X, 359–60.

24 See G. Ferris Cronkhite, "The Railroad," *NEQ*, XXIV

(1951), 306–28, for the use of the railroad in the writings of E, Hawthorne, and Thoreau. E drew upon it "for evidence and illustration to uphold his transcendentalist views of a benevolent World-Soul."

1 Norman Foerster, *Nature in American Literature*, pp. 54–55, refutes this, to my mind convincingly, by reference to Emerson's own poems. "Fortus" is printed, with facsimiles of part of the text and all the illustrations, in *Records of a Lifelong Friendship*.

2 In some moods, E possessed an unsurpassed gift for disposing of his contemporaries. "Allston's pictures," he once wrote, "are Elysian, fair, serene, but unreal. I extend the remark to all the American geniuses: Irving, Bryant, Greenough, Everett, Channing,—even Webster, in his recorded eloquence,—all lack nerve and dagger."

3 E's slighting reference to sculpture in the essay "Art," in which statues are called "stone dolls" and ranked with "toys and trumpery of a theater" (thus disposing of two arts together) was an aberration. There is an even wilder passage in "The Young American"; here sculpture, painting, and architecture are all "effete, having passed into second childhood," with gardening the only fine art left to Americans!

4 See Charles R. Metzger, *E and Greenough, Transcendental Pioneers of an American Aesthetic* (University of California Press, 1954) and cf. Theodore M. Brown, "Greenough, Paine, E, and the Organic Aesthetic," *Journal of Aesthetics and Art Criticism*, XIV (1955–56), 304–17, and further in the same periodical, Percy W. Brown, "E's Philosophy of Aesthetics," XV (1955–56), 350–54, also Donald MacRae, "E and the Arts," *Art Bulletin*, XX (1938), 78–95. The most important single study of E's aesthetic, however, is Vivian C. Hopkins, *Spires of Form*.

5 When Oliver Wendell Holmes was preparing his book on E for the "American Men of Letters" series, he was appalled to discover that E had included in his writings 3393 references to 868 different persons. Shakespeare, with 112 references, led all the rest, and there were only 54 for Jesus, who was passed not only by

Shakespeare but also by Napoleon, Plato, Plutarch, and Goethe; E's other "representative men" achieved 40 and 30, respectively. See the final chapter of Holmes's *RWE* (1885).

6 E's omnipresent sense of balance nowhere shows more interestingly than in his use of quotations and his attitude toward them. Though he may say that he hates quotation and wants to hear what a man himself knows, he was himself an indefatigable quoter, for in spite of all his emphasis on intuition and self-reliance, he knew that there is no such thing as complete originality in a writer and that all literary works are Janus-faced. Alfred the Great achieved more for his countrymen by translating Boethius than he could have achieved by original composition, and the same may be said of Wyclif's translation of the Bible, and of Luther's. E was always interested in quotations included in the writings of others, and part of this interest was because he was interested in the quoter; reading the quotation through his eyes, he found new significance in it. He quotes approvingly from Novalis: "Already my opinion has gained infinitely in force the moment another mind has adopted it." See "Quotation and Originality" in *Letters and Social Aims*, and cf. Ralph H. Orth's discussion in his Foreword to *JMN*, Vol. VI.

7 Cf., e.g., Rusk, *Life*, p. 143.

8 "Concord Edition," Vol. VII, pp. 400ff.

9 Cf. J. D. Yohannan, "E's Translation of Persian Poetry from German Sources," *AL*, XIV (1942–43), 407–20.

10 Harriet Rodgers Zink, "E's Use of the Bible," *University of Nebraska Studies in Language, Literature, and Criticism*, No. 14 (1935), is the fullest study in print of Biblical references in E's writings.

11 In one passage in his journals, E tests readers by their ability to understand Aristotle, Bacon, Giordano Bruno, Swedenborg, and Fourier—surely a mixed bag! The case for Platonic influence in E has been most elaborately stated (many later scholars have found it overstated) in John S. Harrison, *The Teachers of E* (Sturgis & Walton Company, 1910). Frederic Ives Carpenter, *E and Asia*, accuses him of confusing Plato with Neoplatonism.

12 The most elaborate study of E's relation to Plutarch is in Edmund G. Berry's *E's Plutarch* (HUP, 1961). Berry believes that the *Morals* influenced the essays and the *Lives* the biographical papers. At one time, E wished to be a modern Plutarch, "portraying the

essential character of the great men of his own day." See his paper on Plutarch in *Lectures and Biographical Sketches*.

13 "E's Knowledge of Dante," *University of Texas Publication*, No. 4226, July 8, 1942, pp. 171–98. Mathews also thinks E's translation of *La Vita Nuova* a remarkable achievement for a self-taught reader of Italian, working at a time when no complete translation into English had been made. This work, edited by Mathews, was published in *Harvard Law Bulletin*, XI (1957), 208–44, 346–62, and, in book form, by the UNCP, 1960. See, further, Emilio Goggio, "E's Interest in Italy and Italian Literature," *Italica*, XVII (1940), 97–103, and Zoltán Haraszti, ed., *Letters by T. W. Parsons* (Boston Public Library, n.d.).

14 Lowell called Emerson "Plotinus-Montaigne." See the essay on Montaigne in *Representative Men* and the detailed study by Charles Lowell Young, *E's Montaigne* (M, 1941). Young finds a bond between the two writers in their shared conviction that "morality is not alien to human nature, not imposed upon it from without, but consubstantial with it; natural, rational, and something more than either nature or reason."

15 See *ESQ*, No. 20 (1960) and No. 27 (1962).

16 Rusk and others found little or no evidence for Hegelian influence on E. When Cabot lent him a Hegel item he admitted that for him dialectic was in a class with logarithms, and though he retained the volume for some time, he seems finally to have returned it without doing much with it. Later he enjoyed contacts with William T. Harris and other St. Louis Hegelians, but as late as 1870 he was saying that he had no interest in either Hegel or Schelling. Henry A. Pochmann reopened the case for E's interest in *German Culture in America: Philosophical and Literary Influences, 1600–1900* (University of Wisconsin Press, 1961). See also his article, "E and the St. Louis Hegelians," *American-German Review*, X, Feb. 1944, pp. 14–17, and Virginia Moran's reply to Pochmann, "Circle and Dialectic (A Study of E's Interest in Hegel)," *Nassau Review*, I, Spring 1969, pp. 32–42. René Wellek, "E and German Philosophy," *NEQ*, XVI (1943), 41–62, finds that "the specific characteristics of the Germans: their dialectal method, their preoccupation with and special approach to the problem of knowledge, their philosophy of history and of the institutional life of man" do not appear in the

Concord transcendentalists. These merely shared the German enmity toward eighteenth-century empiricism and materialism, and though they found corroboration of their own faith in Germany, they did not really need this, being "deeply rooted in their own spiritual ancestry."

17   In addition to Carpenter's *E and Asia*, see his article, "Immortality from India," *AL*, I (1929–30), 233–42, and Dale Riepe, "E and Indian Philosophy," *JHI*, XXVIII (1967), 115–22. On "Brahma" see, among other studies, Donald Rose, Jr., "E's 'Brahma,' " *ESQ*, No. 39 (1965), pp. 42–43, and Andrew M. McLean, "E's 'Brahma,' as an Expression of Brahman," *NEQ*, XLII (1969), 115–22. See also Leyla Goren, *Elements of Brahmanism in the Transcendentalism of E*, which was originally published in a very small edition, in 1959 and reprinted as a supplement to *ESQ*, No. 34 (1964).

18   "The Influence of Persian Poetry upon E's Work," *AL*, XV (1943–44), 25–41. See E's own "Persian Poetry" in *Letters and Social Aims*.

19   See also Edward Waldo Emerson's general comment on his father's reading of English literature, "Concord Edition," V, 323–24.

20   See, e.g., B. J. Whiting, "E, Chaucer, and Thomas Warton," *AL*, XVII (1945–46), 75–78.

21   Norman Foerster, arguing for E's classical, not romantic, taste, says he liked best the English literature which fell between Elizabeth I and Charles I. But this was far from being classical in any proper sense of the term. E himself had no sympathy with the later apeing of French rules in England. He supports Foerster's view when he calls classical art healthy and romantic, sick. The classical is "the art of necessity; organic" while modern or romantic art "bears the stamp of caprice or chance." Like everything else about E, however, his relationship to romanticism is not simple. Foerster himself grants that he was "constitutionally romantic" in various aspects, and, in the larger sense, transcendentalism itself was a part of the Romantic Movement.

22   See Norman A. Brittin, "E and the Metaphysical Poets," *AL*, VIII (1936–37), 1–21; J. Russell Roberts, "E's Debt to the Seventeenth Century," *AL*, XXI (1949–50), 298–310.

23   If E seems at times inclined to give Bacon a higher place than he deserves in the hierarchy of British writers, Vivian C. Hop-

kins, "E and Bacon," *AL*, XXIX (1957–58), 408–29, makes it abundantly clear that he was not blind to any of Bacon's faults, nor unaware of the problems involved in judging him fairly.

24   See Richard C. Pettigrew, "E and Milton," *AL*, III (1931–32), 45–59.

25   Southey's possible influence upon E is explored by Cameron in his edition of *Indian Superstitions* and in his article, "Young E, Bardism, and Circle Imagery," *ESQ*, No. 2 (1956), pp. 17–18.

26   For the possible influence of Wordsworth upon E, see John Brooks Moore, "E on Wordsworth," *PMLA*, XLI (1926), 179–92; for that of Coleridge, Frank T. Thompson, "E's Indebtedness to Coleridge," *SP*, XXIII (1926), 55–77, and "E's Theory and Practice of Poetry," *PMLA*, XLIII (1928), 1170–84. Thompson argues that E learned the art of lyric poetry from Wordsworth and that of literary criticism from Coleridge; in enlarging his conception of Wordsworth, he was influenced by Coleridge's criticism. E himself makes what amounts to the Coleridgean distinction between fancy and imagination: "Fancy is a wilful, imagination a spontaneous act; fancy, a play as with dolls and puppets which we choose to call men and women; imagination, a perception and affirming of a real relation between a thought and some material fact. Fancy amuses; imagination expands and exalts us." He observes acutely that "Bunyan, in peril for his soul, wrote *Pilgrim's Progress*; Quarles, after he was quite cool, wrote *Emblems*."

27   See Clyde K. Hyder, "E and Swinburne: A Sensational Interview," *MLN*, XLVIII (1933), 180–82.

28   See Frank T. Thompson, "E and Carlyle," *SP*, XXIV (1927), 438–53; Randolph J. Bufano, "E's Apprenticeship to Carlyle, 1827–48," *ATQ*, No. 13, Part I (1972), pp. 17–24.

29   See John T. Flanagan, "E as a Critic of Fiction," *PQ*, XV (1936), 30–45.

30   Annie Fields, "Glimpses of E," *Harper's Magazine*, LXVIII (1884), 457–67, reprinted in Carl Bode, ed., *RWE, A Profile* (Hill and Wang, 1968). There is a curious passage in E's *Journals*, HM edition, VII, 441, in which Carlyle and Dickens are reported to have told E that male continence was a thing of the past in England, to which Dickens added that if his own son were "particularly chaste," he would worry about his health. This passage has always been

suspect from the fact that Dickens nowhere else expressed comparable views, but it remained for Edgar Johnson to point out that since Dickens's oldest son was twelve years old at the time he is supposed to have made this statement, he cannot possibly have expected to be taken literally. There may have been some element in the situation, no longer clear to us, why Dickens and Carlyle wished to shock or tease E, or it may even be that Dickens was michievously attempting a *reductio ad absurdum* presentation of Carlyle's gloomy views. See Johnson, *Charles Dickens, His Tragedy and Triumph* (Simon and Schuster, 1952), II, 645; cf. Edward Wagenknecht, *The Man Charles Dickens* (UOP, 1966), p. 168, and, for the larger issues involved, his *Dickens and the Scandalmongers* (UOP, 1965). Incidentally, Harry Hayden Clark's reference to Dickens's remark, in Myron Simon and Thornton H. Parsons, eds., *Transcendentalism and Its Legacy* (Mich., 1966), p. 60, is garbled.

31 Robert H. Woodward, " 'Seashore' and Bryant: Poetic Theory and Practice," *ESQ*, XIX (1960), pp. 21–22, argues Bryant's influence on E.

32 Edward Everett Hale, *James Russell Lowell and His Friends* (1899), p. 164.

33 See James M. Cox, "E and Hawthorne: Trust and Doubt," *VQR*, XLV (1969), 88–107. B. Bernard Cohen, "E's 'The Young American' and Hawthorne's 'The Intelligence Office,' " *AL*, XXVI (1954–55), 32–43, argues for "a higher degree of rapport [between Hawthorne and E] than has usually been attributed to them by biographers." On another great contemporary writer of fiction, Herman Melville, E had nothing to say, though he owned a copy of *Typee*, but there has been some discussion as to what Melville said or did not say about him. Carl Van Vechten, *Excavations* (K, 1926), pp. 87–88, suggested that E was satirized in *The Confidence Man*, and this idea was developed by Egbert Oliver, "M's Picture of E and Thoreau in *The Confidence Man*," *CE*, VIII (1946), 61–72. Oliver is opposed by William Braswell, "Melville as a Critic of E," *AL*, IX (1937–38), 317–34. Frederic Ives Carpenter believes that Melville also had E in mind in the discussion of Chronometricals and Horologicals in *Pierre* and even that "Cock-a-Doodle-Doo" and "Bartleby" satirize "Self-Reliance."

34 See Bradford's *Biography and the Human Heart* (1932).

35   *ESQ*, No. 10 (1958), p. 38.

36   On Whitman as an Emersonian, see John Brooks Moore, "The Master of Whitman," *SP*, XXIII (1926), 77–89. In 1885, however, Whitman said that the four American poets he admired most were, in order, Bryant, E, Whittier, and Longfellow. Formerly, he added, he had given E first place, but this he had now assigned to Bryant instead. "E's great points are intellectual freedom, perfect style and real manliness; but the tendency of his writing is to refine and sharpen off till the points are lost." See also Carlos Baker, "The Road to Concord: Another Milestone in the Whitman-E Friendship," *Princeton University Library Chronicle*, VII (1945–46), 100–117.

37   The following articles are useful: Haynes McMullen, "RWE and Libraries," *Library Quarterly*, XXV (1955), 152–62; Sherman B. O'Daniel, "E as a Literary Critic," *CLA Journal*, VIII (1964–65), 21–43, 157–89, 246–76; Doris Morton, "RWE and *The Dial*: A Study in Literary Criticism," *Emporia State Research Studies*, XVIII, No. 2 (1969); Merton M. Sealts, Jr., "E on the Scholar, 1833–37," *PMLA*, LXXXV (1970), 185–95.

38   "Fragments on Life."

39   "Saadi."

40   "The Poet."

41   Volume I of *JMN* contains invocations to various powers (see pp. xlv, 4, 11, 91), but this should not be taken too literally. Parenthetically I may mention here that in 1864 E lent some countenance to a notion of Sumner's looking toward the establishment of a kind of American Academy for writing; see *Letters*, V, 395–97. This seems quite out of line with his dislike of standardization.

42   E deliberately employed homely illustrations even in his pulpit days, though he was quite aware that they would be criticized; see McGiffert, *Young E Speaks*, pp. 28, 29, 41, 43. When Alcott first heard him lecture, he was shocked by his departure from neoclassical standards in diction. For some of the words E especially disliked, see "Art and Criticism" in the *Natural History of Intellect* volume. In 1860 he made an amusing blunder when, sending Edith a list of nicknames from Niles, Michigan, he unfortunately made Pike "puke"!

43   See *Early Lectures*, II, xiii–xiv, for a summary of some of the homiletical and other influences which may have been brought to bear on E's style; also A. M. Baumgartner, " 'The Lyceum Is My

Pulpit': Homiletics in E's Earlier Lectures," *AL*, XXXIV (1962–63), 477–86, and, for a defense of E's style, Ronald Beck, "E's Organic Structures," *ESQ*, No. 50, Supplement (1968), pp. 76–77.

44 "E," in *Birds and Poets and Other Papers.*

45 John Townsend Trowbridge, *My Own Story, with Recollections of Noted Persons* (1904), pp. 343–44.

46 See K. W. Dykema, "Why Did Lydia Jackson Become Lidian Emerson?" *AS*, XVII (1942), 185–86, in which the question is discussed against a background of etymological knowledge.

47 That many of Emerson's poems are free verse is now fairly obvious, but Gay Wilson Allen demonstrated it conclusively in his *American Prosody* (ABC, 1935). In his essay on "The Poetry of E" in *The Pageant of Letters* (Sheed and Ward, 1940), Alfred Noyes, a modern British poet of considerable reputation, found E "a far subtler musician in verse" than Poe. See also Kathryn Anderson McEuen, "E's Rhymes," *AL*, XX (1948–49), 31–42.

48 "The Poet."

49 "Merlin."

50 The first important detailed study of "E's Theories of Literary Expression" was that of Emerson Grant Sutcliffe in *University of Illinois Studies in Language and Literature*, Vol. VIII, No. 1 (1923). More recently we have had an excellent, stimulating consideration of E's whole poetic theory in John Q. Anderson, *The Liberating Gods.* Valuable articles on various phases of the subject include Nelson F. Adkins, "E and the Bardic Tradition," *PMLA*, LXIII (1948), 662–77; Seymour L. Gross, "E and Poetry," *SAQ*, LIV (1955), 82–94; Carl F. Strauch, "The Mind's Voice: E's Poetic Style," *ESQ*, No. 60 (1970), pp. 43–57; Sheldon W. Liebman, "The Origins of E's Early Poetics: His Reading of the Scottish Common Sense Critics," *AL*, XLV (1972), 23–33; R. A. Yoder, "Toward the 'Titmouse Dimension': The Development of E's Poetic Style," *PMLA*, LXXXVII (1972), 255–70.

CHAPTER FOUR: FRIENDSHIP

1 "Art" (*Poems*).

2 Oliver Wendell Holmes liked what he called E's "wild strawberry flavor," but the most detailed comentary on this aspect of

his style is in Firkins, *RWE*, pp. 244–49. See also E's own "Art and Criticism" in *Natural History of Intellect,* etc.

3 "Life."

4 Michael H. Cowan's interesting study, *City of the West: E, America, and the Urban Metaphor* (YUP, 1967) sees E's "city" referring "only secondarily to the physical artifact of streets and buildings" and "primarily . . . a metonym for the interaction of its human community."

5 The highest society came to E's lectures in England, though he says they came to hear "the Massachusetts Indian." He was pleased by Lady Byron and much taken by the Duchess of Sutherland, who showed him through her picture gallery, which he hoped the revolution, if it must come, would spare!

6 See John T. Flanagan, "E and Communism," *NEQ*, X (1937), 143–61; John B. Wilson, "E and the 'Communities,' " *ESQ*, No. 43 (1966), pp. 56–61.

7 George William Curtis, *Literary and Social Essays* (H, 1894) describes as a dismal failure an attempt made to bring Concordians together on Monday evenings in 1845. Everyone sat about waiting to hear the finest thing that had ever been said, and E "beamed smiling encouragement upon all parties." Curtis remembered little else beyond "a grave eating of russet apples by the erect philosophers, and a solemn disappearance into night." The experiment lasted for three meetings.

8 Cf. Hubert H. Hoeltje, "E, Citizen of Concord," *AL*, XI (1939–40), 367–78. Having studied town, parish, and church records, Hoeltje concludes that "of all the Concord celebrities . . . certainly E stands out conspicuously as having lived the most active and perhaps the most normal life."

9 The picture may be seen facing p. 184, "Concord Edition," Vol. IX; see also note, p. 463.

10 He probably slanders himself. When an orthodox clergyman, offering a prayer after one of his lectures, implored God to deliver the audience from any more such transcendental nonsense as they had just heard, E inquired the man's name, then commented mildly that he seemed very sincere and plain-spoken. A much more amusing story, perhaps illustrating Emerson's sense of mischief as well as his forbearance, concerns a young preacher who, having referred to "the foolish utterances of Mr. Emerson in his lecture," was

dismayed to notice that the lecturer was in his congregation. The next morning he encountered him on the train. E made a place for him to sit beside him, was extremely kind and cordial, and quite fascinating in his conversation. Just before the young man arrived at his station, E smiled and shook his hand cordially, adding, "And I had the pleasure of hearing you preach yesterday." Mary Hosmer Brown, *Memories of Concord* (The Four Seas Company, 1926).

11   An anonymous contributor to "The Contributor's Club," in *The Atlantic Monthly*, L (1882), 424–25, who introduced herself to E on a train, wrote a charming account of their conversation in which she quoted him as saying, "Perhaps there should not be the word stranger in the language. I do not know any good reason for it." *A Letter of E, Being the First Publication of the Reply of RWE to Solomon Corner of Baltimore in 1842*, with Analysis and Notes by Willard Reed (BP, 1934), shows E's friendly response to a stranger who had written him about a spiritual problem. See also *The Letters of Horace Howard Furness* (1922), I, 29–30. But the testimonies to his friendliness and approachableness are multitudinous.

12   Apparently E was at his best as a social being on this trip. He sought out John Muir at the mill where he was stationed and left a note for him: "Why did you not make yourself known to me last evening?" When they met, he climbed up dangerous ways in the mill, came again and again, as long as he was in the area, and then invited Muir to go with him as far as the Mariposa Grove. They rode twenty-five miles through the Sierra Forest together, and Muir thought he was "enthusiastic like a boy" at the thought of camping out, though apparently this was not done. See William Frederic Badé, *The Life and Letters of John Muir* (1924), I, 252–61. See also Rufus A. Coleman, "Two Meetings with E," *MLN*, LXV (1950), 482–84, and John W. Clarkson, Jr., "E at Seventy," *ATQ*, No. 1 (1969), p. 119. The second item deals with Una Hawthorne.

13   Howe, "RWE As I Knew Him," *Critic*, XLII (1903), 411–13; Hale, *Addresses and Essays* . . . (LB, 1900).

14   *The Journals of Bronson Alcott*, p. 485.

15   "E and the Wisconsin Lyceum," *AL*, XXIV (1952–53), 462–75. "For one thing, he displayed a deepening awareness of the importance of the section and of the role he was playing in the nation's growth."

16   The most famous commentary on E as a public speaker is

Lowell's, in *My Study Windows* (1871). For his lectures in England, see Townsend Scudder, "E's British Lecture Tour, 1847-48," *AL*, VII (1935-36), 15-36, and "E in London and the London Lectures," *AL*, VIII (1936-37), 22-36. British responses are recorded in William J. Sowder, *E's Impact on the British Isles and Canada* (University Press of Virginia, 1966). William Charvat's *E's American Lecture Engagements, A Chronological List* was published separately by The New York Public Library after having appeared serially in their *Bulletin*, Vols. LXIV–LXV; cf. John C. Broderick, LXVI (1962), 347. See also the following articles: Louise Hastings, "E in Cincinnati," *NEQ*, XI (1938), 443-69; Hubert H. Hoeltje, "RWE in Iowa," *Iowa Journal of History and Politics*, XXV (1927), 236-76, and "RWE in Minnesota," *Minnesota History*, XI (1930), 145-59; Brad Luckingham, "The Pioneer Lecturer in the West: A Note on the Appearance of RWE in St. Louis, 1852-53," *Modern Humanities Review*, LVIII (1963), 70-88; Russel B. Nye, "E in Michigan and the Northwest," *MHM*, XXV (1941), 159-72; Eleanor Bryce Scott, "E Wins the Nine Hundred Dollars," *AL*, XVII (1945-46), 78-85; Willard Thorp, "E on Tour," *Quarterly Journal of Speech*, XVI (1930), 19-34; Richard Tuerk, "Los Angeles' Reaction to E's Visit to San Francisco," *NEQ*, XLIV (1971), 477-82; Vern Wagner, "No Tumult of Response: E's Reception as a Lyceum Lecturer," *WHR*, VI (1951-52), 129-35; C. J. Wasung, "E Comes to Detroit," *MHM*, XXIX (1945), 59-72. Alan J. Downer, "The Legendary Visit of E to Tallahassee," *Florida Historical Quarterly*, XXXIV (1955-56), 334-38, assembles evidence that E did not go there. See, further, *Mr. E Lectures at the Peabody Institute* (Peabody Institute Library, 1949); Oral S. Coad, "An Unpublished Lecture by E," *AL*, XIV (1942-43), 421-26; Louis Ruchames, "Two Forgotten Addresses by RWE," *AL*, XXVIII (1956-57), 425-33; Rollo G. Silver, "E as Abolitionist," *NEQ*, VI (1933), 154-58.

17   Vivian C. Hopkins, "Two Unpublished E Letters," *NEQ*, XXXIII (1960), 502-6. Channing's whining complaint about E in David P. Edgell, "A Note on a Transcendental Friendship," *NEQ*, XXIV (1951), 528-32, does not sound convincing to me. See also Robert N. Hudspeth, "A Perennial Springtime: Channing's Friendship with E and Thoreau," *ESQ*, No. 54 (1969), pp. 30-36.

18   E attempts a balanced judgment of Alcott in *JMN*, VIII, 212-15.

19   *Recollections of Seventy Years* (Richard G. Badger, 1909), II, 348.

20   See John Brooks Moore, "Thoreau Rejects E," *AL*, IV (1932–33), 241–56. The most thorough consideration of the relations between the two men, however, is Joel Porte, *E and Thoreau: Transcendentalists in Conflict* (Wesleyan University Press, 1966), which is sympathetic toward Thoreau: "Thoreau represented the side of Emerson—rebellious, unsocial, brooding, and in love with artistic 'idleness'—which the older man increasingly came to dislike and wished to suppress." See also the same writer's "E, Thoreau and the Social Consciousness," *NEQ*, XLI (1968), 40–50.

21   See Max I. Baym, "Emma Lazarus and E," *Publications of the American Jewish Historical Society*, XXXVIII (1949), 261–87. It is unfortunate that we do not know what, if anything, E wrote in reply to Emma's anguished *cri de coeur* after *Parnassus* had appeared, but it does not appear from her *Ce* article cited elsewhere that he can have said anything that made her feel much better.

22   Carl F. Strauch, "Hatred's Swift Repulsions: E, Margaret Fuller, and Others," *SR*, VII (1967–68), 65–103, contains useful data on E's relations with his women friends, but its interpretations, involving the hypothesis of references in Emerson's poems, are highly conjectural. It also, in my judgment, overstates E's coldness. However, *JMN*, VII, 509, shows that E was conscious that he had problems even with Caroline Sturgis and Elizabeth Hoar. See also Introduction, xvi–vii.

23   To follow the progress of E's friendship wtih Margaret Fuller, see *Letters*, II, 336ff.

24   "Margaret Fuller and RWE," *PMLA*, L (1935), 576–94.

25   See John Q. Anderson, "E and Prince Achille Murat," *BPLQ*, X (1958), 27–37.

26   The most curious item in connection with E's interest in other people is the "crush" he developed for a Harvard College classmate, Martin Gay, which seems to have lasted about two years (1820–22). This was not a friendship, for Gay was a considerably grander person than E (or E thought he was), and he apparently never mustered the courage to get acquainted with him. In 1822 he told his journal that he had outgrown his interest in Gay and commented on its oddity; still later, apparently, he struck this passage out and called it "Pish." See *JMN*, I, 22, 52–53, 59. Gay, who came

from Hingham, became a Boston physician and died young. We have no knowledge whether he was ever aware of the effect he had had on E. See, further, on the general subject under consideration here, John Bard McNulty, "E's Friends and the Essay on Friendship," *NEQ*, XIX (1946), 390–97.

CHAPTER FIVE: LOVE

1   O. W. Firkins, *RWE*, pp. 179ff., calls E's treatment of love "Venetian: he writes in dithyrambics: he manifests an abandonment usually reserved for the Over-Soul and its associated topics." He goes on, however, to object to what he considers E's apology for his "self-indulgence (here as so often the apology is the offence)." He also finds the essay self-centered; the woman is practically excluded from her own love affair. "Now when our saint, in some genial hour, has been persuaded, beyond expectation, to enter into our tent and break bread with us, it is disconcerting to hear him say, as he rises from the table, that the act was merely sacramental. We had hoped, God forgive us, that he was a little hungry." E believed that the qualities of supernal excellence which the lover sees in his beloved are real; only instead of being concentrated in her, they are a part of all creation. See "The Choice of Theisms" in McGiffert, *Young E Speaks*.

2   *JMN*, IV, 257.

3   "Quatrains"—"Love" and "Casella."

4   "Destiny."

5   See Edith W. Gregg, ed., *One First Love: The Letters of Ellen Tucker Emerson to RWE* (HUP, 1962), and cf. Henry F. Pommer, *E's First Marriage* (Southern Illinois University Press, 1967).

6   That E opened Ellen's coffin in 1832 has been doubted by Pommer, pp. 55, 116, but the entry of March 29, *JMN*, IV, 7, seems conclusive. Moreover, he seems to have done the same with Waldo in 1857; see *Journals*, HM edition, IX, 102.

7   There is an entertaining account of life at the Emersons' after E's death in Mary Miller Engel, *I Remember the Emersons* (Los Angeles, Times-Mirror, 1941). The table seems to have been

set with little regard to modern dietary worries, and hospitality was generous, though perhaps a little formal; the whole life of the family seems to have been rather highly organized. See, further, Mary Hosmer Brown, *Memories of Concord.*

8   *Autobiography*, I, 147.

9   Cf. Wagenknecht, *Longfellow, A Full-Length Portrait* (LG, 1955), p. 237.

10   Lidian may not have seen the journal entries, but she could hardly have escaped the poems. If, as the editors conjecture, she was Fatima and E's mother "the old Sultana Nevada" in the journal entry given in *JMN*, IX, 11, the coolness and calmness of the latter, as contrasted to Fatima's jaded or agitated state, can hardly have pleased Lidian. Again, one asks whether she was aware (IX, 16) that her husband found in the visit of Caroline Sturgis a rebuke to the "indolences," "indulgences," and lack of "heroic action" in their household? If so, she cannot have enjoyed this either.

11   London, Faber and Faber; New York, M, 1935.

12   "To-Day."

13   Joseph Baim, "The Vision of the Child and the Romantic Dilemma," *Thoth*, VII (1966), 22–30, finds that in E the young child's mind becomes the "symbol of the non-discriminating, non-logical 'all.'" The child lives in the eternal now and discovers transcendent oneness non-intellectually, participating fully in the cosmos and seeing "the miraculous in the common." He praises the Greeks because they achieved childlike vision. All this is in harmony with Matthew 18:3, Boehme, the English metaphysical poets of the seventeenth century, and of course Wordsworth. In Eastern philosophy the child is often identified with Brahma. But Baim does not believe that any of these influences were determinative. Alcott's *Psyche* and E's own love and careful observation of children were more important. There is a good example of E's tenderness in "Memories of RWE—Visiting England," *Christian Science Monitor* Nov. 9, 1955, p. 12, reprinted *ESQ*, No. 2 (1956), pp. 15–16.

14   Many nowadays will shudder at E's taking Waldo to view the corpse of old Dr. Ripley, which the child looked at with "neither repulsion nor surprise, but only with the quietest curiosity." Whatever else might be said about it, this action was at least consistent with E's habit of always facing the facts.

15   Readers of "Threnody" are sometimes puzzled by the

verse which declares of the day of Waldo's death that "Night came, and Nature had not thee," for what can be more natural than death? Yet, in a larger sense, the death of the young *is* unnatural, and the betrayal of all the hopes we have entertained for them seems to make bitter nonsense of life.

16   See Appendix.

CHAPTER SIX: POLITICS

1   On E's attitude toward the West, see, further, Ernest Marchand, "E and the Frontier," *AL*, III (1931–32), 149–74; V. L. O. Chittick, "E's 'Frolic Health,'" *NEQ*, XXX (1957), 209–34; John Q. Anderson, "E and California," *California Historical Society Quarterly*, XXXIII (1954), 241–48. E's interest in folklore is explored by Anderson in "E and the Ballad of George Nidever—'Staring Down' a Grizzly Bear," *WF*, XV (1956), 40–45, and "E and the Language of the Folk," in Mody C. Boatright *et al.*, eds., *Folk Travellers, Ballads, Tales, and Talk* (Texas Folklore Society Publication, No. 25, 1925). In "E's Venture in Western Land," *AL*, II (1930–31), 438–40, H. H. Hoeltje shows that in 1856 E made an unprofitable investment in northwestern Wisconsin.

2   On E's attitude toward the English there is no substitute for reading *English Traits*, but see also B. Bernard Cohen, "E and Hawthorne in England," *BPLQ*, IX (1957), 73–85, and Philip L. Nicoloff, *E on Race and History, An Examination of* English Traits (ColUP, 1961).

3   Once E delayed his return from a lecture trip and went out of his way to explore the Mammoth Cave in Kentucky, in a fourteen-hour trip which involved both risk and hardship for a man of his habits. His account of this, in *Letters*, IV, 211–14, is probably his most elaborate piece of narrative-descriptive writing.

4   See, further, Raymer McQuiston, "The Relation of RWE to Public Affairs," *Bulletin of the University of Kansas*, XXIV, No. 8 (1923); Arthur I. Ladu, "E: Whig or Democrat," *NEQ*, XII (1940), 419–41; Ernest Sandeen, "E's Americanism," *Iowa*, VI (1942), 63–118; M. H. Connor, "E's Interest in Contemporary Political Affairs," *English Journal*, XXXVIII (1949), 428–32. Perry Miller,

"Emersonian Genius and the American Democracy," *NEQ*, XXVI (1953), 27–44, reprinted in Miller's *Nature's Nation* (HUP, 1967), is excellent on the balance between democratic and aristocratic tendencies in E.

5   It is interesting to note that E's position here stands diametrically opposed to what he believed about books and reading: " 'T is an economy of time to read old and famed books. Nothing can be preserved which is not good."

6   See two very important articles: Alexander C. Kern, "E and Economics," *NEQ*, XIII (1940), 678–96; John C. Gerber, "E and the Political Economists," *NEQ*, XXII (1949), 336–57. On E's possible interest in H. C. Carey, see K. W. Cameron in *ESQ*, 13 (1958), 65–83. John O. McCormick, "E's Theory of Human Greatness," *NEQ*, XXVI (1953), 291–314, sees E as an aristocrat.

7   See Lewis S. Feuer, "RWE's Reference to Karl Marx," *NEQ*, XXXIII (1960), 378–79.

8   "Concord Edition," I, p. xxxix.

9   George Santayana, *Interpretations of Poetry and Religion* (S, 1900).

10   Like Ruskin and many others, E did not believe that the unethical man can create perfect beauty in art. Cf. Wendell Glick, "The Moral and Ethical Dimensions of E's Aesthetics," *ESQ*, No. 55 (1969), pp. 11–17.

11   "Emersonian Virtue: A Definition," *AS*, XXXVI (1961), 117–22.

12   Stuart P. Sherman, *Americans* (S, 1922).

13   "To J. W."

14   The fullest study of E and Goethe is that of Frederick B. Wahr (Ann Arbor, George Wahr, 1915). See also his article, "E and the Germans," *Monatshefte für deutschen Unterricht*, XXXIII (1941), 49–63, and, by other hands, Frederick A. Braun, "Goethe as Viewed by E," *JEGP*, XV (1916), 23–34, and Peter Hagboldt, "E's Goethe," *Open Court*, XLVI (1932), 234–44. Vivian C. Hopkins, "The Influence of Goethe on E's Aesthetic Theory," *PQ*, XXVII (1948), 325–43, judged Goethe the greatest single influence leading E away from an exclusively moralistic view of art.

15   E makes some fantastic suggestions about Shakespeare, as when he says that the story in the play gets in the way of the poetry and that therefore it is safer to read the play backwards! He also

says that the truth about Shakespeare must be sought in the plays themselves (in which we are told both that he reveals his personality and that he does not), and not in what has been written about him. On the other hand, he emphatically rejected the legend of the untutored genius. He borrowed the Shakespeare Society Papers from Longfellow and he judged Shakespearean scholarship and criticism to be still in their infancy (he mentioned Coleridge, Lamb, Goethe, Schlegel, Herder, and Jones Very) and wanted Shakespeare and other great poets studied in colleges and universities. His 1841 letter to Christopher Gore Ripley (*Letters*, II, 424ff.) shows a praiseworthy knowledge of contemporary scholarship and is the more remarkable for having been written at Nantasket Beach, without reference to books. Emerson knew that Shakespeare created by inventing a distinctive personal and individual kind of utterance for each realized character. One passage (*JMN*, III, 300) interestingly anticipates George Herbert Palmer's Harvard Ingersoll lecture, *Intimations of Immortality in the Sonnets of Shakespeare* (1912). He flirted with Delia Bacon's Baconian heresy but did not embrace it; see Vivian C. Hopkins, *Prodigal Puritan, A Life of Delia Bacon* (HUP, 1950). He has one amusing misquotation from *Hamlet*, in which he makes "Lethe's wharf" "lazy wharf." But his principal triumph in this field came when, relying upon his own often execrated ear, he made up his mind that Shakespeare was not the sole author of *Henry VIII*. See Robert P. Falk, "E and Shakespeare," *PMLA*, LVI (1941), 532–43; Thomas A. Perry, "E, The Historical Frame, and Shakespeare," *MLQ*, IX (1948), 440–47.

16   E finds that Shakespeare, unlike Massinger and Beaumont and Fletcher, never confounds moral values (Bacon, too, is "worldly" compared to him), and that even his fun is spiritual, with his license set in a moral framework. He so distinguished Cleopatra from the common voluptuary as to make even luxury sublime, as, in the grandeur of her death, she makes suicide lovely. He rightly rejects the "tavern gossip" about Shakespeare's roistering, etc. that has come down to us as unsubstantiated and incompatible with "the gentle and all accomplished sage" revealed in the plays, yet curiously leaves the impression that he believed Shakespeare's life to have been far more "profane" than we have any reason to suppose it was. See Wagenknecht, *The Personality of Shakespeare* (UOP, 1972), especially pp. 100–101 and Ch. VII.

17 At the end of E's essay on Milton (*Natural History of Intellect*), there is an "apology" for the divorce pamphlets, as "a sally of the extravagant spirit of the time" and a touching revelation of the suffering of Milton's own "angelic soul" under one of the "unavoidable evils" of life. There is not the slightest suggestion that Milton may have been right or even that his basic thesis is reasonably debatable. There is a detailed study of E's attitude toward Shakespeare, Bacon, and Milton in William M. Wynkoop, *Three Children of the Universe* (The Hague, Mouton & Co., 1966).

18 "Ode Inscribed to W. H. Channing."

19 "Power."

20 Emerson certainly did not believe in a fire-and-brimstone hell; when Julia Ward Howe tried to convince him of the existence of Satan, he merely replied, "Surely the Angel must be stronger than the Demon!"—Laura E. Richards and Maud Howe Elliott, *Julia Ward Howe, 1819–1910* (1915), I, 70. Yet I should hesitate to say that he denied the possibility of damnation, any more than Milton did; indeed he once declared that where orthodoxy builds on fear of sin, liberalism builds on love of goodness, and that these are both half truths, with Universalism representing the view of uninstructed persons whose instincts are right but whose thinking power is weak.

21 When E discussed the horrors of cannibalism while carving a roast, the vegetarian Alcott amusingly caught him out by asking why, if meat was to be eaten at all, we should not have the best!

22 At the close of his freshman year, E composed a drinking song for his fellow classmen. See Tremaine McDowell, "A Freshman Poem by E," *PMLA*, XLV (1930), 326–29.

23 (OUP, 1951).

24 The identification is made in *Letters of Emerson to a Friend*, p. 73n. In harmony with the passage quoted are others in the journals in which he points out that it would require men of great spiritual power to make nonresistance work and that a goody-goody cannot be expected to overcome a pirate, even by spiritual means.

25 See two important articles by John Q. Anderson, "E and 'Manifest Destiny,'" *BPLQ*, VII (1955), 23–31; "E on Texas and the Mexican War," *WHR*, XIII (1959), 191–99. On the possibility of E's connection with the Young America movement, see R. E. Spiller, in the new HUP edition of E's *Collected Works*, I, 220–21.

26 In 1862 E had argued for emancipation on the practical ground that the South might beat the North to it, thus gaining recognition from Europe and dooming the Union cause. This is all perfectly logical on paper, but there was not the slightest chance that the situation posited could ever come about.

27 The two most careful considerations of the John Brown matter are by Gilman M. Ostrander, "E, Thoreau, and John Brown," *Mississippi Valley Historical Review*, XXXIX (1952–53), 713–26, and John J. McDonald, "E and John Brown," *NEQ*, XLIV (1971), 377–96. Ostrander sums up the modern biographer's portrait of Brown as that of "an embezzler, a murderer, a cattle thief, and an inveterate liar," and though McDonald is somewhat less severe, both writers describe E and Thoreau as seeing in Brown a transcendental hero, "divinely guided in paths of lawlessness" and "mystically obeying the higher law." For Hawthorne's attitude, see Wagenknecht, *Nathaniel Hawthorne, Man and Writer* (OUP, 1961), especially pp. 124, 213. For an all-out contemporary attack on the mood of the Phi Beta Kappa address of 1867 see Beriah Green's letters in *The National Anti-Slavery Standard*, as reprinted in *ESQ*, No. 51 (1968), pp. 26–32.

28 "Music."

29 "Saadi."

30 "Beauty." A number of books and articles bearing on the subjects under consideration in this section should be listed here. For the objections of Henry James, Sr., to E's approach to evil and allied subjects, see William James, ed., *The Literary Remains of the Late Henry James* (1885). James saw E as "devoid of spiritual understanding" because his nature was so angelic that he had never been tempted. Coventry Patmore, *Principle in Art* (George Bell, 1890), though less generous, was fundamentally in agreement, and William James himself, though influenced by E, still felt a danger to morality in his thinking. Some of these ideas were later more gently expressed by George A. Gordon, "E as a Religious Influence," *Atl*, XCI (1903), 577–87, and D. Elton Trueblood, "The Influence of E's 'Divinity School Address,'" *HTR*, XXXII (1939), 41–56. Harry Bamford Parkes found E a force for moral and spiritual disintegration in "E," *Hound and Horn*, V (1933), 581–601, and in his books, *The Pragmatic Test* (Colt Press, 1941) and *The American Experience* (K, 1947), and Randall Stewart attacks E from the religious point of

view in *American Literature and Christian Doctrine* (Louisiana State University Press, 1958). More philosophically minded considerations of the problem will be found in Newton Arvin, "The House of Pain: E and the Tragic Sense," *Hudson Review*, XII (1959), 37-53, reprinted in *American Pantheon* (Delacorte Press, 1966), and in Zacharias Thundyil, "E and the Problem of Evil," *HTR*, LXII (1969), 51-61. Robert Stafford Ward, "Still 'Christians,' Still Infidels," *Southern Humanities Review*, II (1968), 365-73, attacks the neo-orthodox attack on E and stresses the elements of agreement between E's view of evil and those of Catholicism and Calvinism. On war and peace specifically, see Chester E. Jorgenson, "E's Paradise Under the Shadow of Swords," *PQ*, XI (1932), 274-92, and two studies by William A. Huggard, "E and the Problem of War and Peace," *Iowa*, Vol. V, No. 5 (1938), and "E's Philosophy of War and Peace," *PQ*, XXII (1943), 370-75. See also Philip Butcher, "E and the South," *Phylon*, XVII (1956), 279-85.

31 See Henry Nash Smith, "E's Problem of Vocation," *NEQ*, XII (1939), 52-67, reprinted in Konvitz, *The Recognition of RWE*.

32 For a detailed account of "The Evolution of E as an Abolitionist," see Marjory M. Moody, *AL*, XVII (1945-46), 1-21; cf. Spiller, *Collected Works*, I, 142-43. It should be pointed out, however, that, for a man who, even before he had become an abolitionist, always insisted on Negro rights, E has some amazing passages on Negroes scattered through his journals. Sometimes he even doubts their humanity; they belong to fossil formations and must shortly perish! These passages coexist with others quite inconsistent with them. In 1826 Emerson compared the manners of ragged Negroes in Charleston with those of Boston aristocrats. In 1844 he was convinced that nothing could keep the black man down if he had within himself the capacity to rise. In 1846 he refused to appear before the New Bedford Lyceum because Negroes were discriminated against there. When his children were assigned "The Building of a House" as a subject for a theme, he told them to be sure to say that no house could be perfect nowadays without a hiding place for runaway slaves. When emancipation came, he was impressed by the sobriety and moderation of the Negroes, and in 1867 he observed that it did not make sense to complain of the faults of a race that you were attempting to exclude from the privileges open to others. One whole journal of E's was devoted to compiling materials for a history of

liberty which he never wrote; see John C. Broderick, "E and Moor-field Storey: A Lost Journal Found," *AL*, XXXVIII (1966-67), 177-86. Also consult Louis Ruchames, "E's Second West Indian Eman-cipation Address," *NEQ*, XXVIII (1955), 383-88.

CHAPTER SEVEN: THE OVERSOUL

1 See Baritz, *City on a Hill*, for a very good discussion of this last point. Unitarianism, on the other hand, must have contributed, or at least importantly strengthened, the emphasis upon the dignity of human nature which was another important aspect of E's think-ing and teaching. Randall Stewart calls this "the deification of man" and sees it as "radically anti-Christian" and as having importantly tended toward making Americans intolerable to themselves and to other nations. H. B. Parkes reproaches E with having borrowed from the European past the weapons with which he cut his ties to it, but though he simplifies many things, he is useful in pointing out Calvinistic survivals in E, and he also shows how some of his ideas were anticipated by church fathers, mystics, and heretics, clear back to the early Christian centuries. Howard Mumford Jones, *Belief and Disbelief in American Literature* (UCP, 1967) is much more sym-pathetic toward E, but the most important study in this area is Perry Miller's brilliant paper, "From Edwards to E," *NEQ*, XIII (1940), 589-618, reprinted in his *Errand Into the Wilderness* (HUP, 1956). See also Lawrence Willson, "The Gods of New England," *PS*, IX (1955), 141-53, and McGiffert, *Young E Speaks*, especially pp. xxx-xxxi, 113-14, 231-32, 239, 241-42.

2 See especially, in this connection, *Young E's Transcendental Vision*. Perry Miller's anthology, *The Transcendentalists* (HUP, 1950) is of course indispensable. Neither Paul F. Boller, Jr.'s, *Ameri-can Transcendentalism, 1830-1860: An Intellectual Portrait*, an-nounced for publication by P in the summer of 1973, nor Lawrence Buell's *Literary Transcendentalism: Style and Vision in the American Renaissance* (Cornell Univ. Press, 1974) appeared early enough to be consulted for this study. Representative of many articles dealing with a variety of thinkers believed to have influenced E are Merrel R. Davis, "E's 'Reason' and the Scottish Philosophers," *NEQ*, XVII

(1944), 209–27, which concerns the philosophers he studied in college, especially Dugald Stewart, and Clarence P. Hotson, "Sampson Reed, A Teacher of E," *NEQ*, II (1929), 249–77. When E discovered this Swedenborgian druggist, it was, he said, like encountering a revelation, and he called his book the best thing of its kind since Plato.

3 Robert Detweiler, "The Over-Rated 'Over-Soul,'" *AL*, XXXVI (1964–65), 65–68, argues that the term was not very important to E, and that "if we continue to use it as a convenient catch-all for E's brand of Transcendentalism, we should be aware that we are radically oversimplifying and at once obscuring his thought."

4 F. DeWolfe Miller, *Christopher Pearse Cranch and His Caricatures of New England Transcendentalism* (HUP, 1951).

5 Cf. Charles Berryman, "The Artist-Prophet: E and Thoreau," *ESQ*, No. 43 (1966), pp. 81–86.

6 "The Bohemian Hymn."

7 For a strong statement of the case against E's antipersonalism, especially with reference to Jesus, see Frances G. Peabody, "RWE and the Doctrine of the Divine Immanence," in *Pioneers of Religious Liberty* (AUA, 1903).

8 Quatrain in "Life." See Karl Keller, "From Christianity to Transcendentalism: A Note on E's Use of the Conceit," *AL*, XXXIX (1967–68), 94–98, for a very interesting interpretation of these lines.

9 See Harold Fromm, "E and Kierkegaard: The Problem of Historical Christianity," *MR*, IX (1968), 741–52.

10 Except in the George Herbert-like poem "Grace," which Carpenter thinks inharmonious with "Self-Reliance," E says little about the traditional Christian idea of Divine Grace; cf. McGiffert, p. 255. See C. P. Hotson, "A Background for E's Poem 'Grace,'" *NEQ*, I (1928), 124–32; G. R. Elliott, "On E's 'Grace' and 'Self-Reliance,'" *NEQ*, II (1929), 93–104; Hyatt H. Waggoner, "'Grace' in the Thought of E, Thoreau, and Hawthorne," *ESQ*, No. 54 (1969), pp. 68–72.

11 See McGiffert, pp. xviii–xix, 56, 120ff.

12 Lowell refused to print this stanza in the *Atlantic*. The identification of the person referred to in the third verse is uncertain; see E. W. Emerson's note, "Concord Edition," IX, 485–86.

13 Maurice Maeterlinck, *On E and Other Essays* (DM, 1912).

14 *Young E Speaks*, especially pp. 238, 243–45, 251.

15 Henry Demarest Lloyd, *Mazzini and Other Essays* (P, 1910), p. 79.

16 *Recollections*, II, 493.

17 But cf. Hopkins, *Spires of Form*, pp. 178ff.

18 On spiritualism, see John B. Wilson, "E and the 'Rochester Rappings,' " *NEQ*, XLI (1968), 248–58. Patrick F. Quinn, "E and Mysticism," *AL*, XXI (1949–50), 397–414, denies E any significant mystical experience.

19 See Conrad Wright, "E, Barzillai Frost, and the Divinity School Address," *HTR*, XLIX (1956), 19–43, for the view that E's intense dislike of the preaching of the Concord minister named influenced the famous address.

20 For E's relations with and attitude toward William Ellery Channing, see Lenthiel H. Downs, "E and Dr. Channing: Two Men from Boston," *NEQ*, XX (1947), 516–34.

21 Apparently she would have liked to be buried by Episcopal rites, and E said he would have given them to her if it had been practicable. See K. W. Cameron, "Early Background for E's 'The Problem,' " *ESQ*, No. 27 (1962), pp. 37–46. Cameron also finds the suggestion of "unconscious repudiation" of his father and of his father's church in E's never preparing a memorial of him and, apparently, destroying most of his sermons.

22 E's first published work was "Thoughts on the Religion of the Middle Ages," published in *The Christian Disciple*, New Series, IV (1822), 401–8; see *JMN*, I, 304ff.

23 See *JMN*, VIII, 181–82, and IX, 467–68; Richard D. Birdsall, "E and the Church of Rome," *AL*, XXXI (1959–60), 273–81.

24 Yukio Irie, *E and Quakerism* (Tokyo, Kenkyusha, 1967), is the book-length study in the field indicated. See also Frederick B. Tolles, "E and Quakerism," *AL*, X (1938–39), 142–65, and Mary C. Turpie, "A Quaker Source for E's Sermon on The Lord's Supper," *NEQ*, XVII (1944), 95–101.

25 E as a critic of Swedenborg has been elaborately considered by Clarence Paul Hotson in "E's Biographical Sources for 'Swedenborg,' " *SP*, XXVI (1929), 23–46; "E and the Swedenborgians," *SP*, XXVII (1930), 517–45; "George Bush: Teacher and Critic of E," *PQ*, X (1931), 369–83; "The Christian Critics and Mr. E.," *NEQ*, XI (1938), 29–47, and other articles, many of them in New Church periodicals; see listing in Leary. J. Keith Torbert, "E and Sweden-

borg," *Texas Review*, II (1916–17), 313–26, and Carl F. Strauch, "E
Rejects Reed and Hails Thoreau," *HLB*, XVI (1968), 257–73, also
apply here.

26 Augustus Hopkins Strong, *American Poets and Their The-
ology* (Griffith and Rowland Press, 1916), gives us the judgment of
American fundamentalism on E's heresies. Still orthodox and Christian but much less hidebound is Elmer James Bailey, *Religious
Thought in the Greater American Poets* (Pilgrim Press, 1922). Robert
C. Pollock, "RWE: The Single Vision," in Harold C. Gardiner, ed.,
American Classics Reconsidered: A Christian Appraisal (S, 1958) is
a highly sympathetic and penetrating evaluation by a Catholic scholar.
See also William A. Huggard, "E's Glimpses of the Divine," *Per-
sonalist*, XXXVI (1955), 167–76; Carl F. Strauch, "E's Sacred Sci-
ence," *PMLA*, LXXXIII (1958), 237–50; Harold L. Berger, "E and
Carlyle: The Dissenting Believers," *ESQ*, No. 38 (1965), pp. 87–89.

WHAT EMERSON IS

1 Carl F. Strauch, "The Daemonic and Experimental in E," *Personalist*, XXXIII (1952), 40–55: "If E is ever to regain something of
the critical stature he possessed before and after his death, I hazard
the prophecy that it will be through a revaluation of his works, and
especially his poetry, as the expression of an ambivalent personality
precariously maintaining his equipoise in a continuous process of
mastering the elements that for him constituted life." See also
Strauch, "E's Sacred Silence," *PMLA*, LXXIII (1958), 237–50; Ray
Benoit, "E and Plato: The Fire's Center," *AL*, XXXIV (1962–63),
487–98; Harry Hayden Clark, "Conservative and Mediatory Em-
phases in E's Thought," in Simon and Parsons, *Transcendentalism
and its Legacy*, and, in the same volume, Albert Gilman and Roger
Brown, "Personality and Style in Concord." In Douglas C. Stevenson, "E and the Agrarian Tradition," *JHI*, XIV (1953), 95–115, what
has been called E's "johnny-cake side" is seriously studied. Finally,
attention should be called to the valuable symposium published in
ATQ, No. 9, Parts 1 & 2 (1971) and separately as *E's Relevance Today*, ed. by Eric W. Carlson and J. Lasley Dameron (Transcendental Books, 1971). The contributors, including Alfred S. Reid,

William B. Barton, Mary Edrich Redding, Vivian C. Hopkins, and others, enter very high claims for him. Though it is unlikely that any single reader will accept all the views expressed, it must still be maintained that the effect of the inquiry is to show that E is far from being a back number.

APPENDIX A

A NOTE ON EMERSON
SCHOLARSHIP AND THE
AIM AND METHOD OF THIS BOOK

1 See also Whicher's article, "E's Tragic Sense," *AS*, XXII (1952–53), 285–92.

2 See especially Vol. I, pp. xxvii–viii, and J. E. Parsons's introduction to Vol. VIII.

3 "Frost and E: Voice and Vision," *MR*, I (1959), 5–23.

4 "E's Transformation in the 1820's," *AL*, XXXIX (1968–69), 133–54.

5 Lydenberg, "E and the Dark Tradition," *Critical Quarterly*, IV (1962), 352–58; see also R. A. Yoder, "E's Dialectic," *Criticism*, XI (1969), 313–28; Harold Bloom, "E: The Glories and the Sorrows of American Romanticism," *VQR*, XLVII (1971), 546–63.

6 *Critic*, XLII (1903), 437–40. See also Charles Gray Shaw, "E the Nihilist," *International Journal of Ethics*, XXV (1914–15), 68–86.

7 *A Biography of RWE, Set Forth in His Life Essay* (William Harvey Miner Co., Inc., 1921).

SELECTED BIBLIOGRAPHY

For abbreviations employed in this section, see the beginning of the "Notes." Many articles and some books cited in the notes are not relisted here.

E bibliography is plethoric, and a full listing would require a very large book. George Willis Cooke, *A Bibliography of RWE* (1908) is useful as far as it goes, but must now be supplemented by the bibliography volumes of Spiller *et al.*, *Literary History of the United States* (M, 1948, 1959), Lewis Leary's bibliographies of *Articles on American Literature* (DUP, 1954, 1970), the current indexes in *PMLA* and elsewhere, and the bibliographies in such works as *Eight American Authors, A Review of Research and Criticism* (Modern Language Assn., 1956) and Frederic Ives Carpenter's *RWE: Representative Selections* (ABC, 1934) and *E Handbook* (Hendricks House, 1953).

The standard edition of E's writings is still the "Centenary Edition" (called the "Concord Edition" in its subscription form), with notes by Edward Waldo Emerson (1903–1904), but this will certainly be superseded by the new edition of *Collected Works*, under the general editorship of Alfred R. Ferguson, now in course of publication by HUP. In 1972 the same publisher completed the publication of a three-volume set of *The Early Lectures of RWE*, ed. by Robert E. Spiller and others; a set of the later lectures will follow. E's portion of the *Memoirs of Margaret Fuller Ossoli*, in which he collaborated with W. H. Channing and James Freeman Clarke, is not included in his collected works; this originally appeared in two volumes in 1859, and Roberts Brothers brought out a one-volume edition in 1884. E's substantial poetic anthology, *Parnassus*, dates from 1874. *Uncollected Writings: Essays, Addresses, Poems, Reviews and Letters*

(Lamb Publishing Company, 1912) and *Uncollected Lectures: Reports of Lectures on American Life and Natural Religion, Reprinted from* The Commonwealth, ed. by Clarence Gohdes (William Edwin Rudge, 1932), should not be overlooked, but more important is the collection of sermons by Arthur Cushman McGiffert, Jr., *Young E Speaks: Unpublished Discourses on Many Subjects* (1938). Edward Everett Hale brought out *Two Unpublished Essays: The Character of Socrates; The Present State of Ethical Philosophy* (Lamson, Wolffe & Co., 1896) and *RWE, Together with Two Early Essays of E* (Brown & Company, 1899). E contributed an introduction to Volume I of *The Hundred Greatest Men: Portraits of the Greatest Men of History*, etc. (Sampson Low, Marston, Searle, and Rivington, 1879). See also Merton M. Sealts, Jr., and Alfred R. Ferguson, eds., *E's* Nature—*Origin, Growth, Meaning* (DM, 1969); Carl F. Strauch, "E's Phi Beta Kappa Poem," *NEQ*, XXIII (1950), 65–90; *Indian Superstitions*, ed., with a Dissertation on E's Orientalism at Harvard, by K. W. Cameron, *ESQ*, No. 32 (1963). *The Living Thoughts of E*, ed. by Edgar Lee Masters (LG, 1940) is interesting, but the best book of selections is Stephen E. Whicher, *Selections from RWE: An Organic Anthology*, "Riverside Editions" (1957).

The ten-volume edition of E's *Journals* (1909–1914), ed. by Edward Waldo Emerson and W. E. Forbes, has long been standard, but is now being superseded by the definitive edition of *The Journals and Miscellaneous Notebooks of RWE* (cited in my notes as *JMN*), edited by a shifting board of scholars. HUP brought out Vol. I in 1960, and nine more have appeared since, but Vol. X was too late to be consulted in the preparation of this volume.

The great collection of *Letters* is that of Ralph L. Rusk (6 vols. ColUP, 1939), an heroic piece of editing. The most extensive previously published collection was *The Correspondence of Thomas Carlyle and RWE*, first published in two volumes in 1883. The definitive modern edition is that of Joseph Slater, *The Correspondence of E and Carlyle* (ColUP, 1964). See also *A Correspondence between John Sterling and RWE, with a Sketch of Sterling's Life by E. W. Emerson* (1897); Charles Eliot Norton's collection of E's letters to Samuel Gray Ward: *Letters from RWE to a Friend* . . . (1899); Frederick W. Hollis, ed., *Correspondence Between RWE and Herman Grimm* (1903); H. H. Furness, ed., *Records of a Lifelong Friendship, 1807–1882: RWE and William Henry Furness* (1910);

Howard F. Lowry and R. L. Rusk, eds., *E-Clough Letters* (Rowfant Club, 1934). See also *RWE to Elizabeth Hoar* (Ysleta, Texas: Edwin B. Hill, 1942); *Thoreau's Pencils: An Unpublished Letter from RWE to Caroline Sturgis, 19 May, 1944* (Houghton Library Brochure, No. 4, 1944); Herbert F. West, ed., *Mr. E Writes a Letter about Walden* (Thoreau Society Booklet, No. 9, 1954), and the following articles: K. W. Cameron, "A Sheaf of E Letters," *AL*, XXIV (1952–53), 476–80; R. W. Cummins, "Unpublished Letters to Louis Prang and Whittier," *AL*, XLIII (1971–72), 257–59; Howard M. Fish, Jr., "Five E Letters," *AL*, XXVII (1955–56), 25–30; C. Carroll Hollis, "A New England Outpost: As Revealed in Some Unpublished Letters of E, Parker and Alcott to Ainsworth Spofford," *NEQ*, XXXVIII (1965), 65–85; Walter M. Murphy, "A Letter by E," *AL*, XXXVI (1964–65), 64–65; Barbara D. Simison, "The Letters of RWE: Addenda," *MLN*, LV (1940), 425–27; A. Warren Stearns, "Four E Letters to Dr. Daniel Parker," *Tuftonian*, I, Nov. 1940, pp. 6–9; William White, "Two Unpublished E Letters," *AL*, XXXI (1959–60), 334–36, and "Thirty-Three Unpublished Letters by RWE," *AL*, XXXIII (1961–62), 159–78; Nathalia Wright, "RWE to Horatio Greenough," *HLB*, XII (1958), 91–116.

The authorized biography of E is James Elliot Cabot, *A Memoir of RWE*, 2 vols. (1887). The definitive modern biography is Ralph L. Rusk, *The Life of RWE* (S, 1949). The following studies, biographical and critical, of widely varying value, all appear between independent covers:

John Albee, *Remembrances of E* (Robert G. Cooke, 1901); Bronson Alcott, *E* (Cambridge, privately printed, 1865) and *RWE, An Estimate of his Character and Genius* (A. Williams, 1882); John Q. Anderson, *The Liberating Gods: E on Poets and Poetry* (Miami, 1971); Joel Benton, *E as a Poet* (M. L. Holbrook, 1883); Augustine Birrell, *E, A Lecture* (P. Green, 1903); Jonathan Bishop, *E on the Soul* (HUP, 1964); Sarah K. Bolton, *RWE* (Crowell, 1904); Frederic Ives Carpenter, *E and Asia* (HUP, 1930); Elisabeth Luther Cary, *E, Poet and Thinker* (P, 1904); André Celières, *The Prose Style of E* (Paris, Impressions Pierre André, 1936); Moncure D. Conway, *E at Home and Abroad* (1882); Michael H. Cowan, *E, America, and Urban Metaphor* (YUP, 1967); George Willis Cooke, *RWE: His Life, Writings, and Philosophy* (1881); Samuel McChord Crothers, *E, How To Know Him* (Bobbs-Merrill, 1921); William F. Dana,

The Optimism of RWE (CUC, 1886); August Derleth, *E, Our Contemporary* (Crowell-Collier Press, 1970); Newton Dillaway, *Prophet of America: E and the Problems of Today* (LB, 1936); Edward Waldo Emerson, *E in Concord* (1889);

O. W. Firkins, *RWE* (1915); Charles Howell Foster, *E's Theory of Poetry* (Iowa City, Midland House, 1939); Richard Garnett, *Life of RWE* (Walter Scott, 1888); Robert M. Gay, *RWE, A Study of the Poet as Seer* (D, 1928); Henry David Gray, *E: A Statement of New England Transcendentalism as Expressed in the Philosophy of its Chief Exponent* (Leland Stanford, Jr., University Publications, University Series, 1917); Alfred H. Guernsey, *RWE: Philosopher and Poet* (Appleton, 1881); Walter Harding, *E's Library* (University Press of Virginia, 1967); David Greene Haskins, *RWE, His Maternal Ancestors with Some Reminiscences of Him* (CUC, 1887); J. Arthur Hill, *E and His Philosophy* (William Rider, 1929); Hubert H. Hoeltje, *Sheltering Tree: A Story of the Friendship of RWE and Amos Bronson Alcott* (DUP, 1943); Vivian C. Hopkins, *Spires of Form, A Study of E's Aesthetic Theory* (HUP, 1951); Alexander Ireland, *RWE: Recollections of His Visits to England . . .* (Simpkin, Marshall, 1882); Howard Mumford Jones, *E Once More* (BP, 1953); David Lee Maulsby, *The Contribution of E to Literature* (Tufts College Press, 1911); Edwin D. Mead, *E and Theodore Parker* (AUA, 1910) and *The Influence of E* (AUA, 1903); Régis Michaud, *E, The Enraptured Yankee* (H, 1930); Josephine Miles, *RWE* (University of Minnesota Press, 1964); John Morley, *RWE, An Essay* (M, 1884);

Swami Paramanda, *E and Vedanta* (2nd ed., Boston, Vedanta Centre, 1918); Sherman Paul, *E's Angle of Vision: Man and Nature in American Experience* (HUP, 1952); Bliss Perry, *E Today* (Princeton Univ. Press, 1931); George Searle Phillips (January Searle), *E: His Life and Writings* (Holyoake & Co., 1855); V. Ramakrishna Rao, *E: His Muse and Message* (University of Calcutta, 1938); J. Russell Reaver, *E as Mythmaker* (UFP, 1954); Phillips Russell, *E, The Wisest American* (Brentano's, 1929); Frank B. Sanborn, *RWE* (Small, Maynard, 1901) and *The Personality of E* (Charles E. Goodspeed, 1903)—also, Sanborn, ed., *The Genius and Character of E: Lectures at the Concord School of Philosophy* (1885); Townsend Scudder, *The Lonely Wayfaring Man: E and Some Englishmen* (OUP, 1936); James B. Thayer, *A Western Journey with Mr. E* (LB, 1884); William Roscoe Thayer, *The Influence of E* (CUC,

1886); Lawrance Thompson, *E and Frost, Critics of Their Times* (Philobiblion Club, 1940); Stephen E. Whicher, *Freedom and Fate: An Inner Life of RWE* (Univ. of Pennsylvania Press, 1953); George Edward Woodberry, *RWE* (M, 1907). See also *The Centenary of the Birth of RWE, as Observed in Concord, May 25, 1903, under the Direction of The Social Circle in Concord* (1903) and John D. Gordan, "RWE, 1803-1882: Catalogue of an Exhibition from the Berg Collection," *BNYPL*, LIX (1953), 392-408, 433-60. The memorial number of the London *Bookman*, June 1903, has an article by Edward Waldo Emerson and a fine collection of pictures.

Warren Staebler, *RWE* (Twayne, 1973), did not appear until after this book had been completed.

There follows a representative sampling of books which either contain sections on E or which, though devoted to other or larger subjects, contain significant references to him:

A. Bronson Alcott, *Concord Days* (RB, 1872); Louisa May Alcott, "Reminiscences of RWE," in James Parton, ed., *Some Noted Princes, Authors, and Statesmen of Our Time* (Henry Bill Publishing Co., 1886); Quentin Anderson, *The Imperial Self: An Essay in American Literary and Cultural History* (K, 1971); Arthur Bryant, *The American Ideal* (LG, 1936); John Burroughs, *Birds and Poets* (1877), *Indoor Studies* (1889), and *The Last Harvest* (1922); Henry Seidel Canby, *Classic Americans* (HB, 1931); F. I. Carpenter, *American Literature and the Dream* (Philosophical Library, 1955); John Jay Chapman, *E and Other Essays* (S, 1898); Arthur Christy, *The Orient in American Transcendentalism, A Study of E, Thoreau, and Alcott* (ColUP, 1932); James Freeman Clarke, *Nineteenth Century Questions* (1897); L. C. Collns, ed., *The Posthumous Essays of John Churlton Collins* (Dent, 1912); George E. DeMille, *Literary Criticism in America* (Dial Press, 1931); John Dewey, *Characters and Events: Popular Essays in Social and Political Philosophy*, ed. by Joseph Ratner (2 vols., Holt, 1929);

Charles Carroll Everett, *Essays Theological and Literary* (1902); Charles Feidelson, Jr., *Symbolism and American Literature* (UCP, 1953); Annie Fields, *Authors and Friends* (1896); Norman Foerster, *American Criticism* (1928); Martin Green, *Re-Appraisals* (N, 1965); Thomas Wentworth Higginson, *Contemporaries* (1899); Henry Hazlitt, "E," in John Macy, ed., *American Writers on American Literature* (Liveright, 1931); M. A. DeWolfe Howe, *American*

Bookmen (DM, 1898); Holbrook Jackson, *Dreamers of Dreams: The Rise and Fall of Nineteenth Century Idealism* (Farrar, Straus, n.d.); Henry James, *Partial Portraits* (M, 1888); Alfred Kreymborg, *Our Singing Strength* . . . (Coward McCann, 1929); Ludwig Lewisohn, *Expression in America* (H, 1932);

John Macy, *The Spirit of American Literature* (D, 1913); F. O. Matthiessen, *American Renaissance: Art and Expression in the Age of E and Whitman* (OUP, 1941); Bliss Perry, *In Praise of Folly and Other Papers* (1923); William Lyon Phelps, *Some Makers of American Literature* (Marshall Jones Company, 1923); John Paul Pritchard, *Return to the Fountains: Some Classical Sources of American Criticism* (DUP, 1942) and *Criticism in America* (UOP, 1956); Arnold Smithline, *Natural Religion in American Literature* (College and University Press, 1966); Leslie Stephen, *Studies of a Biographer*, Vol. IV (Smith, Elder, 1907); Wilson Sullivan, *New England Men of Letters* (M, 1972); Tony Tanner, *The Reign of Wonder* (Cambridge University Press, 1965); Henry van Dyke, *Companionable Books* (S, 1922); Leon H. Vincent, *American Literary Masters* (1906); Hyatt H. Waggoner, *American Poets from the Puritans to the Present* (1968); Austin Warren, *New England Saints* (Mich, 1956); René Wellek, *A History of Modern Criticism, 1750–1950* (YUP, 1965); Edwin P. Whipple, *American Literature and Other Papers* (1887).

There is an excellent sampling of writing about E in Milton R. Konvitz, ed., *The Recognition of RWE: Selected Criticism Since 1887* (Mich, 1972). Much of the material reprinted or extracted by Konvitz is not listed separately here. It need hardly be said that E appears in a fairly high percentage of American biographical writing of the nineteenth and twentieth centuries. I have mentioned such works only when it was necessary to refer to them in the notes.

During recent years, Kenneth W. Cameron has been publishing, generally through Transcendental Books, Hartford, a large number of collections of materials important for E research. These include *A Commentary on E's Early Lectures (1833–1836) with an Index Concordance* (1961); *Concord Harvest: Publications of the Concord School of Philosophy and Literature, with Notes on its Successors and its Resources for Research in E, Thoreau, Alcott, and the Later Transcendentalists* (1970); *An E Index of Names, Exempla, Sententiae, Symbols, Words and Motifs in Selected Notebooks of RWE*

(1958); *E the Essayist, An Outline of his Philosophical Development through 1836, with Special Emphasis on the Sources and Interpretation of* Nature, *etc.* (1945); *E's Workshop: An Analysis on his Reading in Periodicals through 1836, with the Principal Thematic Key to his Essays, Poems, and Lectures, Also Memorabilia of Harvard and Concord* (1964); *E Among his Contemporaries: A Harvest of Estimates, Insights, and Anecdotes from the Victorian Literary World and an Index* (1967); *Index-Concordance to E's Sermons* (1963); *RWE's Reading* . . . (1941); and *Young E's Transcendental Vision, An Exposition of his World View, with an Analysis of the Structure, Backgrounds, and Meaning of* Nature *(1836)* (1971). Some of this material has also appeared in the *ESQ,* which Cameron has been editing and publishing since 1955; since 1969 he has also been editing and publishing the *ATQ.* Out of the immense wealth of material here published or republished, I have listed only selected items separately.

The following articles concern various phases of E's influence upon or resemblance to various later writers and critics: Robert Bloom, "Irving Babbitt's E," *NEQ,* XXX (1957), 448–73; Gene Bluestein, "E's Epiphanies," *NEQ,* XXXIX (1966), 447–60; William E. Bridges, "Transcendentalism and Psychotherapy: Another Look at E," *AL,* XLI (1969–70), 157–77; Harry M. Campbell, "E and Whitehead," *PMLA,* LXXV (1960), 577–82; Frederic I. Carpenter, "Points of Comparison between E and Henry James," *NEQ,* II (1929), 458–74, and "William James and E," *AL,* XI (1939–40), 39–57; Martin Christadler, "RWE in Modern Germany," *ESQ,* No. 38 (1965), pp. 112–25; Reginald L. Cook, "E and Frost, A Parallel of Seers," *NEQ,* XXXI (1958), 443–69; Robert Detweiler, "E and Zen," *AQ,* XIV (1962), 422–38; Fred Erisman, "Transcendentalism for American Youth: The Children's Books of Kate Douglas Wiggin," *NEQ,* XLI (1968), 238–47; Grace R. Foster, "The Natural History of the Will," *AS,* XV (1945–46), 277–87; C. Hugh Holman, "Hemingway and E: Notes on the Continuity of an Aesthetic Tradition," *Modern Fiction Studies,* I, Aug. 1955, pp. 12–15; Hermann Hummel, "E and Nietzsche," *NEQ,* XIX (1946), 63–84; Paul Lauter, "E through Tillich," *ESQ,* No. 31 (1963), pp. 49–55; E. C. Lindeman, "E's Pragmatic Mood," *AS,* XVI (1946), 57–64; Rudolf Schottlaender, "Two Dionysians: E and Nietzsche," *SAQ,* XXXIX (1940), 330–43; Paul C. Wermuth, "Santayana and E," *ESQ,* No. 31 (1963), pp. 36–40.

The closing sections of this bibliography list articles on E in various aspects which have not been mentioned elsewhere:

Richard P. Adams, "E and the Organic Metaphor," *PMLA*, LXIX (1954), 117–30, and "The Basic Contradiction in E," *ESQ*, No. 55 (1969), pp. 106–10; Nelson F. Adkins, "E's 'Days' and Edward Young," *MLN*, LXIII (1948), 269–71; Charles Akers, "Personal Glimpses of our New England Poets," *NEM*, n.s. XVII (1897–98), 446–56; John Q. Anderson, "E and 'The Moral Sentiment,'" *ESQ*, No. 19 (1960), pp. 13–15; Carlos Baker, "E and Jones Very," *NEQ*, VII (1934), 90–99; Nina Baym, "From Metaphysics to Metaphor: The Image of Water in E and Thoreau," *SR*, VI (1966–67), 231–43; Frank Bellew, "Recollections of RWE," *LiM*, XXXIV (1884), 45–50; James Binney, "E Revisited," *Midwest Quarterly*, XII (1970–71), 109–22; Walter Blair and Clarence Faust, "E's Literary Method," *MP*, XLII (1944–45), 79–95; Paul F. Boller, Jr., "E and Freedom," *Univ. of Houston Forum*, IV, Spring 1966, pp. 4–14; Percy H. Boynton, "E in his Period," *International Journal of Ethics*, XXXIX (1928–29), 177–89; Gamaliel Bradford, "E," *New Princeton Review*, n.s. V (1888), 145–63; Lionel Braham, "E and Boehme: A Comparative Study in Mystical Ideas," *MLQ*, XX (1959), 31–35; Stuart G. Brown, "John Jay Chapman and the Emersonian Gospel," *NEQ*, XXV (1952), 147–80; Kenneth Burke, "I, Aye, Ay—E's Early Essay on 'Nature': Thoughts on the Machinery of Transcendance," *SR*, LXXIV (1966), 875–94;

K. W. Cameron, "History and Biography in E's Unpublished Sermons," *ESQ*, No. 12 (1958), pp. 2–9, and "E's Fight for his Walden Woodlots," *ESQ*, No. 22 (1961), pp. 90–95; Hazen C. Carpenter, "E, Eliot, and the Elective System," *NEQ*, XXIV (1951), 13–34, and "E and Christopher Pearse Cranch," *NEQ*, XXXVII (1964), 18–42; John W. Chadwick, "E," *Arena*, XV (1895), 12–16; Thomas H. Clark, "An E Reminiscence," *SAQ*, IV (1905), 284–86; James Freeman Clarke, "Memoir of RWE, LL.D.," *Proceedings of the Massachusetts Historical Society*, II, Second Series (1866); John Clendenning, "E and Bayle," *PQ*, XLIII (1964), 79–86; Henry Steele Commager, "Tempest in a Boston Tea Cup," *NEQ*, VI (1933), 651–75; Stephen L. Conroy, "E and Phrenology," *AQ*, XVI (1964), 215–17; Moncure D. Conway, "E, The Teacher and the Man," *Critic*, XLII (1903), 404–11; Morton Cronin, "Some Notes on E's Prose Diction," *ASp*, XXIX (1954), 105–13; John B. Crozier, "The Key to E," *Fortnightly Review*, n.s. CX (1921), 229–42, 383–95; Carl Dennis, "E's Poetry of Mind and Nature," *ESQ*, No. 58 (1970), pp. 139–53; G. R. Elliott, "E as Diarist, A Middle-Aged View," *University of Toronto Quarterly*, VI (1937), 299–308; C. H. Faust, "The Background of the Unitarian Opposition to Transcendentalism," *MP*, XXXV (1937–38), 297–324; O. W. Firkins, "Has E a Future?" *MLN*, XLV (1930), 491–500; Charles H. Foster, "E as American Scripture," *NEQ*, XVI (1943), 91–105; Robert L. Francis, "The Architectonics of E's *Nature*," *AQ*, XIX (1967), 39–52; Gerhard Friedrich, "A Note on E's *Parnassus*," *NEQ*, XXVII (1954), 397–99; William H. Furness, "Random Recollections of E," *Atl*, LXXI (1893), 344–49; Jean Gorely, "E's Theory of Poetry," *Poetry Review*, XXII (1931), 263–73; Clark Griffith, " 'Emersonianism' and 'Poeism': Some Versions of the Romantic Sensibility," *MLQ*, XXII (1961), 125–34; Theodore L. Gross, "Under the Shadow of Our Swords: E and the Heroic Ideal," *Bucknell Review*, XVII, March 1969, pp. 22–34; Robert T. Harris, "*Nature*: E and Mill," *WHR*, VI (1951–52), 1–13; John E. Hart, "Man Thinking as Hero: E's 'Scholar' Revisited," *ESQ*, No. 55 (1969), pp. 102–6; T. W. Higginson, "The Personality of E," *Outlook*, LXXIV (1903), 221–27; Vivian C. Hopkins, "E and Cudworth: Plastic Nature and Transcendental Art," *AL*, XXIII (1951–52), 80–98;

Henry James, Sr., "E," *Atl*, XCIV (1904), 740–45; Ellwood Johnson, "E's Psychology of Power," *Rendezvous*, V, Spring 1970, pp. 13–25; Joseph Jones, "E and Bergson on the Comic," *Comparative Literature*, I (1949), 63–72; Pendleton King, "Notes of Conversations with E," *LiM*, XXXIII (1884), 44–50; H. L. Kleinfield, "The Structure of E's Death," *BNYPL*, LXV (1961), 47–64; Alfred J. Kloeckner, "Intellect and Moral Sentiment in E's Opinions of 'The Meaner Kinds' of Men," *AL*, XXX (1958–59), 322–38; Ralph C. Larosa, "E's Search for Literary Form: The Early Journals," *MP*, LXIX (1971–72), 25–35; Sheldon W. Liebman, "The Development of E's Theory of Rhetoric, 1821–1836," *AL*, XLI (1969–70), 178–206; C. Grant Loomis, "E's Proverbs," *WF*, XVII (1958), 257–62; David Macrae, "E: A Personal Reminiscence," *Spectator* XC (1903), 972–73; Herambachandra Maître, "E from an Indian Point of View," *HTR*, IV (1911), 403–17; Bruce McElderry, Jr., "E's Second Address on the American Scholar," *Personalist*, XXXIX (1958), 361–72; Donald M. Murray, "E's 'Language as Fossil Poetry': An Analogy from Chinese," *NEQ*, XXIX (1956), 204–15; Leonard Neufeldt, "The Vital Mind: E's Epistemology," *PQ*, L (1971), 153–70; Franklin B. Newman, "E and Buonarroti," *NEQ*, XXV (1952), 524–35; Egbert S. Oliver, "E's 'Days,' " *NEQ*, XIX (1946), 518–24; Karl A. Olsson, "Fredrika Bremer and RWE," *Swedish Pioneer Historical Quarterly*, II (1951), 39–52;

Saul K. Padover, "RWE: The Moral Voice in Politics," *Political Science Quarterly*, LXXIV (1959), 334–50; Bernard J. Paris, "E's 'Bacchus,' " *MLQ*, XXIII (1962), 150–59; Robert C. Pollock, "A Reappraisal of E," *Thought*, XXXII (1957–58), 86–132; Horatio N. Powers, "A Day with E," *LiM*, XXX (1882), 477–80; J. Russell Reaver, "Mythology in E's Poems," *ESQ*, No. 39 (1965), pp. 56–63; Alfred S. Reid, "E and Bushnell as Forerunners of Jamesian Pragmatism," *Furman University Bulletin*, n.s. XVIII, Nov. 1965, pp. 18–30; E. J. Rose, "Melville, E, and The Sphinx," *NEQ*, XXXVI (1963), 249–58; Earl Rovit, "E: A Contemporary Reconsideration," *AS*, XLI (1971–72), 429–38; Ralph L. Rusk, "E and the Stream of Experience," *CE*, XIV (1953), 373–79;

Frank B. Sanborn, "E in His Home," *Arena*, XV (1895), 16–21; Mildred Silver, "E and the Idea of Progress," *AL*, XII (1940–41), 1–19; Joseph Slater, "Two Sources for E's First Address on West Indian Emancipation," *ESQ*, No. 44 (1966), pp. 97–100; Henry Nash Smith, "E's Problem of Vocation: A Note on 'The American Scholar,' " *NEQ*, XII (1939), 52–67; William J. Sowder, "E's Early Impact on England: A Study in British Periodicals," *PMLA*, LXXVII (1962), 561–72, "E's Rationalist Champions: A Study in British Periodicals," *NEQ*, XXXVII (1964), 147–70, and especially "E's Reviewers and Commentators: Nineteenth Century Periodical Criticism," *ESQ*, No. 53 (1968); Robert E. Spiller, "E and Humboldt," *AL*, XLII (1970–71), 546–48; William T. Stafford, "E and the James Family," *AL*, XXIV (1952–53), 433–61; Randall Stewart, "The Concord Group, A Study in Relationships," *SeR*, XLIV (1932), 434–46; Floyd Stovall, "The Value of E Today," *CE*, III (1941–42), 442–54; Carl F. Strauch, "The Year of E's Poetic Maturity: 1834," *PQ*, XXXIV (1955), 353–77, "The Background of E's 'Boston Hymn,' " *AL*, XIV (1942–43), 36–47, "E as a Creator of Vignettes," *MLN*, LXX (1955), 274–78, "The Importance of E's Skeptical Mood," *HLB*, XI (1957), 117–39, "E as Literary Middleman," *ESQ*, No. 19 (1960), pp. 2–9, "E and the Longevity of the Mind," *ESQ*, No. 54

(1969), pp. 60–68, and "E's Use of the Organic Method," *ESQ*, No. 55 (1969), pp. 18–24; Virginia Wayman, "A Study of E's Philosophy of Education," *Education*, XXXVI (1935–36), 474–82; Thomas Whitaker, "The Riddle of E's 'Sphinx,' " *AL*, XXVII (1955–56), 179–95; Stanley T. Williams, "E: An Affirmation," *TSL*, II (1957), 41–50.

INDEX

Wells, H. G., 179
Whicher, Stephen E., 235–36
Whipple, Edwin P., 21, 84
Whitman, Walt, 3, 63, 93–94, 130, 137, 177–78, 266
Whittier, John Greenleaf, 3, 83, 91, 162
Wilde, Oscar, 212
Wilkinson, Garth, 77
Williams, Stanley T., 77
Willis, Nathaniel Parker, 21
Willson, Forecythe, 92
Winters, Yvor, 49

Women, E's attitude toward, 136–44
Woodberry, George Edward, 6
Woodbury, Charles J., 85, 253
Woolf, Virginia, 141
Wordsworth, William, 15, 82, 85, 101, 104, 182, 256–57, 264
Wright, Frank Lloyd, 68
Writing, E's views on, and writing habits, 95–106

Yohannan, J. D., 81–82
Young, Charles Lowell, 36, 262